Science and Policy in Natural Resource Management

Understanding System Complexity

Despite many well-intentioned policies and changes to our management practices, our natural resources continue to decline. The roles and interplay between science and policy in the regional broadacre agriculture landscape are examined here, offering readers a thorough understanding of the complex interactions that occur across spatial scales to produce the regional-scale impacts. The fundamental causes of resource degradation, social decline and environmental pollution are addressed, examining the cross-scale drivers from the individual farm level to the global level of commodity systems. Broadacre agriculture is a common land use throughout all continents of the world and is driven by the same type of dynamics, and this case study of the Western Australian agricultural region can be used to clearly demonstrate the principles for other commodity systems. Aimed at academics and researchers through to policy analysts, this book will inspire innovation and action in sustainable natural resource management.

HELEN F. ALLISON is a researcher into complex systems and has experience working with terrestrial and aquatic systems in tropical, temperate and Mediterranean climates in Australia, Europe and South Africa. She is a Post-Doctoral Fellow at Murdoch University in Perth, Western Australia.

RICHARD J. HOBBS is Professor of Environmental Science at Murdoch University, where he teaches Environmental Restoration. He is the author of over 230 refereed publications, many magazine articles and unrefereed publications, and author/editor of 12 books.

His particular interests are in vegetation dynamics and management, fragmentation, invasive species, ecosystem restoration, conservation biology and landscape ecology.

Science and Policy in Natural Resource Management
Understanding System Complexity

HELEN E. ALLISON

RICHARD J. HOBBS

Murdoch University, Perth, Australia

CAMBRIDGE
UNIVERSITY PRESS

CAMBRIDGE UNIVERSITY PRESS
Cambridge, New York, Melbourne, Madrid, Cape Town, Singapore, São Paulo

Cambridge University Press
The Edinburgh Building, Cambridge CB2 2RU, UK

Published in the United States of America by Cambridge University Press, New York

www.cambridge.org
Information on this title: www.cambridge.org/9780521858830

First published 2006

Printed in the United Kingdom at the University Press, Cambridge

A catalogue record for this publication is available from the British Library

ISBN-13 978-0-521-85883-0 hardback
ISBN-10 0-521-85883-6 hardback

Contents

Illustrations

Tables

Foreword

This is probably the first study that has used resilience, the adaptive cycle and panarchy as a major part of the conceptual foundation for the work. Resilience (as used here) has been explored in the literature for about 30 years, the adaptive cycle originated about 18 years ago and both have been integrated within the panarchy concept for only a few years. The authors combine these concepts with soft systems science conceptual modelling tools to review and assess the character of agricultural development from an integrated perspective of economic, social and ecological changes over about 100 years. They then apply these methods in a strategic analysis of the Western Australian agricultural region.

In the process the authors explore the significance of paradigms of science and policy that come from renewable resource management and practice. These emerge from and create different modes of scientific enquiry, different philosophical foundations of theory, and different modes of management. The latter range over time from traditions of command and control, to integrated management and adaptive management, to the synthetic kind of understanding and action that comes from recent work on complex adaptive systems. The authors find that the earlier approaches of science and management have been part of the cause of the erosion of the system because of their inability to lead to remedial policy and action. They are conceptually limited and too constrained. All elements are necessary but insufficient. The science of complex adaptive systems, however, is very different from traditional disciplinary, reductionist science. It is integrated across disciplines; it assumes non-linearities, multi-stable states and operations interacting over multiple scale ranges. In this case these are over scales from the individual farm to the global market for wheat. It argues for 'just sufficient' parsimony to find the simple sets of explanation for the complex behaviour.

Change is seen as being both regular and abrupt. Uncertainty is high and an integral part of the concepts and methods. Versions of booms and busts are common, as are continual efforts to partially or wholly recover and redesign. The purpose is not only to reduce uncertainty where possible, but equally, to live with and learn from unexpected results. Models are useful but transient in their usefulness. Systems of people and nature adapt so that an evolutionary change perspective is essential. That is, the system you start with need not be the same as the one you have or will have.

The authors review and assess all that history of approach, science and policy with great clarity, knowledge and sense. They write extremely well and clearly. I really have not seen a better review and assessment than the one they have done. And they do it by vividly exploring the strategic events and processes in the region over a hundred-year period.

Because their analysis is strategic, it aims to define the problems and directions for response. Although any strategic analysis needs data, narrower analysis and models, those do not appear directly in this book. Instead, they are drawn on from the extensive literature available. Therefore few graphs, tables of numbers or graphs from models appear here. Those exist elsewhere in the published literature and reports, allowing the authors to use them and concentrate on their strategic study. I believe they have taken exactly the right course for their strategic purpose.

The authors have extensively reviewed the literature emphasising social and ecological knowledge, and some economic theories and studies as well. Their survey is really admirable. Parts of that survey deal with resilience, adaptive cycles and panarchy. They present an accurate description and assessment of the theories and practices from which the concepts were developed. I find the accuracy of their review to be surprising, since so many such reviews still appearing in the narrower literature are simply wrong, or incomplete or narrowly disciplinary. I found it to be simply excellent.

The authors add to that a review and assessment of economic cycles that, together with the cycles observed in the agricultural developments, clearly shows the degree of influence of internal causes vs. external commodity and international market causes. They show through the use of the adaptive cycle and soft modelling diagrams how the system is dominated by external economic commodity forces outside Western Australia. That is the panarchy in operation. In contrast, endogenous (local) forces that drive other social and ecological elements are not strong enough to be contributing to the evolution of a sustainable system. That has led to progressive resource impoverishment, major destruction of native vegetation, increasing salt concentration of soils, biodiversity loss and social decline. Technological quality and innovation for agriculture has continually advanced and the value of wheat has regularly declined. Some policy reform is possible that might add perennial vegetation, introduce crop diversity and add new agricultural innovations. Some of these would be useful. But the essential story and analysis leads to the conclusion that the deleterious changes in the agricultural region are irreversible.

The critical change or transformations now needed are global – in trade, in international markets that involve changes in the World Trade Organisation and in geopolitical relations and trade agreements. These need to better integrate economic, social and ecological elements than occurs at present. The authors are right, but such integration occurs so slowly that the beneficiaries will not likely be Western Australia, but other places and other times. It represents a major focus for research, action and policy. That represents a true transformation – partly the double loop learning they refer to, but more transformational learning across scales.

The example of Western Australian agriculture is of great value as the lessons learnt can be applied elsewhere, since the authors end appropriately on questions of institution and governance. The authors do offer a set of actions that are now appropriate. The key ones involve imaginative ways to communicate the story within the region; major changes in education; advances in interactive modelling methods and practices. They offer suggestions for the directions needed in such circumstances – ones that essentially focus on transformation of governance – on institutional reform, on recognition of multiple values on a panarchy of scales across time and space. And they recognise that fundamental change has to wait for the critical time for transformation to be possible. Prepare for it, but wait for it.

C. S. (Buzz) Holling

Preface

'I strongly advise you to stay within the discipline' was the advice from the Head of School in the mid 1970s, when the first author Helen Allison was proposing to take a course in History and Philosophy of Science, conducted in another department, as an option in her Zoology Honours year at Aberdeen University. The reason she was told was that timetabling was difficult and it couldn't be done. In retrospect confining her education to the accepted scientific paradigm would preserve the credibility of the established set of protocols proposed by the zoology discipline thus avoiding any potential for her to ask probing questions on theoretical issues, controversies and paradoxes.

Now 30 years later this book is the result of a course-altering event during the research for a Ph.D. dissertation by Helen, when she discovered an alternative to reductionism. On reading the book *Complexity: The Emerging Science at the Edge of Order and Chaos* (Waldrop, 1992) Helen wondered why she had not been exposed much earlier in her career to the integrating ideas of complexity and self-organising adaptive systems. However, on reflection it is not surprising, given the tacit agreement and protocols of the scientific paradigm. Helen is grateful to the author M. Waldrop who introduced her to the new sciences for the twenty-first century.

Now it is becoming acceptable to talk about diverse epistemologies, different ways of understanding the world, alternative worldviews and different ways of investigation. We now recognise that the complex problems of human societies require new approaches in science to understand the fundamental drivers of their dynamics and to be able to intervene with appropriate policies. Novel approaches and greater integration of the sciences have been advocated by an increasing number of people, including the second author Richard Hobbs. These approaches are receiving much greater attention while still remaining fragmented and marginalised not only within academic institutions but in the thinking that still informs policy for natural resource management.

In this book we wish to share with the reader what we have learnt about these new sciences integrated with our combined 60 years experience on natural resource management. We also wish to challenge the reader to think both broadly and deeply on the issues that are facing broadacre agricultural systems 'What are the big or distal drivers that are impacting on these types of regions?' To investigate what these drivers might be we have to go beyond the single discipline, and look at relationships between factors and find the tools that can help us investigate these broad integrative relationships.

Acknowledgements

We are greatly indebted to C. S. (Buzz) Holling, Lance Gunderson and Tim Haslett who recognised the importance of this work in its original form, and to Alan Crowden for having the confidence in it to support our approach to Cambridge University Press.

We wish to express our appreciation to two institutions for supporting this research in various ways. Firstly, our thanks to Murdoch University, Western Australia, for financial support by way of a University Scholarship to Helen over the period 2000–3. Secondly, our thanks to Land & Water Australia, in particular Dr Nick Schofield, manager of the Innovation Program, who facilitated our grant approval which provided support for the final transformation of the dissertation into this book.

This book is the result of the generosity of many people who gave their time and contributed in many ways, helping us to integrate the many exciting and new ideas being explored to help understand and manage intractable problems in social-ecological systems.

Helen would like to thank colleagues past and present for their generous contributions of information and time: Associate Professor Frank Murray, Murdoch University, supported my initial proposal, and patiently followed my path of discovery of alternative ways of understanding; Dr Jennifer Robinson, Murdoch University, for her eclectic intellect, robust arguments, forthright approach and discussions on system dynamics; Charlie Nicholson, CALM, a former manager, original thinker and always a systems thinker; Dr Neil Pettit, Washington University, for encouragement and incisive comments on the final draft; Dr Julia Hobson, Murdoch University, who provided positive feedback on drafts of my papers; Dr Bryan Jenkins, Murdoch University, for his participation, energy and interest in conceptualising models; the members of the Task Force for the Review of Natural Resource Management and Viability of Agriculture in Western Australia (Dr Paul McLeod, Dr Libby Mattiske,

Dr George Gardiner, Norman Flugge and Margaret Agnew) for whom I was Executive Officer, for sharing their progressive views on the future of natural resource management and policy; Will Fey for choosing to coach me in system dynamics 'his way'; Dr Tim Haslett, Monash University, and his students who took me under their wing at my first system dynamics conference and who very kindly provided me with his system dynamics modelling course notes 'Mastering ithink'; Professor Nimal Jayaratna, Curtin University Business School, who encouraged the extension of my enquiring mind in the genre of systemic analysis; others include Dr Michael Booth, Dr Frank Harman and Dr David Annandale of Murdoch University; Dr David Egan, Curtin University Business School; Dr Sarah Lumley, University of Western Australia; Dr William Hutchinson, Edith Cowan University; Aldo Zagonel, University of Albany, SUNY; Dr Andrea Hinwood, Edith Cowan University and Deputy Chair of the Environmental Protection Authority; Dr Brian Walker, The Resilience Alliance; Kristen Blann, University of Minnesota; Annie MacBeth, Futurist; Peter Curry and Dr Denis Saunders.

There are also innumerable friends and colleagues who have encouraged me in my endeavour, including Dr Sue Moore, Murdoch University, who gave me the final encouragement I needed to start my Ph.D., and Dr Viki Cramer, who always made herself available for academic, diverse and interesting discussions; friends who reminded me that there was a world outside of my research and provided support in their own ways: Agriculture Breakfast Group (Ross George Agriculture WA, Dr Donald Burnside URS, Martin Wells, John Duff, Nic Watson, Commissioner for Soil Conservation, Dr David Bennett and others mentioned individually elsewhere); Wednesday morning beach swimming group, a constant source of inspiration on summer and winter mornings; Envirodrinks colleagues; my dear friends Lindy Brookes and Joe Tonga who on numerous occasions provided me with dinner, bed and breakfast; Peter Krawec; Kellie and Peter Pendoley; Helen Fordham; Dr Ann Hamblin; and to all those not named individually.

Thanks for support and friendship goes to fellow students in the wind tunnel that we postgraduates called home for the duration of our candidature. I am grateful for the support of the staff in the Division of Science and Engineering: Jeanne Clarke, Frank Salleo, Colin Ferguson, Sarah Xu, Susan Flay, Heather Gordon and Lindsay Lincoln, and in the Division of Research and Development, Ann Randell and Karen Olkowski. Thanks go to Alan Rossow and Kevin Hardman for drafting the maps and some of the more difficult figures and to Ted Lamont and Richard Krumins, Murdoch University, for advice on the tricks to making acrylic moulds when I struggled with a three-dimensional acrylic model of the adaptive cycle.

Finally, special thanks to Jay Whitely, a fellow Ph.D. colleague and friend, who gave so willingly of his time, provided much humour, and guided me in the art of LaTeX for the document preparation, and Dr Iain Allison, Senior Science Adviser, Glasgow University, who supplied me from an early age with his brotherly advice and encouragement, introduced me to *Zen and the Art of Motorcycle Maintenance: An Inquiry into Values* (Pirsig, 1976) and *Sophie's World: A Novel About the History of Philosophy* (Gaarder, 1994) and who holds no responsibility for the consequences of those actions and the content of this work. All errors and interpretation are our sole responsibility.

In addition to the above, Richard would also like to thank the many people who have shaped his thinking in this area and provided him with the confidence to pursue this new and challenging way of working, including Brian Walker, Ted Lefroy, Buzz Holling, Viki Cramer and Sue Moore. I'd also like to thank my wife Gillian and my two children Katie and Hamish for keeping me grounded and reminding me that there is a real world out there, as well as putting up with my long hours holed up in the study and periods away from home.

The original text for the dissertation was proofread by Jan Knight of Flying Edits.

Parts of this book appeared in a paper published in *Ecology and Society* **9**(1): 3, www.ecologyandsociety.org/vol9/iss1/.

We are grateful to the following for permission to reproduce copyright material: Figures 4.1 and 4.2 from *Sociological Paradigms and Organisational Analysis: Elements of the Sociology of Corporate Life* by G. Burrel and G. Morgan (1979) reprinted by permission of Harcourt Education; Figures 4.4 and 4.5 reprinted by permission of K. Blann; Figure 4.3 by R. Quinn and J. Rohrbaugh (1993) reprinted by permission of *Management Science*; Figures 5.1 and 5.2 from *Understanding and Evaluating Methodologies* by N. Jayaratna (1994) reprinted by permission of The McGraw-Hill Companies; Figure 5.4 reprinted by permission of J. Ravetz; Figures 5.5, 6.5 and 8.1 from *Panarchy*, edited by Lance H. Gunderson and C. S. Holling, Copyright 2002 Island Press, reproduced by permission of Island Press, Washington, DC; Figures 7.1, 7.2 and 7.4 from *Commodity System Challenges Moving Sustainability into Mainstream of Natural Resource Economics*, reprinted by permission of The Sustainability Institute; extract in the Epilogue from *Zen and the Art of Motor-cycle Maintenance* by R. M. Pirsig, published by Vintage, reprinted by permission of The Random House Group Ltd.

Abbreviations

ABARE	Australian Bureau of Agriculture and Resource Economics
ABS	Australian Bureau of Statistics
AEAM	Adaptive Environmental Assessment and Management
AM	Adaptive Management
CCP	Command and Control Policy
CVA	Competing Values Approach
EPA	Environmental Protection Authority
EPPs	Environmental Protection Policies
ESD	Ecologically Sustainable Development
ESRC	Economic and Social Research Council, UK
EVAO	Estimated Value of Agricultural Output
ICM	Integrated Catchment Management
NAP	National Action Plan on Salinity and Water Quality Australia
NIMSAD	Normative Information Model-based Systems Analysis and Design
OCM	Office of Catchment Management
PRIME	Planning, Research, Implementation, Monitoring and Evaluation Framework
SES	Social-Ecological System
WA	Western Australian

1

Introduction

A common perspective until recently was that our problem-solving
abilities have been improving over the years. In the area of resource
and environmental management, for example, there was a great deal of
faith in our growing scientific understanding of ecosystems, our bag of
increasingly sophisticated tools and technologies, and the application
of market mechanisms to problems such as air pollution control and
fishery management through individually allocated quotas. However,
the experience over the last few decades does not support such
optimism. A gap has developed between environmental problems and
our lagging ability to solve them.

Fikret Berkes, Johan Colding and Carl Folke, 2003

1.1 Introduction and motivation

Despite some impressive progress over the past 30 years, protecting the
natural environment is still one of today's top global issues and sustainable
use is a widely accepted goal for the management of renewable resources
(Rosenberg *et al.*, 1993). The global scale of the negative impacts on the
environment from human use are now well documented (Daily, 1997; ESRC
Global Environmental Change Programme, 2000; McNeill, 2000). It is
believed that these changes are so vast, pervasive, intractable and yet so
important that they require our immediate attention (Jasanoff *et al.*, 1997;
Lubchenco, 1998). However, global problems are the product of human
actions across spatial scales, from the local through the regional and national
scales to the global scale, and across temporal scales, in which time delays
between cause and effect contribute to fluctuations and instability in the
system. Recognition of the increasing number of interacting agents, the inter-
relatedness in time and space, across hierarchies, and oscillations in variables

in the system all serve to increase the complexity of these problems as knowledge of the interacting process increases difficulties for decision-making (Funtowicz and Ravetz, 1993). Therefore, protecting the environment has been recognised as a broader and more challenging task than it once seemed (Holling *et al.*, 2002b).

In Australia human use of the environment has been changing ecosystems for at least 60 000 years and for possibly as long as 140 000 (White, 1994). However, the rate of change has increased since European settlement began about 200 years ago. Agriculture has played an important role in the development of Australia and has had both positive and negative impacts on the society and the environment. In the late 1950s Australian agricultural products accounted for more than 80% of the value of Australia's exports, contributing not only to the local, regional and national economies, but also to the country's history and culture. Since then the proportion of exports contributed by agriculture has markedly declined as the Australian economy has become increasingly diverse. Farmer terms of trade have followed a negative trend, contributing to negative social impacts in rural areas associated with declining farm numbers, such as fewer jobs, reduced services and rural disadvantage (Tonts and Black, 2002). The direct contribution of agriculture to gross domestic product is now around 3%, having remained stable throughout the last decade despite the continuous increase in total agricultural production (National Land and Water Resources Audit, 2002; Australian Bureau of Statistics, 2003).

Most Australian ecosystems have experienced some change, although the most extensive and intensive changes have occurred in temperate, Mediterranean and coastal ecosystems developed for agriculture rather than the tropical and semi-arid regions. For example, two such areas are the Western Australian (WA) agricultural region (Figure 1.1) and the Murray–Darling Basin in eastern Australia (Figure 1.2). The WA agricultural region is the focal region in this study and the Goulburn Broken Catchment (Figure 1.2), which comprises 2% of the Murray–Darling Basin, is used as comparison for resilience analysis in Chapter 6.

In Western Australia, an area that has undergone extensive change is the WA agriculture region (Figure 1.1). In this region, which covers approximately 18 million hectares (180 000 square kilometres), widespread areas of native vegetation have been cleared and replaced to a large extent with annual cropping systems. The climate is a dominant factor that dictates the predominant land use and type of cropping system. These cropping systems provide grain, wool, meat and other commodities that are part of the Australian domestic and global economies.

Fig. 1.1. Map showing the WA agricultural region and the Brockman Line. The Brockman Line was an outcome of the Royal Commissions in 1917–18 identified as what was believed to be the inland safe rainfall limit for wheat growing. *Source:* derived from Burvill (1979)

The Murray–Darling Basin is a large, very shallow drainage basin covering more than one million square kilometres with only one exit flowing out of Lake Alexandrina in South Australia (Murray–Darling Basin Ministerial Council, 2000a). Changing patterns of land use have caused impacts on groundwater throughout the catchment, some of which are felt hundreds

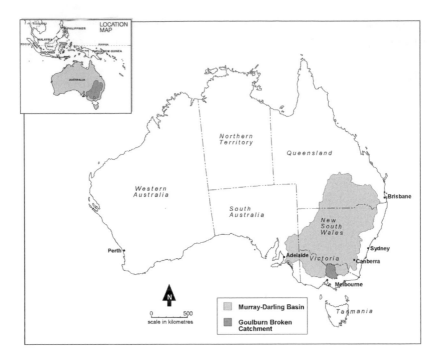

Fig. 1.2. Map showing the location of the Goulburn Broken Catchment within
the Murray–Darling Basin.

and even thousands of kilometres downstream. The Murray–Darling Basin
generates about 40% of the national income derived from agriculture and
grazing. It supports one-quarter of the nation's cattle herd, half of the sheep
flock, half of the cropland and almost three-quarters of its irrigated land.
The Murray–Darling Basin contains more than twenty major rivers as well
as important groundwater systems and is an important source of fresh water
for domestic consumption, agricultural production and industry, a supply now
being threatened. The development that made the economic productivity of the
Murray–Darling Basin possible has also caused many biophysical changes.
Broadscale clearing has reduced biodiversity and threatens the potential of
economic production in the future. Groundwater levels are now rising in many
parts of the Murray–Darling Basin causing widespread and serious salinity
problems.

Agricultural land use in Western Australia, like that in eastern Australia,
has had direct and indirect, negative and unintended effects on the quality of
land and water resources, shown by declining trends in many of the indicators
of the quality of these resources (National Land and Water Resources Audit,

2001a,b, 2002). Agriculture in south-western Western Australia produces agricultural goods worth over $4.5 billion (AUD) annually for local and export markets. Systems in which interactions occur across broad scales, from the individual farmer level to the global level through export into commodity markets, have been defined as large-scale systems (Gunderson *et al.*, 2002c), hence the WA agricultural region is considered to be a large-scale system. Clearing of native vegetation is causing saline groundwater to rise, impacting on land and water resources and rural infrastructure (Government of Western Australia, 1996a).

The WA agricultural region comprises around 18 million hectares of land of which the predominant land use is broadacre agriculture. Within this region 16 million hectares is in private ownership and is extensively cleared. Very little native vegetation remains either in the formal conservation system or on private land. Land set aside for nature conservation is restricted to a system of over 600 small nature reserves covering about 1.1 million ha (Department of Conservation and Land Management, 2005). On private land native vegetation remains as small and scattered remnants covering 1.3 million ha. Few of these remnants are fenced from sheep and cattle and most are being affected by hydrologic forms of land degradation (George *et al.*, 1996). In the whole of the south-west of Western Australia an estimated 4.3 million hectares or 16% have a high potential to developing soil salinity from shallow watertables (National Land and Water Resource Audit, 2000). Production from this salinised land has either been lost or reduced. It is estimated that the total value of this loss is in the order of $1.4 billion (AUD) (Government of Western Australia, 1996a). Of the Australian total, 70% of soil salinity is in Western Australia, 36% of Western Australia's potential water resources are saline or brackish, and few freshwater ecosystems remain unaffected, contributing to biodiversity loss. Without action it is estimated that the area that may become salt affected will rise to 33% over the next 50 to 300 years depending on the landscape characteristics (Hodgson *et al.*, 2004). The current trend towards a drier climate in the region may alter the predictions about the area that will potentially become salt affected.

The trends reported for indicators of natural resource degradation and social capacity in WA agriculture are consistent with the national trends and those of modern agricultural societies in Europe (Pretty *et al.*, 2001; National Land and Water Resources Audit, 2002; Tonts and Black, 2002), which raises the question of the long-term sustainability of modern agriculture in certain contexts (Hill, 1998). For example, farms have become fewer in number, larger in size, and in Europe farms have also been abandoned. It is anticipated that in the marginal agricultural areas of the WA agricultural region, farmland may become abandoned and research is currently investigating the potential for secondary native vegetation re-establishment to occur in these areas (Hobbs *et al.*, 2003). Interest in managing the negative unintended effects of agricultural land use throughout the last century is reported to be linked to the culture of the day, Australian society's values and government policy (Burvill, 1979; Frost and Burnside, 2001; Government of Western Australia, 2002a). Despite the implementation of policies designed to address natural resource degradation, these problems remain intractable to the current policy and decision-making methods.

In order to change to more sustainable land management practices, people require the willingness, capacity and the understanding to make the necessary decisions (Gallopin, 2002). Understanding the dynamics of the interactions of human and ecological systems poses problems for the traditional scientific paradigm and ecological theory on which current policy and management of human use of natural resources are based (Kay *et al.*, 1999; Holling, 2000). The prevalent analytic traditional scientific (normal science) paradigm and associated intellectual perspectives are extremely limited as a means to understand and inform policy (Brewer, 1986; Jasanoff, 1990) when people's history, values and worldviews are involved in solving what have become known as complex problems. Hence in natural resource management systems (which have three interrelated systems, the social, the economic and the ecological systems) researchers are increasingly calling for a new paradigm; firstly, to help understand how these systems interact, and secondly, how to manage them (Holling, 1995; Costanza *et al.*, 1997; Lubchenco, 1998; Patterson and Williams, 1998).

The critical issue confronting problems in science, whether it is environmental change and degradation, population, or social capacity, is how to accommodate the changing role of science and technology and the responsibilities of science to the confronting decisions that society has to make (Capra, 1983; Jasanoff *et al.*, 1997); particularly as normal science is unable to deal effectively with either the need to accommodate diverse perspectives and values, or the uncertainty of future system behaviour. Normal scientific methodology with its emphasis on precision, accuracy, probability and definitions of proof is difficult to apply as situations become more variable, less controllable and less predictable as complexity increases. In response to these complex problems science is developing new theories to help the cause–effect relationships. Three sets of overarching ideas have been identified as important to the future paradigm of science to address these critical issues. They come under the headings of complex causes, interdisciplinary research and the related issue of breadth of expertise of individual scientists (Jasanoff *et al.*, 1997), concepts investigated in this book.

The emerging paradigm comes under the rubric of complexity (Waldrop, 1992; Manson, 2001) and post-normal science (Funtowicz and Ravetz, 1993), focussing on new and adequate ways of dealing with and managing uncertainty. Situations in which facts are uncertain, values are in dispute, stakes are high and decisions are urgent require very different practices from normal science (Bateson, 1979; Funtowicz and Ravetz, 1992; Gibbons *et al.*, 1994; Tognetti, 1999; Robertson and Hull, 2003). Based on the earlier research of Bateson (1979), Funtowicz and Ravetz (1992) proposed the adoption of a post-normal science paradigm while emphasising that normal and post-normal science paradigms are complementary.

Post-normal science provides a means of enquiry within the social context that is concerned with the relationship between humans and their environment in a hierarchical framework of systems, because ecological systems provide the means for growth, or constraints, for social systems at different scales (Tognetti, 1999). In these situations systems approaches are replacing the reductionist methodology of traditional science. Systems approaches in principle are concerned with the structure of the elements in a system and their interactions to investigate the patterns of behaviour of that system and the interactions between systems. A key feature of the systems approach is the requirement for making the assumptions explicit; for example, it is assumed that a system exhibits emergent properties, which means that at any defined level of complexity the system's behaviour cannot be solely explained by reference to the lower levels (Clayton and Radcliffe, 1996). Other important assumptions are those of hierarchical control and communication, which are involved with regulation and feedback control.

Since the 1970s it has been suggested that a new approach to natural resource management is required to address emerging challenges (Holling, 1973). There is an expanding literature that investigates the application of the principles of a systems approach to natural resource problems within the social context (Emery, 1969; Meadows *et al.*, 1972; Vayda and McCay, 1975; Holling, 1978; De Greene, 1993; Gunderson *et al.*, 1995; Holmes and Wolman, 2001). This literature has developed the theory of resilience applied to linked social, economic and ecological systems, henceforth referred to as social-ecological systems (SES). The aim of resilience theory is to analyse the complex structural–functional and causal relationships in order to improve natural resource policy and management to create SESs which can reorganise and adapt following changes or perturbations (Walker, 2000; Gunderson and

Holling, 2002; Gunderson and Pritchard, 2002; Walker *et al.*, 2002; Costanza and Jorgensen, 2002; Berkes *et al.*, 2003).

Based on these emerging theories a key aim in this book is to develop an understanding of the dynamics of natural resource management in the WA agricultural region. We explore the central theme of how to define, formulate and conceptualise natural resource problems through the application of complex systems theory, resilience theory and the adaptive management cycle, organisational analysis and qualitative system dynamics in the WA agricultural region. The purpose is to identify the means to build resilience to deal with uncertainty and change into the WA agricultural region, a system made up of people and nature. This will be achieved through the examination and application of the above interconnected theories. The obstacles to changing land management practices lie in two fundamental areas, firstly, in decisions and choices that the individual makes and, secondly, in the collective decisions and choices that society makes. We explore the theories on which natural resource management is based and the consequences of that understanding at the collective level. The social theory of individual decisions and choice is outside the bounds of this book although social capacity is discussed briefly in Chapter 7.

We adopt an interdisciplinary systems approach within the post-normal science paradigm, using basic laws, principles, concepts and findings across ecology, economics, history, social sciences and other disciplines to address the issues. Particular attention is paid to the parallels identified among multiple disciplines in order to highlight the linkages among disciplines that enable new insights and understanding to be gained. In bringing together ideas from a variety of disciplinary areas, there seems to be a notable amount of coherence (both within and between disciplines) and mutual theoretical support of the conceptual elements within resilience theory.

1.2 Structure of this book

We draw from diverse literatures in the sciences, the philosophy of science, ecology, social science, organisational theory, organisational ecology and economics in order to make comparisons, integrate and synthesise information in these disciplines. By drawing on diverse literatures one can observe a convergence of research on complex systems. We show how theories from diverse literatures are being applied to problem situations that have similar characteristics, namely complexity and uncertainty.

We have developed a guiding framework for a strategic analysis (Figure 1.3). It provides the reader with an overview of the book chapters and

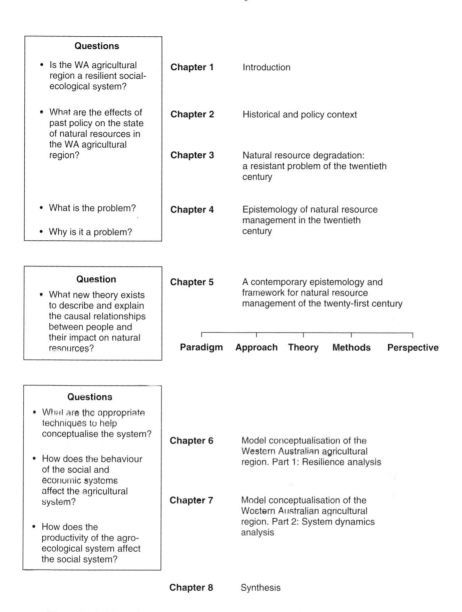

Fig. 1.3. Guiding framework showing the key questions and the progression through the book with the chapters identified.

shows the questions to be addressed. This book is composed of eight chapters. Chapter 1 provides an introduction to the issues, sets the context and poses a number of questions and sub-questions to be addressed. In this introductory chapter we establish the breadth and interdisciplinary nature of this book while focussing on the particular issues of complexity and uncertainty in problems of natural resource management in the agricultural context.

How we understand 'the problem' and go about the process of problem-solving in complex issues is introduced as an issue for science and policy, particularly when people's values are concerned and need to be taken into account in the problem-solving process. Natural resource management decisions must be taken with serious regard for whole contexts, including important cultural, social and political dimensions that have contributed to the current state of the system and condition of our natural resources. Any natural resource problem caused by human actions is a result of prior events and processes that develop and are portrayed as historical patterns over generations or even centuries. Rarely will the experience of one generation be able to unravel the origin of an event or a process fully enough to make decisions to explicitly influence future system behaviour. The way we interpret what we see is based on history, our mental models and other techniques created to help make sense of what we see. In Chapter 2, we provide the historical and policy context of the WA agricultural region and an evaluation and assessment of natural resource management. The historical account spans the 116-year history, between 1889 and 2005, of the development of agriculture in Western Australia and the evolution of policy for natural resource management relating to agriculture. In Chapter 3, we describe the key features of the negative impacts or unintended effects of the management of agricultural landscapes in Australia with a focus on the WA agricultural region. One of our central concerns is that if society is not to repeat the same problems with each successive policy as those encountered with command and control policy and with the integrated and adaptive management approaches as currently practised, then it is apparent that we will need to approach the problem-solving process in a very different manner to past measures.

It is important that we critically analyse the applicability of past measures to addressing natural resource problems not only from a methodological perspective but also from a paradigmatic perspective. The key characteristics of the current dominant paradigm and methodology of science and its relation to social action and organisational analysis are described in Chapter 4. The key characteristics of alternative frameworks are examined for organising competing values and alternative worldviews of how 'reality' may be understood. We outline the tenets of traditional or normal science philosophy and its influence on natural resource management and policy. Command and control and integrated and adaptive management are then appraised as approaches to policy implementation. This is done by comparing the epistemology and methodology of these approaches.

Following on from how we have understood natural resource management in the past, in Chapter 5, we review the systems literature relevant to the new and evolving basis for understanding natural resource problems. We develop a heuristic framework composed of the paradigm, approach, theory, perspective and methods that we adopt and subsequently apply to the WA agricultural region. The framework, based on systemic notions, is designed to explore the fundamental causal relationships in systems made up of people and nature.

In Chapters 6 and 7 we integrate the information from Chapters 2 to 5 and explore what the findings may mean for the future dynamics of the WA agricultural region. In Chapter 6, we apply resilience theory to analyse and evaluate the WA agricultural region's resilience and capacity for change and renewal. In Chapter 7, we use qualitative system dynamics, at the highly aggregated level, to develop further insights into understanding the phenomenon known as 'the counterintuitive behaviour of social systems' and 'policy resistance'. These phenomena describe the tendency for interventions to be delayed, diluted or defeated by the response of the system to the intervention itself (Meadows and Robinson, 1985; Forrester, 1995). In addition we integrate system dynamics with resilience theory to identify high leverage policy points in the system that might be used to effect fundamental and lasting change. In Chapter 8 we provide the synthesis, conclusions and potential extensions that arise from this work.

2

Historical and policy context

Rather than float in an unconnected present, environmental history can
provide some context and story as to how we got here. ... So we can
proceed, believing that environmental history can speak to
environmental policy, to some extent at least.

Stephen Dovers, 2000

2.1 Introduction

Some societies may count their history in thousands of years, for example
Aboriginal society has been a component of Australian landscapes for between
60 000 and 140 000 years (White, 1994) whereas European explorers visited
these shores around 500 years ago, with significant settlement and changes
in land use for less than 200 years in Western Australia.

Over the long period of Aboriginal occupation there have been great
changes in the geography of Australia. Some 30 000 years ago the country
was mainly a green and pleasant land in which giant animals roamed, lakes
were full, and mountains were snow covered. Conversely 15 000 years ago
the land had a larger desert core. Around 10 000 years ago the climate and
vegetation patterns reached approximately their present condition. Through
all this time sea levels were also fluctuating. At their lowest point Australia
formed one giant land mass from the bottom of Tasmania through to New
Guinea (Figure 1.2). Archaeological research has shown the kinds of adaptive responses that Aboriginal people made to these changes (Horton, 1994)
emphasising the dynamic nature of Aboriginal culture and technology.

Although it was once thought that Aboriginal Australians made little and
only simple use of the land, and had little attachment to it, we now understand more of the complex interrelationships that they have with the land

and how they have changed it. Structural and organisational, and practical and technical aspects were closely interwoven; tribal territory size, social structure and totemic beliefs were linked to methods of resource exploitation such as the use of fire, animal hunting, harvesting of plants, the construction of fish traps and the building of dams and canals. Their traditional land use systems brought about significant changes in the structure of Australian ecosystems (Stephens, 1986; Horton, 1994) prior to European settlement.

From the 1600s various Dutch explorers visited Australia's shores, for example Dirk Hartog in 1616, Volkesson in 1658 and Willem de Vlamingh in 1696. The first of the British explorers, Captain James Stirling, arrived in Western Australia in 1827 while exploring the 'great southern land'. Settlement followed rapidly when land grants were offered by the British government, which required settlers to reach Western Australia before October 1829. The small colony struggled for the first 60 years to 1889 when dramatic changes began to take place, and this is where our account of the history of the WA agricultural region begins.

This review and evaluation of natural resource management and policy starts where there is adequate history of the interaction between people and nature at a regional scale to identify patterns of change that have elicited policy responses. This chapter provides a review of the 116-year history, between 1889 and 2005, of the development of the WA agricultural region and an analysis of policy for natural resource management relating to agriculture. Although the focus is on the WA agricultural region, it is set within the state and national contexts to show the relationships among policies at the various political hierarchical levels.

Agriculture is a dominant use of the landscape in many western societies. In Australia 60% of the continent has been modified for agriculture including pastoral and cropping activities (National Land and Water Resources Audit, 2002). The WA agricultural region comprises approximately 18 million hectares or about 12% of the State of Western Australia, where rainfall is sufficient to support cropping. Agricultural development has had to overcome many difficulties to maintain productivity and this history is well documented (see for example, Rintoul (1964); Bolton (1972); Burvill (1979); Davidson (1981); Beresford *et al.* (2001)).

Agricultural land management methods, particularly those of annual cropping, continue to cause changes in ecosystems resulting in extensive degradation of land and water both on and off farm. The widespread modification of the landscape into agro-ecosystems has had major negative impacts on the soil, water, biodiversity and ecosystem services of Western Australia.

Consequently land degradation has been the subject of numerous Common-wealth and State enquiries from the first Commission of Agriculture report in 1891 (Western Australian Commission on Agriculture, 1891) and has been reviewed elsewhere (Department of Environment, Housing and Community Development, 1978; Burvill, 1979; Chisholm and Dumsday, 1987; Legislative Assembly, Western Australian Parliament, 1990; McTainsh and Boughton, 1993). In response to the early symptoms of soil erosion, Australia has devel-oped various soil conservation policies since the first statute was proclaimed in 1893.

History reveals three eras in policy development: command and control policy (CCP), integrated natural resource management policy approaches, including strategic regional approaches and the emerging market-based policy, depicting a trend from a reduction in regulation to a market-driven approach (Industry Commission, 1998; Pannell, 2000a; Department of Agriculture, Fisheries and Forestry-Australia, 2002). Much has been written as separate issues about:

1. the history of land development;
2. natural resources management relating to agriculture in Australia; and
3. increasingly about the problems of policies required to effect improvement in complex natural resource management.

However, little attention has been paid to the integration of these three factors in a dynamic analysis. The aims of this chapter are (1) to present a summary of the historical background of the development of the WA agricultural region, (2) to examine the evolution of policy from the initial specific soil conservation policies to the current multi-objective sustainable natural resource management policies; and (3) to provide the context for the application of emerging theories of the behaviour and dynamics of the WA agricultural region.

2.2 Historical periods

In the history of Western Australia, agriculture and natural resource policies were reactive in response to reports on the declining condition of soil, land or water. Of the numerous reports, Royal Commissions and enquiries into soil conservation and land management in Australia only those considered to be the most significant and influential in either changing the direction of policy or identifying the direction of change are discussed in this review and are presented in Figure 2.1. This figure shows the links between Australian Government and State policies.

A comprehensive history of the development of agriculture in Western Australia is given by Burvill (1979), agricultural development of WA valley floors by Frost and Burnside (2001), the economic history of Australian farming by Davidson (1981), the development of salinity by Beresford *et al.* (2001) and Bekle (2002), land clearing for agriculture in the period 1970 to 1990 by the Australian Greenhouse Office (2000) and an audit of land and water resources by National Land and Water Resources Audit (2001a,b,c,d,e). These publications have been used extensively in this analysis.

In the development of agriculture in Western Australia, Burvill (1979) identified six distinct temporal periods between 1829 and 1979. These are labelled as:

1. The First Sixty Years (1829–89);
2. The Move Forward (1889–1929);
3. Depression and the War (1929–45);
4. Recovery (1945–9);
5. The Rural Boom (1949–69); and
6. A Troubled Decade (1969–79).

We have added three periods to cover the period from 1979 to 2005, labelled Environmental Awareness (1980–90), The Decade of Landcare (1990–2000) and The Turn of the Century (2000–5). We have used these temporal periods as they are convenient categories for conducting this historical analysis and are used as the basis for resilience analysis in Chapter 6.

2.2.1 The First Sixty Years (1829–89) and The Move Forward (1889–1929)

For the first sixty years of the WA colony's history, pastoral activities were developed ahead of agriculture and only 28 000 hectares were developed for cropping by the 1880s. This figure rose to 5.8 million hectares by 1929, the end of the period labelled The Move Forward. After the discovery of gold in Western Australia in the 1880s and the establishment of responsible government in 1890, the WA Government saw a need to diversify the economy through the development of an agricultural industry. The WA Government was proactive in financing and establishing the necessary infrastructure to encourage farming, including land subdivision and railways. Generally the railways were constructed along the valley floors and consequently the land adjacent to the railways was cleared for agriculture first (Frost and Burnside,

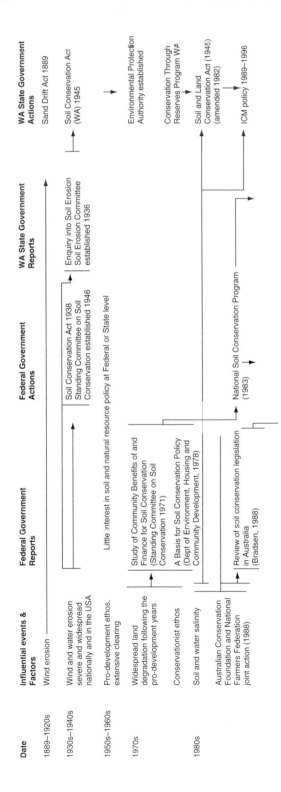

Fig. 2.1. Influential events and factors in the history and policy of natural resources relating to agriculture 1889–2005. (Continued on next page)

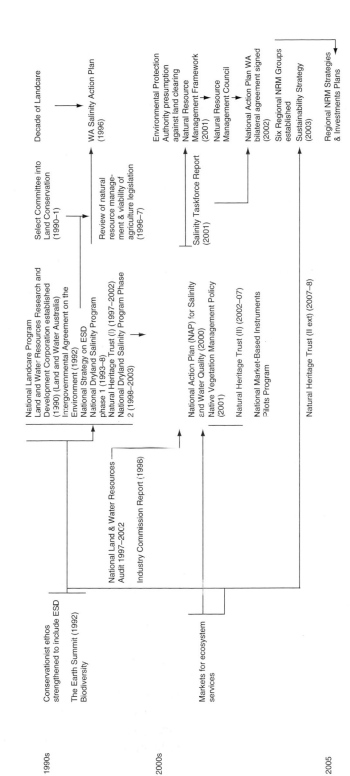

1990s

Conservationist ethos
strengthened to include ESD

The Earth Summit (1992)
Biodiversity

Decade of Landcare

Select Committee into
Land Conservation
(1990–1)

Environmental Protection
Authority presumption
against land clearing

National Landcare Program
Land and Water Resources Research and
Development Corporation established
(1990) (Land and Water Australia)
Intergovernmental Agreement on the
Environment (1992)
National Strategy on ESD
National Dryland Salinity Program
phase 1 (1993–8)
Natural Heritage Trust (I) (1997–2002)
National Dryland Salinity Program Phase
2 (1998–2003)

WA Salinity Action Plan
(1996)

Review of natural
resource manage-
ment & viability of
agriculture legislation
(1996–7)

National Land & Water Resources
Audit 1997–2002

Industry Commission Report (1998)

Natural Resource
Management Framework
(2001)

Natural Resource
Management Council

National Action Plan WA
bilateral agreement signed
(2002)

Six Regional NRM Groups
established

Sustainability Strategy
(2003)

Salinity Taskforce Report
(2001)

2000s

National Action Plan (NAP) for Salinity
and Water Quality (2000)
Native Vegetation Management Policy
(2001)

Natural Heritage Trust (II) (2002–07)

National Market-Based Instruments
Pilots Program

Markets for ecosystem
services

Regional NRM Strategies
& Investments Plans

Natural Heritage Trust (II ext) (2007–8)

2005

Fig. 2.1. (cont.)

2001). The proclamation of the Homesteads Act 1893 and the Land Act 1898 were the first statutes involved in the allocation of land for agriculture. These set out the concessions and conditions for obtaining farmland, enabled land use planning and accelerated the rates of land released for agriculture. In these early days lack of infrastructure was a major impediment to agricultural development, a situation which the Government attempted to address. Much of the available finance of the WA Government was consumed in the construction of the Eastern Railway, from Fremantle to York, and so when the potential for agriculture was recognised in the south of the State, the capital to construct the Great Southern Railway was raised in London by Sir Anthony Horden, a wealthy New South Wales businessman, by floating a private consortium, the West Australian Land Company (the Company) (Burke, 1991). The Company was granted almost three million acres of land by the Crown in exchange for building the railway that ran from Albany in the south to Beverley where it joined the Eastern Railway. However, unable to attract immigrants and unable to sell the land for development, the Company got into financial difficulty and the WA Government was forced to raise capital to buy back the land it had granted to the Company. The WA Government issued inscribed stock in London in 1896 for 1.1 million pounds sterling (Burke, 1991). Burke (1991) contended that the loans policy and debt contributed to the great hardships suffered by the early settlers.

The first WA Government report on agriculture was released in 1891 (Western Australian Commission on Agriculture, 1891). It documented the extent of cropping and identified soil capability in potential areas examined for agriculture. This report noted that there were extensive tracts of sand plain and ironstone country that were useless for farming and intersected the good soil in the areas in and around Perth as far as Williams in the south-east, and Albany in the south and New Norcia in the north (Figure 1.1). Since this first agricultural report, there has been a plethora of reports and scientific advice to Government containing similar warnings of the limited agricultural potential of many areas and the potentially detrimental effects of agricultural practices to natural resources.

Agriculture faced many problems throughout its history, two of which were vermin and drought. In the young life of the colony of Western Australia the threat of rabbits led to a Royal Commission as early as 1901, which resulted in the first statutory requirement for landowners to control vertebrate pests, the Vermin Boards Act 1909, and also in the building of the No. 1 and No. 2 Rabbit Proof Fences in an attempt to control the expansion in area of rabbits. These attempts were unsuccessful as rabbits were already west of the fence lines.

Again in 1916 a Royal Commission was appointed to review agriculture (Royal Commission on the Agricultural Industries of Western Australia,

1917) and the agricultural potential of the mallee lands in the south-east of Western Australia (Royal Commission on the Agricultural Industries of Western Australia, 1918). Following this review a map was prepared defining the area considered to be the safe rainfall limit for growing wheat. This line became known as the Brockman Line after the Surveyor-General F. S. Brockman and is shown in Figure 1.1 (Burvill, 1979). Even then agriculture extended beyond this line, causing concern for the long-term viability of agriculture in these areas. In addition, these two reports identified a number of other ecological and social factors that were considered to be problems. For example, the Royal Commission (Royal Commission on the Agricultural Industries of Western Australia, 1917) was critical of a lack of institutional and regulatory frameworks for agriculture, based on the fact that farmers failed to repay loans, and the failure of the Western Australian Government to provide adequate supervision of and support to farmers. Soil salinity was already apparent in the mallee region but was discounted as a concern in the report of 1918 (Royal Commission on the Agricultural Industries of Western Australia, 1918). However, within another 10 years soil salinity was shown again to be a problem in certain soil types.

Soldier settlement schemes in the years following the First World War (and later the Second World War) were responsible for large-scale land allocation for agriculture. Western Australia set aside 5.67 million hectares for over 5000 returned servicemen on blocks of land often too small and unproductive to support a family. Many of these were subsequently restructured by farm amalgamation. The rates of land clearing between 1890 and 2001 are shown in Figure 2.2. On average approximately 164 500 hectares a year were cleared, although the rates varied in response to a number of factors identified in the following sections.

2.2.2 Depression and the War (1929–45)

During this period a combination of social, economic and ecological factors caused many farmers to face bankruptcy and abandon their farms. Wheat prices dropped from $23 per ton to $8 per ton in the early 1930s. Simultaneously the wool price dropped, removing the opportunity for farmers to move between the production of these two commodities, which was the normal strategy for the commonly practised ley-farming method. Consequently the rate of clearing dropped by about 75% from 143 750 hectares a year before 1929 to 36 789 hectares a year between 1930 and 1945. The record low prices for commodities combined with the previous years' over-investments in

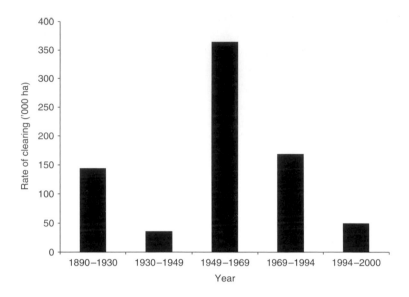

Fig. 2.2. Rates of clearing of native vegetation in the WA agricultural region between 1890 and 2000. *Sources:* Burvill (1979); Beeston *et al.* (1994)

capital expenditure and rapid expansion of the area cropped, to take advantage of the high prices, were major economic problems, but these were only part of the problem that affected farmers in the early 1930s. Environmental issues such as the dry seasons in the mid 1930s and in 1940, and pest infestations of grasshoppers, rabbits and emus compounded the poor economic returns. Following the devastating effects of the 1930s, the effects of war followed in the 1940s imposing technical difficulties. Superphosphate fertiliser was rationed and labour, motor vehicles and tractors were in short supply, causing those regions inland of the Brockman Line (Figure 1.1) to become economically marginal during years of low rainfall.

2.2.3 Recovery (1945–9) and The Rural Boom (1949–69)

Major scientific advances in countering trace metal deficiency during the short period of four years between 1945 and 1949 (Recovery) allowed farmers to expand their activities into the lighter sandy soils and increased rates of land clearing were also possible using new technology. The War Service Land Settlement Scheme which began in 1949 was responsible for new areas of Crown land being developed and 1134 farms were created and offered to returned servicemen. This scheme continued through The Rural Boom until

1968. Even in this period of recovery, the effects of climatic variability beset the WA agricultural region. Following a widespread dry period in the 1930s, there were wetter than average seasons in 1945 and 1946, resulting in floods causing extensive water erosion.

In stark contrast to the poor conditions (economic, environmental and technical) in the period labelled Depression and the War (1929–45), the 20 years of The Rural Boom were the only period of untroubled prosperity (Frost and Burnside, 2001). At this time a combination of four key factors in the economic, social, ecological and technological systems encouraged very high rates of clearing. These were cheap fuel, increasing technology in the form of heavy machinery and the use of heavy chain to clear native vegetation, high wheat and wool prices and government policy encouraging the clearing of one million acres a year.

The prices for wheat and wool escalated in the period after the war in the early 1950s. In 1950–1 wool was approximately ten times the value it was during the war and wheat reached five to eight times its value in 1930 to 1944. As a result of these four factors the rates of clearing (Figure 2.2) increased by a factor of ten, doubling the area cleared from 6.48 million hectares in 1949 to 13.77 million hectares in 1969, to capitalise on the high commodity prices.

The WA Government encouraged extensive clearing under its one million acres a year land development policy. For example it entered into an agreement with an American group, the Chase Syndicate in 1956, to develop 600 000 hectares of sand plain in the Esperance district, well beyond the Brockman Line (Figure 1.1). The initial agreement failed because of inappropriate clearing and sowing methods and it was renegotiated with the Esperance Land Development Company (Burke, 1991), which proceeded with the land clearing and agricultural development.

The Rural Boom was sustained by ecological and technical factors. Favourable rains for a ten-year period from 1958 to 1968 combined with technological advances in fertilisers operated to overcome soil deficiencies, which encouraged the expansion of agriculture into areas with proportionately more second and third class soils. Third class soils were classified as marginal and it was not expected that landholders would clear them although invariably they did (Australian Greenhouse Office, 2000). These third class soils are in contrast to the higher capability first class soils. Once the limiting factors of soil deficiencies had been overcome, climate rather than soil capability was in most instances the limiting factor in agricultural production (Passioura, 2002). Expansion into areas with poorer soils and less reliable rainfall, outside of the Brockman Line (Figure 1.1), were the cause for many difficulties in the following decades, particularly in extended periods of dry climatic conditions.

Technological innovations in other areas of the agricultural industry occurred, production of new chemicals for the control of pests and weeds, new crop varieties and farm machinery that together increased the intensity of agricultural production, largely masking increasing levels of soil degradation and its effects on production (Bradsen, 1988).

2.2.4 A Troubled Decade (1969–79)

The Rural Boom from 1949 to 1969 produced record numbers of sheep and quantities of wheat in Australia. Globally there was an oversupply of these commodities beyond the demand of world markets. In response to the oversupply the Australian Government intervened by introducing wheat quotas in 1969, which caused wheat production to drop by one-third between 1969 and 1972.

In the late 1970s new trends in agriculture emerged that were accompanied by new constraints. The general trend in agriculture was towards increased specialisation, more technically complex and more intensive agriculture. The lack of infrastructure that had constrained agriculture in the past was replaced by the limitation of unreliability of the growing season due to annual rainfall variability, particularly in the newer, less favourable areas developed after 1950 in the pro-development years. Widespread dry climatic conditions affected many areas in 1969, 1976 and 1977–8. During the 1970s and the following two decades, reports on the environmental impacts of agriculture recorded and reiterated the problems, originally raised much earlier in the twentieth century, of the increasing extent and severity of land and water degradation. The problem of development of agriculture in marginal areas, exacerbated by unreliable rainfall, was a concern raised much earlier by the Royal Commission in 1917 (Royal Commission on the Agricultural Industries of Western Australia, 1917). The biophysical constraints were becoming more obvious and salinity was becoming a publicly acknowledged concern.

From 1970 onwards increasing mechanisation displaced the ley-farming method, and replaced the role of livestock in agricultural systems with increasingly energy intensive practices. Gains in production arose from the combined effects of mechanisation, new crop varieties, fertilisers, pesticides and herbicides that masked and more than offset losses from reduced land area from soil salinity and loss of soil productivity due to soil acidity and sodicity (discussed in Chapter 3). Intensive agriculture also had its economic disadvantages, and many small farmers found it difficult to pay the high prices required for the inputs needed to ensure high productivity in order to compete in the marketplace, compared with the economies of scale of larger farm enterprises. Declining farmer terms of trade (falling prices of agricultural commodities in comparison to the price of farm inputs) compounded the problem, making it increasingly difficult for small farmers to maintain their livelihoods solely by engaging in agricultural activities (Barr, 2000). Large numbers of farmers left agriculture during A Troubled Decade (Figure 2.3). The number of agricultural establishments in Western Australia fell from approximately 23 000 to 17 800 establishments between 1968 and 1976, the trends being mirrored throughout Australia (National Land and Water Resources Audit, 2002).

Soil conservation began to re-emerge as a matter of national importance and concern, triggered by a rising conservationist ethos and increased land degradation caused by two decades of pro-development agricultural policies in the 1950s and 1960s. By the end of the 1970s it was estimated that just over half of Australia's agricultural land was degraded (Department of Environment, Housing and Community Development, 1978) causing pressure to be exerted by conservation interests to allocate areas for biodiversity protection through the conservation reserves program (Conservation Through Reserves Committee WA, 1974) (Figure 2.1).

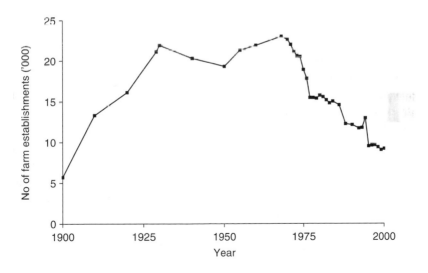

Fig. 2.3. Farm numbers in the agricultural region of Western Australia between 1900 and 2000. Sources: 1900–76, Burvill (1979); 1977–94, WA Year Books; 1995–2000, ABARE (2002). The data were compiled from three sources and some variation in absolute numbers can be detected between sources caused by changes in definitions between reports.

The publication of the report *Study of Community Benefits of, and Finance for, Soil Conservation* (Standing Committee on Soil Conservation, 1971) recorded strong attitudinal changes towards land degradation, resulting seven years later in the collaborative report on the National Soil Conservation Study (Department of Environment, Housing and Community Development, 1978) between the Australian Government and State Governments. This summary report examined three aspects of soil conservation:

1. the nature of land degradation that had arisen as a result of the interplay between the activities of humans and the natural environment;
2. relationships between land users and government; and
3. present and potential government intervention mechanisms.

It established the basis for action by state governments in soil conservation in response to the Australian Government's offer of funds, thus encouraging and ensuring the states' direct involvement in soil conservation.

2.2.5 Environmental Awareness (1980–90)

In Western Australia the climate is variable, and periods of drought and excessively wet times are the norm rather than the exception. In response to land degradation exacerbated by climatic events, enquiries into agriculture were a regular occurrence. As land degradation became more serious there was a trend towards incremental expansion of the powers of the original statutes or regulatory policy or their replacement with statutes of a similar genre (Bradsen, 1988). For example, the Soil Conservation Act 1945 was amended in 1982 to expand its scope to cover soil and water salinity and other forms of land degradation. This expansion in the scope of the Act was reflected in its new title, the Soil and Land Conservation Act 1945.

In the history of agriculture, 1988 was a landmark year in the public awareness of environmental issues for two reasons. Firstly, Bradsen (1988) completed an authoritative report on soil and land conservation and policy that had its inception in soil conservation studies of the mid 1970s. Bradsen examined (1) the philosophical basis, the origins, developments and the overall effectiveness of the legislation, and (2) the historical and contemporary role of the Australian Government along with the constitutional issues involved, and recommended some changes to increase the effectiveness of the legislation. Bradsen (1988) believed that the 'acid test' for any piece of legislation was its effectiveness. Soil conservation legislation throughout Australia was severely criticised because of its lack of effectiveness, as the evidence showed that the scale of the land degradation problem was increasing. The scale, extent and costs of natural resource degradation are described in Chapter 3.

One of the central issues in the philosophy of the legislation concerns whether the public interest in soil conservation should prevail over the private right of landholders to use, or abuse, their land. In the years prior to the 1930s, the soil conservation statutes made it clear that landholders were not free to choose whether or not to deal with these problems. However, in the reviews of legislation that took place post the 1930s (including the Soil and Land Conservation Act 1945), the ethic adopted was that contained in the contemporary US policy that made soil and land management essentially optional. For example, under the Soil and Land Conservation Act 1945 it is only required that a land user gives a Notice of Intention to clear native vegetation as opposed to an application to clear. The important distinction is that under a Notice of Intention to clear native vegetation the onus of responsibility lies with the Government to object to the proposed clearing within 90 days, otherwise the applicant may proceed. The applicant had the right to clear unless the Commissioner of Soil Conservation objected on soil and land conservation grounds.

The second important event in 1988 was the cooperative agreement between the Australian Conservation Foundation and the National Farmers Federation to combat the problems of land degradation at the national policy level. The joint action between these two groups, which previously had taken opposing positions on land conservation policy, was an unprecedented effort to try to solve an intractable, national-scale problem. As a consequence of this alliance and in collaboration with the Australian Government, the National Soil Conservation Strategy was released in 1989 aimed at mitigation of land degradation.

2.2.6 The Decade of Landcare (1990–2000)

The Decade of Landcare was a time of change in terms of recognition of the scale of natural resource problems, non-government organisation pressure on governments and government action in response to the environmental and social pressures. These changes included integrated land management (including adaptive management), strategic regional approaches and statutory policy in the form of Environmental Protection Policies (EPPs).

As the environmental movement increased its pressure, the Australian Government declared the 'Decade of Landcare' initiative in the 1989 State-ment on the Environment under the National Landcare Program, a voluntary community participatory program supported by funding through the National

Table 2.1. *The five goals and performance of the Decade of Landcare Plan*

	Goal	Goal achieved
1.	The whole community aware of the problem of land degradation and the benefits of sustainable land use.	Yes
2.	Continuing development and implementation of sustainable land use principles and practices.	Yes
3a.	All public and private land users and managers understanding the principles of sustainable land use; and	Yes
3b.	Applying them in their use and management decisions.	No
4.	All Australians working together in partnership for sustainable land use.	No
5.	Effective and appropriate economic, legislative and policy mechanisms in place to facilitate the achievement of sustainable land use.	No

Sources: derived from Cary and Webb (2000); Thompson and Heffer (2000)

Heritage Fund. A large number of initiatives were introduced under this umbrella scheme in this period, for example, Greening Australia, the Billion Trees Program, Save the Bush, Native Vegetation Remnant Program, Salt-watch and Nature Guarantee, all aimed at mitigating the various manifestations of natural resource degradation.

During the Decade of Landcare the rate of land clearing dropped from 188 000 hectares a year between 1977 and 1994 to about 42 800 hectares a year between 1994 and 2001. Increased emphasis and broadening of criteria for clearing controls to include environmental impacts assessed by environmental agencies, and the reduced availability of uncleared land on high class soils were the two main factors that reduced the rate of clearing at this time.

The Decade of Landcare Plan (the Landcare Plan) set out five goals, shown in Table 2.1, all of which are social goals that targeted changes in land manager behaviour. This led to later criticism of the Landcare Plan for the lack of appropriate indicators, monitoring and auditing for environmental outcomes (Brussard *et al.*, 1998; Kington, 2000; Pannell and Glenn, 2000). Consequently there were no means to evaluate the effectiveness of natural resource policy in terms of 'onground' improvements to account for the use of public funds (Bardsley *et al.*, 2001). It has been suggested that although these 'goals' are valuable tools, they are process orientated and they are not themselves goals but have frequently become ends in themselves for Landcare in Western Australia (Wallace, 2003). This confusion between means and ends has been attributed to the complexity of most natural resource management issues, the lack of technical solutions and the long timescales over which management must be applied. A discussion on the dichotomy of means and ends in organisation is given in Section 4.4.2. Subsequently, the National Land and Water Audit was initiated in 1997 to comprehensively assess the condition of Australia's natural resources.

Despite this failing, the Landcare Plan was an important strategy that helped to inform and change attitudes of many land managers in relation to the need to change current land management practices. The participatory nature of the Landcare Plan proved to be its strength through facilitating the sharing of information and increasing social capital (Thompson and Heffer, 2000), thus substantially achieving goals 1 and 3 of the Landcare Plan. However, changes to more sustainable land use practices have been shown to require more than a change in attitude.

To record changes in Australian farmers' attitudes to environmental issues during the Decade of Landcare, a social study was undertaken over the 10-year period (Reeve, 2001), in which farmers were interviewed twice, once in 1991 and again in 2001. The study showed that while there had not been large changes in opinions and attitudes, there were many statistically significant changes which, taken together, presented a fairly cohesive picture of attitudinal change. Overall, it appeared that rural environmental issues were better understood than they were in 1991. It was found that farmers had gained a fuller appreciation of the policies of environmental organisations but their support for these organisations had declined. For many issues, more farmers appeared to be aware of the complexities and uncertainties in these issues; however, it seemed that fewer were inclined to believe that there were simple solutions.

An attempt to develop a systems approach for Landcare was proposed in Western Australia in the early 1990s (Hartley *et al.*, 1992). However, its introduction and adoption proved difficult because of lack of understanding and support for the alternative paradigm, as experienced elsewhere (Light, 2000). Further attempts to incorporate the principles of systems approaches and alternative worldviews were promoted in the Sustainable Rural Development Kit, in which it was identified that 'economic development and material wealth cannot be separated from, and sometimes will be in conflict with, environmental quality and social cohesion.' (Dore *et al.*, 2000). The kit provided information on alternative paradigms, approaches, methodologies, tools, techniques and resources, which by 2000 were gaining increased recognition in the literature and to some extent in practice, by those who understood the new paradigm. In a review of the Landcare Plan, Toyne and Farley (2000), its original architects, identified two key features that contributed to its failure to achieve its goals. Firstly, there was a clear deficiency with the policy environment of the Landcare Plan; of major importance was its failure to properly articulate its place in the bigger picture, that is the context. Toyne and Farley claimed that the policy was not integrated as it claimed to be but that structural adjustment, market systems, macroeconomic policy and economic incentives were all disconnected from Landcare policy. Secondly, there were the agency/structure issues such as state governments' responsibilities, regional structures, service provision and incentives that undermined the process. The National Action Plan on Salinity and Water Quality Australia (the NAP) (Commonwealth of Australia, 2001), discussed in Section 2.2.7, was developed to try to overcome the latter deficiency. The Decade of Landcare produced widespread voluntary action, but was criticised because there was a lack of strategic direction and integration, the resources were spread too thinly, the 'vegemite approach' (Pannell, 2000b) and because activity was confused with effectiveness. Pannell (2001) believed that Landcare was 'an interesting experiment' and recommended that it was essential for Landcare to move forward, based on the uncertainty and risk of failure of remedial land management activities currently being undertaken to address the problem of soil salinity.

Community landcare, on its own, is unlikely to be effective for solving off-site environmental problems caused by agriculture. The potential contribution and strength of community landcare is playing only a local part in a wider catchment management environment where a fuller range of policy instruments will be required. If this greater range of structures is not present, as land degradation problems become more intractable, community landcare members will find their personal contributions to be ineffective in the overall scheme of catchment management (Cary *et al.*, 2002). This finding is consistent with new scientific research on the hydrological processes in Western Australia, which shows the insidiousness of the problem and that mitigation is often more difficult than it seems (Marsh, 2001).

Integrated natural resource management

Implementing the concept of sustainable natural resource management posed major challenges to the community and Government, particularly the need to integrate information across the ecological, economic and social systems. Integrated approaches to natural resource management policy that focussed on process, community participation and education were introduced in the 1980s and became the favoured approach in the 1990s. Because of the difficulty of understanding the construct of sustainability there were numerous attempts to produce a model of integrated natural resource management for sustainable outcomes that could be implemented. These integrating approaches have been described in the literature using a variety of terminologies in addition to integrated natural resource management. These include integrated catchment management (ICM) (Hollick and Mitchell, 1991), adaptive environmental assessment and management (Holling, 1978; Walters, 1986; Lee, 1993; Gunderson *et al.*, 2002a); an ecosystem approach (Van Dyne, 1969; Lackey, 1998; Sexton, 1998; Stein and Gelburd, 1998); landscape management (Hobbs, 1997); integrated resource management approach (Mitchell, 1979; Bellamy and Johnson, 2000); catchment management approach (Blackmore, 1995); and natural resource management from a systems approach (Grant, 1998). In Western Australia, ICM was adopted as an integrating approach through WA Government policy in 1987 and from 1990 was facilitated by the Office of Catchment Management (OCM) (Office of Catchment Management, 1995). Many catchment management groups were formed under this policy and are still in existence in 2005. In 1994 the integrating function of the OCM was essentially lost when the function was assigned to joint implementation by the four natural resource agencies, the Department of Agriculture, the Department of Conservation and Land Management, the Environmental Protection Authority and the Waterways Commission. Lack of institutional integration of functions dealing with natural resource management, identified by Toyne and Farley (2000) as one of the major impediments of the Landcare Plan, has continued to be one of the major constraints to improved natural resource management in Western Australia.

In the late 1980s and 1990s there was continuing pressure on the WA Government to respond to changing societal values on natural resource degradation, and various attempts to influence policy are catalogued here. The WA Parliament established the Select Committee on Land Conservation (Select Committee) in 1989 to enquire comprehensively into land conservation including the role of the other natural resource management agencies. The Select Committee's objective was to adopt a community-orientated approach that balanced self-help and regulation. The sentiments and the philosophy of the Final Report (Legislative Assembly, Western Australian Parliament, 1991), however, were not necessarily mirrored by WA politics and the final report and the recommendations did not gain approval from everyone concerned with agriculture (Legislative Assembly, Western Australian Parliament, 1991), resulting in many of the recommendations not being endorsed by the WA State Government.

The introduction of the concept of Ecologically Sustainable Development (ESD) in the late 1980s and its subsequent adoption into the Australian National Strategy on ESD (Commonwealth of Australia, 1992) influenced future environmental policy. The principles of ESD were the basis for the review of WA agricultural legislation undertaken by the Task Force for the Review of Natural Resource Management and Viability of Agriculture in Western Australia (Task Force), appointed in 1995. Its purpose was to recommend a framework for the Agricultural Portfolio's future involvement with natural resource management. The Task Force reviewed five statutes administered by the Department of Agriculture concerned with the management of natural resources and the viability of agriculture. These statutes were the Soil and Land Conservation Act 1945, the Agriculture Act 1988, the Rural Adjustment and Finance Corporation Act 1993, the Agricultural and Related Resources Protection Act 1976 and the Agricultural Protection Board Act 1950. The Task Force noted in its discussion paper and draft report (Task Force for the Review of NRM and Viability of Agriculture in Western Australia, 1996, 1997) the need for a comprehensive review of natural resource legislation across agencies to address the lack of integration of policy, rather than an independent review within the agricultural sector. However, the scope for such a comprehensive review was beyond the terms of reference of the Task Force.

The Task Force incorporated the principles of ESD into its recommendations and addressed other issues such as stewardship, duty of care, equity and regional decision-making. For the first time in the history of natural resource management policy in Western Australia, the issues of risk and uncertainty related to natural resource management were raised as important issues. A draft report was tabled in Parliament but the Minister for Agriculture did not adopt the recommendations. The reasons stated in the Ministerial Statement (House MLA, 1997) at the time the draft report was tabled were that actions had been taken by the Department of Agriculture as well as the whole of government that complemented the draft report and the Department of Agriculture had significantly refocussed its activities to respond to clients' needs. For example, at this time the National Dryland Salinity Program Phase I (1993–8) had increased the focus on finding solutions for soil salinity through establishing focus catchments of which the Upper Kent River Catchment was the Western Australian example. In 1996 the State Government had also published a Salinity Situation Statement and Salinity Action Plan for Western Australia (Department of Agriculture, 1996) and established research and technical groups to investigate the issues (Figure 2.1).

However, commentators criticised the decision to terminate the Task Force before the preparation of the final report and the reasons given by the Minister for Agriculture. It was proposed that the report threatened the primacy of the Department of Agriculture as the lead agency in agricultural land management (Capp, 1997a) and that it drew criticism from agricultural lobby groups and producer organisations (Parker, 2002). The former position is supported by the Ministerial Statement (House MLA, 1997) which stated that 'More than \$40 million is now directed at sustainable agriculture outcomes, ensuring that the Department of Agriculture remains the State's lead agency in agricultural land management.' On the second point there were objections from the agricultural lobby groups that feared any restrictions on their 'right to farm'. These were addressed in the Ministerial statement: 'As Minister for Primary Industry I am committed to a sustainable agricultural industry in this State's [sic] and to the fundamental principle of individual landholders remaining responsible for managing their own land.' This position was criticised for a number of reasons including the lack of resolution between private and public rights and the need for overarching legislation for sustainable land management (Australian Institute of Agricultural Science and Technology, 1997; Capp, 1997b). Nonetheless there were other advocates for integrated natural resources management and within two years, as scientific research gave more worrying prognosis of the changes in the hydrological cycle, scale of soil salinity and other degrading processes, the Deputy Premier Hendy Cowan announced that a new organisation to oversee natural resource management was back on the agenda (Capp, 1999). However, it was not until 2002 that the Natural Resource Management Council was appointed in Western Australia.

The Industry Commission (1998) comprehensively reviewed the impacts associated with agriculture in Australia within the context of ecologically sustainable land management. The Commission's recommendations were built around three pillars:

1. the requirement to devise a new approach to the regulatory regime to ensure that resource owners and managers take into account the environmental impacts of their decisions (duty of care);
2. to create or improve markets for key natural resources; and
3. to encourage conservation on private land.

They also identified that underlying and fundamental to the effectiveness of policy is the generation and dissemination of environmental knowledge to all participants, also emphasised by Bradsen (1988) and enshrined in two of the five goals of the Landcare Plan (Table 2.1).

These three reports (Legislative Assembly, Western Australian Parliament, 1991; Task Force for the Review of NRM and Viability of Agriculture in Western Australia, 1997; Industry Commission, 1998) included the need to underpin sustainable agriculture with legislation. However, many land managers see legislation as a negative mechanism. It was proposed that the negativity was based on the notion that clearer and more uniform policies might place limits on the freedom of action of individuals in the interests of promoting the common goal of sustainable regional land management (Task Force for the Review of NRM and Viability of Agriculture in Western Australia, 1997).

In December 1999, the Australian Government produced a discussion paper as the background to developing a national framework for managing natural resources in rural Australia (Commonwealth of Australia, 1999). The central theme was the development of an integrated framework based on fundamental changes in natural resource management. This fundamental change was described as: 'Moreover, degradation problems cannot be tackled in isolation. We need to look beyond individual problems – be they salinity, farm viability or loss of native species – and take account of the links within and between natural systems and the interplay of economic, social and biophysical factors that influence natural resource decision-making. An integrated approach is needed.' (Commonwealth of Australia, 1999). It is interesting to reflect that the first reference on the need to take account of the relationships between ecological, economic and social factors in the agricultural context in Australia was identified 21 years earlier in 1978 in an inquiry on soil conservation (Department of Environment, Housing and Community Development, 1978), before the publication of *Our Common Future* (World Commission on Environment and Development, 1989) and the rise of the construct of sustainability.

Statutory policy

Statutory Environmental Protection Polices (EPPs) provided for under the Environmental Protection Act 1986 (EP Act) may be used to address cumulative impacts of development, including agricultural development. These have been used to manage water quality problems in coastal catchments, for example, the Environmental Protection (Peel Inlet–Harvey Estuary) Policy (1992) and the Environmental Protection (Swan and Canning Rivers) Policy (1998). Only one (the Environmental Protection (South West Agriculture Zone Wetlands) Policy (1998)) has been invoked in the broadacre agricultural region. The purpose of this policy is to prevent the further degradation of valuable wetlands and to promote the rehabilitation of wetlands in the South West Agricultural Zone of the State. However, it was not widely adopted as it required voluntary nomination of wetlands to trigger action for their protection, and land managers in general were reluctant to invite any restrictions on their land use through the nomination of wetlands.

The Environmental Protection (South West Agriculture Zone Wetlands) Policy (1998) used the Natural Resource Zones of the South West Land

Division (Allison *et al.*, 1993) as a basis for decision-making. This zoning scheme was developed originally as a means to aid the Environmental Protection Authority in the assessment of applications of Notices of Intent to clear native vegetation on environmental grounds. The scheme was a general biophysical framework that could be adopted for other natural resource decision-making processes. A natural resource zone was defined as an area of land where people can affect changes in the landscape by their activities, for example, part of a river catchment. It was considered to be an area that people could relate to and feel a sense of belonging, particularly in terms of vegetation and landforms (Allison *et al.*, 1993). Although an EPP was proposed by the WA Conservation Council to address the cumulative impacts of land clearing at this time, there was little political support for restricting land clearing on the basis of environmental protection and natural resource degradation, and the development of an EPP for the protection of native vegetation was never progressed.

2.2.7 The Turn of the Century (2000–5)

In 2000 the Environmental Protection Authority (2000) (EPA) took a strong position with a presumption against land clearing in the south-west of Western Australia for agricultural purposes and in recent years most applications, referred to the EPA by the Commissioner of Soil Conservation, have been recommended against. The increased importance placed on environmental criteria to proposed clearing is shown by the significant changes in legislation. New legislation came into effect in July 2004 that cancelled the process of Notice of Intent to clear native vegetation handled by the Commissioner of Soil Conservation. In its place clearing of native vegetation requires an application for a Clearing Permit to the EPA, with the onus of responsibility on the applicant to supply the information on soil and nature conservation grounds, on which the application may be assessed.

Strategic regional approaches

The outcome of the 1999 Australian Government discussion paper (Commonwealth of Australia, 1999), discussed above, was the policy *Our Vital Resources: A National Action Plan for Salinity and Water Quality in Australia* (NAP) (Commonwealth of Australia, 2001). Although the NAP incorporated some of the elements recommended in the discussion document (such as the requirement for regional management plans, targets, standards, capacity building, property rights for water and the identification of market-based systems) as promising measures for water and salinity management, it fell short of the integrated framework for natural resource management conceived in the discussion document. As its name suggested it had a narrower focus on salinity and water quality. To counter criticism on the narrow scope, the NAP was identified as an initial step and left the broader issues of conservation of biological diversity for future attention, and any commitment to future action (and therefore Australian Government funding) was conditional on bilateral agreements with the States and Territories. The goal of the NAP was to motivate and enable regional communities to target action to prevent, stabilise and reverse trends in soil salinity affecting sustainability of production and the viability of infrastructure, to improve water quality and secure reliable water allocations for human uses, industry and the environment. The Australian Government established a framework for investing in natural resource management in partnership with State and Territory Governments through binding agreements, specifically Intergovernmental Agreements covering the National Action Plan for Salinity and Water Quality (NAP) and the extension of the Natural Heritage Trust (NHT2). The framework included the requirement to establish regional integrated natural resource management strategies that are jointly accredited by the Australian Government and the relevant State or Territory Government. Fifty-six regions were identified covering all of Australia and a natural resource management plan was developed for each.

The Australian Government committed $700 million to the NAP over seven years 2002–8. State and Territory Governments collectively matched this funding providing a total of $1.4 billion. Bilateral Agreements provide for the allocation of $1.4 billion over seven years through the NAP between the States and Territories, and $300 million over four years for NHT2. Western Australia's contribution of $158 million is matched by $158 million from the Australian Government and the total amount will be largely delivered through the six Western Australian natural resource management regional groups between 2005 and 2008. In addition there will be significant levels of funding to community and industry groups through the Envirofund and the National Landcare Program. The funding through these programs is additional to ongoing State funding for natural resource funding of $240 million in 2003–4 and similar amounts in ongoing years.

The WA Government signed a bilateral agreement with the Australian Government in 2002 (Government of Western Australia, 2002b) to initiate the NAP in Western Australia, coordinated and delivered by the newly formed Natural Resource Management Council through the WA State Natural Resource Policy (Government of Western Australia, 2001). The WA Government's framework took a broader approach than the NAP to assist in achieving sustainable natural resource management. This was a purposeful move towards a partnership model based on the principles of ESD. It had as its goal the conservation and sustainable management of the State's natural resources, with efficient and effective partnerships between all levels of government, industry and the community as an important tool to achieve its goals. One of the key objectives was to establish a framework for a coordinated and integrated approach by the four key agencies (Department of Agriculture, the Department of Conservation and Land Management, the Department of Environmental Protection and the Water and Rivers Commission) as required by the NAP, that is, the integrating function once performed by the OCM for 1990–4. The framework also laid out the structure of partnerships between the State Government and the six regional natural resource management groups already established in Western Australia, thus linking the three hierarchical institutional levels responsible for natural resource management, national, state and regional levels. The lack of coordinated institutional arrangements has often been identified as a major impediment to the effective implementation of natural resource management in Australia (Young and Gunningham, 1997; Mobbs and Dovers, 1999; Toyne and Farley, 2000; Dovers, 2001) and salinity in Western Australia (Kington, 2000) and, therefore, the NAP was seen as a promising step to fill the gap. The partnership model was designed to encompass regional-scale issues from a strategic management perspective in an integrated participatory approach. This relatively new process evolved from the ICM approach of the late 1980s and considerable effort was directed towards developing partnership models to deal with the challenges that arose in this approach; for example, the change from individual level to group level agricultural extension activity. The delivery of natural resource management through this program of regionalisation constitutes an attempt at an adaptive management process at the landscape scale.

The WA Government released a draft State Sustainability Strategy in September 2002 (Government of Western Australia, 2002a) and the final strategy in September 2003 (Government of Western Australia, 2003) (the Strategy) with the express purpose of comprehensively addressing sustainability through simultaneous environmental, social and economic improvement. The Strategy identified that natural resource management policies contained only some elements of sustainability focussing on the integration of the biophysical sciences and economics. The Strategy recognised the importance of improving the way in which community values may be incorporated into policy. It also addressed briefly the opportunity for increasing the sustainability of agriculture under the rubric of sustainable use of natural resources, while recognising and acknowledging the enormity of the task. The opportunities included low-input agriculture to meet future market needs, accreditation systems and mechanisms to create value for ecosystem services.

2.3 Drivers of change

There are multiple drivers of change that operate across different spatial and temporal scales (individual, regional, state, national and global) that positively and negatively influence land users in their management practices. In different eras of history certain driving forces, based on social values, can be identified that were most influential; for example, British agricultural practices and traditions, and pro-development attitudes predominated in agriculture until the 1970s (Burke, 1991). Periods of development were characterised by high levels of public or private inputs, in the form of government investment in infrastructure, land surveys, research into agricultural problems, restructuring of land lot sizes, rural adjustment and private investment through intensifying agricultural practice. Burvill (1979) concluded that the key motivation in agriculture was profit maximisation and stated: 'Farming in 1979 in Western Australia is still relatively young by world standards. It is export-orientated and profit-orientated. Although some farmers have pride in their livestock and their crop yields, the general ethic is a desire to maximise a positive balance of farm output over farm inputs, thus increasing farm income.'

In an analysis of the history of the WA agricultural region focussing on valley floors, Frost and Burnside (2001) identified three factors that were critical to the pro-development ethos:

1. government policy drove most of the development in the agricultural region, a factor also identified by Kington (2000);
2. prosperity in the 1950s and the 1960s (also described by Burvill (1979)); and
3. a culture of innovation and change (see also Burvill (1979); Barr and Cary (2000)).

More recently it was also proposed that fluctuating prices for commodities, particularly over extended periods, may be the primary driver to alter land use (National Land and Water Resources Audit, 2001c). The characteristics of commodity systems and their influence on social, environmental and economic variables are discussed in greater detail in Chapter 7.

The origins of interest in land degradation as an environmental issue, as opposed to an agricultural issue, may be traced to the changes taking place in international policy that resulted in the United Nations Conference on the Human Environment and the Stockholm Convention in 1972. The emerging conservationist ethos and widespread land degradation influenced the Australian Government to renew its interest in soil conservation (Figure 2.1). In contrast to the drivers of change that existed pre-1970, Australian Greenhouse Office (2000) identified five categories that were important in agricultural areas post-1970 for the realisation of either immediate or future returns. These were infrastructure, market forces, incentives, innovations and environmental and social influences. It was recognised that these five factors are interrelated but no attempt was made to examine the interrelationships.

Barr (2000) recognised that in general Australian farmers responded quickly to technological change when suitable social and economic conditions existed, although this was modified by individual landowners' characteristics. For example, changes to alternative commodities and the adoption of innovations were modified by characteristics such as the land user's disposition, the type of innovation and the information transfer processes (Guerin, 2000). In relation to factors that influence conservation practices, a review of landowners' perceptions to soil erosion hazard in South Australia found that some of the characteristics of the land user's disposition that correlated positively with farmer readiness to adopt soil conservation methods were: younger age, higher education, higher gross income, greater ownership of machinery, more top dressing and less guardedness to strangers (Williams, 1976), the last characteristic demonstrating less conservative characteristics. In the WA agricultural region the average age of farmers is increasing (discussed in Chapter 6) and may be a negative influence on the adoption of alternative land management practices in those land managers.

Inappropriate agricultural methods, profit maximisation and short-term gain were identified as the other driving forces in the history of agriculture in Western Australia that contributed to the degradation of the natural resources on which the industry depends, causing the Commonwealth of Australia (2002) to state, 'Degradation of natural systems occurs because our economy makes it cheaper to degrade Australia than to look after it'.

2.4 Concluding remarks

This chapter discussed the historical and policy context for natural resource management in the WA agricultural region. It was shown that a development-driven WA Government was responsible for extensive land clearing for agriculture in Western Australia in the years pre-1970, often contrary to scientific advice on the problems of soil degradation including rising watertables, waterlogging and soil salinity. However, in the 1980s and 1990s the severity and extent of soil salinity and the prognosis of future negative trends in other natural resource indicators caused a rapid proliferation and evolution of Australian and State Government policies designed to 'solve the problem'.

The current legislation aimed at addressing land degradation is a result of incremental amendments of soil conservation legislation, one building on the other as the previous version failed to cope with the problems that arose. The regulatory powers of the statutes were expanded as new forms of degradation or extent of degradation became publicly and politically obvious, in an endless search for solutions to perverse, undesirable and unintended outcomes of earlier policies. The apparently intractable nature of natural resource degradation caused by agricultural land use has also been ascribed to the views of the role and image of the agriculture industry as a 'virtuous and noble undertaking' (Botterill and Chapman, 2002), and natural resource management was often undertaken with unfounded optimism (Pannell, 2001).

A growing awareness of land degradation problems and increasing dissatisfaction with agricultural statutes and policy to manage these problems led to deregulation and the development of non-statutory policy that emerged in the 1980s to address broader environmental goals. These took two general forms: firstly, a shift towards integrated land management policy approaches delivered through regional partnerships and coordination among four State Government agencies; and secondly, a quest for new and innovative market-based instruments. Lack of institutional collaboration at all levels of government had negative effects on natural resource management, and the bilateral agreements of the NAP in the early years of the twenty-first century were promoted as the latest policy attempt at collaboration. The amendment to the EP Act that came into effect in 2004 signalled the importance given to Western Australia's native vegetation not only because of its biological diversity and uniqueness, but also because of the part it plays in ecosystem processes. The rhetoric and promises of solutions to natural resource problems through the application of the command and control policies (CCP) and integrated natural resource management policy have not come to fruition (Patterson and Williams, 1998; Bellamy and Johnson, 2000; Wallace, 2003). It is proving difficult to translate policy into practice and the delivery of integrated natural resource management over the past 20 years remains an elusive objective. Despite policy measures designed to mitigate the negative impacts of land management practices, it is considered that most broadscale agricultural systems are not sustainable using current management practices.

Land and water degradation caused by agricultural practices, implemented under a suite of complex and conflicting policies, are Australia's most serious and widespread environmental problems (Lefroy and Hobbs, 1997; CSIRO, 2000; Barr and Cary, 2000; National Land and Water Resources Audit, 2002). The current status of natural resources in the WA agricultural region is the direct result of the day-to-day management decisions made by land managers that span the history of the region. These decisions have been shaped by policies designed to achieve multiple and often conflicting goals that have changed through time. Reflecting on the WA agricultural region over the past 116 years, we can now interpret our past actions against Australia's National Land and Water Resources Audit (National Land and Water Resources Audit, 2001a,b,c,d,e, 2002), which shows natural resources to be degrading, as discussed in Chapter 3.

3

Natural resource degradation: a resistant problem of the twentieth century

I'm truly sorry man's dominion, Has broken nature's social union
Robert Burns, 1785

3.1 Introduction

The ultimate responsibility for achieving sustainable natural resource management resides with the government. It is the government's responsibility to establish the policy, legislation and administrative structures, which was discussed in Chapter 2, to enable and facilitate the community's sustainable use of natural resources. The primary responsibility for the management and use of natural resources remains a matter for the owners of the natural resources, consistent with government policy. Within any framework of policies and institutions for land management it is land managers who have the responsibility to interpret government policy in order to implement actions to meet policy objectives. Land managers have the most direct impact on the quality of natural resources through their management practices.

Within the framework of policies the traditional approach by governments to land management was command and control policy (CCP), which was largely replaced by integrated natural resource management approaches in the 1980–90s. The Landcare movement of the 1990s was responsible for information transfer on sustainable land management practices and persuading agricultural producers of the need for change (Cary *et al.*, 2002). However, the policy framework was unable to satisfactorily address long-term and large-scale natural resource problems.

Agricultural producers are keen to adopt new practices that yield greater short-term returns. In most cases these increased returns do not fully account for the long-term detrimental effects on the natural resources affected by their use (van Bueren and Pannell, 1999; Pannell *et al.*, 2001). Issues such as soil salinity bring land management in agriculture directly to the attention of the community and illustrate the complexity, size, costs and sometimes dramatic nature of land management issues. The central issues of natural resource degradation and the associated costs, as a resistant problem for policy, are examined in this chapter.

3.2 Natural resource degradation

Past warnings of actual and potential natural resource degradation went unheeded generally, as a national concern, until the National Soil Conservation Strategy was released in 1989. Since then the Landcare movement has made little progress in effecting behavioural change and ecological change, with CSIRO (2000) reporting that 'Australia's current use of natural resources is not sustainable' at the national level. It is now widely recognised by industry, government and the general community that primary producers must manage their land in a sustainable way (Commonwealth of Australia, 1999). However, practices are slow to change.

At the turn of the century the Australian Government acknowledged the severity of degradation of Australia's natural resources and initiated the Australian National Land and Water Resources Audit (the Audit) in 1997 (National Land and Water Resources Audit, 1997). The Audit was the most comprehensive assessment undertaken in Australia of the bio-physical condition and use of natural resources along with social and economic information. The aim of the Audit was to provide information as the basis for decision-making for natural resources at the national, state and local levels. The Audit was funded through the National Heritage Trust ($34 million over four years to June 2001) and collected information on the extent of degradation, as well as social and economic indicators in seven themes (Table 3.1) (National Land and Water Resources Audit, 2001a,b,c,d,e). Dryland (soil) salinity and vegetation cover, condition and use, and other degrading processes are briefly examined here.

In Western Australia human activity through the removal of extensive areas of native vegetation has altered the region's microclimate (Lyons, 2002) and the hydrological cycle, thus causing watertables to rise (McFarlane *et al.*, 1993), and contributed to the reduction in biodiversity (Burbidge, 1988). The process of land use change for agriculture has resulted in three main categories of land and water degradation within the WA agricultural region (Table 3.2).

Salinity is often cited as the major threat to agricultural production (see for example, Government of Western Australia, 1996a; Beresford *et al.*, 2001;

Table 3.1. *The seven themes of Australian National Land and Water Resources Audit*

Themes
1. Surface and groundwater management, availability, allocation, use and efficiency of use.
2. Dryland (soil) salinity.
3. Vegetation cover, condition and use.
4. Rangeland monitoring; land use change, productivity, diversity and sustainability of agricultural enterprises.
5. Capacity of, and opportunity for farmers and other natural resource managers to implement change.
6. Waterways, estuarine, catchment.
7. Landscape health.

Source: National Land and Water Resources Audit (1997)

Table 3.2. *Categories of land and water degradation*

1. The effect of native vegetation removal (waterlogging, soil salinity, native vegetation decline, loss of biodiversity, loss of ecosystem services) (Wood, 1924; Legislative Assembly, Western Australian Parliament, 1990; Young *et al.*, 1996; Murray–Darling Basin Ministerial Council, 2000a; National Land and Water Resources Audit, 2001a).
2. Soil degradation (wind erosion, water erosion, soil structure decline, soil compaction, acidity, sodicity, water repellent properties) (Legislative Assembly, Western Australian Parliament, 1990; National Land and Water Resources Audit, 2002).
3. Water degradation (degradation of creeks and rivers, siltation, salinisation and eutrophication) (Bartlett *et al.*, 1996; National Land and Water Resources Audit, 2001e; Commonwealth of Australia, 2001).

National Land and Water Resources Audit, 2001a) and to native vegetation and ecosystems. The symptoms of soil salinity are often visibly obvious, showing up as the appearance of salt scalds and a decline in tree health and death in drainage lines. The current prognosis for much of the soil salinity in the WA agricultural region is that there is no solution and that a new hydrological equilibrium will be reached, little affected by either any possible economically viable revegetation strategies (Pannell, 2000a) or technical intervention (Hodgson *et al.*, 2004). The responsiveness of groundwater systems to management is generally much less than previously assumed, particularly for off-site effects (Hodgson *et al.*, 2004). Rising watertables and soil salinity are a major threat to native vegetation in the fragmented ecosystems of the WA agricultural region, based on our current understanding of hydrological processes (Cramer and Hobbs, 2002). In addition, two other degrading processes, increasing soil acidity and sodicity, pose significant economic burdens to agricultural production (National Land and Water Resources Audit, 2002). Taken together these three degrading processes – salinity, soil acidity and sodicity – are considered to be the major contributors to the increase in the extent of unproductive land and the loss of production in Australia (National Land and Water Resources Audit, 2001a).

The changes in land use have had private impacts for land managers but also there are significant public impacts both on- and off-site on ecosystems, in the form of the loss of biodiversity, loss of ecosystem services, reduced quality of water resources and damage to public infrastructure (Bartlett *et al.*, 1996; Pannell, 2001). The south-west of Western Australia has the highest biological diversity in Australia and is one of the 25 biodiversity hotspots in the world (Keighery, 2000; Myers *et al.*, 2000; Hopper *et al.*, 2001). Broadscale clearing has reduced the amount of native vegetation to less than 10% of its original area and the remaining vegetation is highly fragmented. There is a high density of rare and geographically restricted plant species and fauna that are rare or at risk within the WA agricultural region. About 24 species of plants, 13 species of mammals, and 2 species of birds had disappeared from the region by 1980 and many of these species are now extinct (Kitchener *et al.*, 1980). Many other species have experienced significant reductions in range and abundance over the WA agricultural region (Saunders and Ingram, 1995) and at April 2003, 185 were listed as threatened and 18 as extinct in the wild (Burbidge, 2004).

3.2.1 Costs of land degradation

There are two main categories of the costs of land degradation, economic loss due to land degradation and cost to mitigate the effects, but in practice, there are few agreed data on the economic cost of agricultural practices. Pretty *et al.* (2001) reviewed the policy challenges and priorities for the costs and benefits of intensive agriculture in Europe and the USA. The costs and benefits are difficult to measure because of their diffuse nature and the lack of methods to place value on goods and services that are not traded in the marketplace, such as aesthetic values. Some of these previously non-market goods and services, for example carbon sequestration and water purification, are now part of developing programs to place a market value on them. The greatest challenge is to find ways to integrate such policy tools into effective packages that will increase the supply of desired environmental and social goods while ensuring that farmers' livelihoods remain sustainable.

The lack of agreed methods in valuation has resulted in a wide range for the estimated costs reported to control land degradation and in the estimated time for the 'problems to be solved'. The reported estimates may also reflect a political optimism about land managers' abilities to effect the required changes. The analysis of cost in this chapter is for national as well as the various individual state figures in order to get a comprehensive view of the problem, as figures are not always available for Western Australia on a state basis. The aim is to show how estimates have changed over time to demonstrate the complexity and uncertainty of making such an analysis and predictions. The estimated economic losses and costs to mitigate land degradation have risen dramatically since estimates were first made 30 years ago (Tables 3.3 and 3.4). Estimates can also vary depending on the methods used and variables included (Standing Committee on Soil Conservation, 1971; Department of Environment, Housing and Community Development, 1978; Government of Western Australia, 1996b; Virtual Consulting Group and Griffin nrm Pty Ltd, 2000).

These estimates were made with the assumptions that there was adequate information on which to make the analysis and that there were the means to control the degrading processes and environmental effects. The first report (Standing Committee on Soil Conservation, 1971) estimated that the annual Australian Government assistance that would be required between 1976 and 2000, for New South Wales alone, was $3 million annually to control degradation, a figure now considered a very low estimate. In a second report the Department of Environment, Housing and Community Development (1978) examined the previous report (Standing Committee on Soil Conservation, 1971) and concluded that it would take about 100 years to achieve control of soil degradation in the non-arid regions of Australia at a cost of $350 million. It was considered that this situation was undesirable and that the Federal and State Governments should expand their soil conservation activities in order to achieve control within the shorter time period of 30 years, probably based on political expediency rather than scientific analysis.

These figures appear low when compared with the estimate in 1996 by the WA State Government, who calculated that $30 billion would be needed over 30 years to 'fix the problem' of salinity (Government of Western Australia, 1996a). In 1996, at the inception of the WA Government's policy, *Restoring Nature's Balance, the War on Salt*, it was estimated that Western Australia was losing around $64 million a year in agricultural production because of

Table 3.3. *Estimated economic losses due to land degradation*

Date	State/National	Estimates ($billion AUD) annually	Issue
1996[a]	WA	0.064	salinity
1999[b]	National	2	soil sodicity
2000[c]	National	1.5–2	salinity, soil erosion, acidity waterlogging, loss of soil structure and water quality
2000[c]	National (yield gap)	0.187 in 2000 0.288 in 2020	salinity
2000[c]	National (yield gap)	1.6	acidity
2000[c]	National (yield gap)	1	sodicity
2000[c]	National	0.089 in 2002 0.150 in 2020	infrastructure
2000[c]	National (yield gap)	2.787	salinity, acidity and sodicity

Yield gap: the difference between the value of the yield on land assuming no soil health problems and the value of the yield on land with soil health problems
Sources:
[a] Government of Western Australia (1996a)
[b] Australian Academy of Science (1999)
[c] National Land and Water Resources Audit (2002)

Table 3.4. *Estimated annual costs and time to mitigate land degradation*

Date	State/National	Estimates ($billion AUD) annually	Time (Years)	Issue
1971[c]	NSW	0.003	24	land degradation
1978[d]	National	0.675	30	land degradation
1996[a]	WA	30	30	salinity
2000[b]	National	65	10	land degradation

[a] Government of Western Australia (1996a)
[b] National Land and Water Resources Audit (2002)
[c] Standing Committee on Soil Conservation (1971)
[d] Department of Environment, Housing and Community Development (1978)

salinity alone (Government of Western Australia, 1996a). In 1999 it was estimated that soil sodicity cost Australian agriculture as much as $2 billion each year in lost production (Australian Academy of Science, 1999). In 2000 the annual economic losses in Australia to the combined problems of salinity, soil erosion, acidity, waterlogging, loss of soil structure and water quality were estimated to be $1.5 to $2 billion annually (Virtual Consulting Group and Griffin nrm Pty Ltd, 2000; Thompson and Heffer, 2000). In terms of cost to mitigate land degradation it was estimated that a capital investment of $60 billion with an ongoing maintenance program of $0.5 billion would be needed to implement the required changes over a 10-year period, a total investment of around $65 billion (Virtual Consulting Group and Griffin nrm Pty Ltd, 2000).

The management objective for agro-ecosystems was, in earlier times, to maximise the sustainable yield for the maximum economic return. In its submission to the WA State Sustainability Strategy (Government of Western Australia, 2002a), the Department of Agriculture stated that the lack of effec- tiveness of policy was related to the community's goals and values at the time, which were in favour of the pro-development ethos with little regard for natural resource conservation (Government of Western Australia, 2002a). The consequence of changing social values has led to an increasing importance being placed on the management of agricultural landscapes for multiple objec- tives in the ecological (Hobbs, 1998) and social systems (Lee, 1993). There is increasing support for the integration of the role of social systems in natural resource degradation on the basis that conservation problems nearly always have their roots in social systems (Allen and Gould, 1986). For example, increasing importance is being placed on a range of objectives including the maintenance of biodiversity and ecosystem services (carbon sequestration, water purification and flood mitigation) and ecosystem health for human well- being as well as intrinsic value. However, the conservation ethos that emerged in the 1970s has had little effect on reversing natural resource degradation over the past 30 years.

As a major global land use, agriculture plays a leading multi-functional role in both the maintenance and loss of ecosystem services. For example, an agricultural system that depletes organic matter or erodes soil while producing food imposes costs that others must bear (a negative externality in economic language); but one that sequesters carbon in soils (a positive externality) contributes to the global good by mediating climate change, and to the private good by enhancing soil health. Similarly, a system that protects on farm beneficial biota for pest control contributes to stocks of biodiversity, while systems that eliminate biota do not. Only a few of these positive and negative external effects have been properly measured or costed (Pretty *et al.*, 2001).

The maintenance of ecosystems is crucial to providing ecosystem services that are essential to the existence of humanity, an issue extensively reviewed elsewhere (Wilson, 1988; Young *et al.*, 1996; Daily, 1997; Pretty *et al.*, 2001).

It is concluded that the extent and increasing rates of change in natural resource degradation may exceed the ability of ecosystems to adapt (Holling *et al.*, 2000; Costanza and Farber, 2002; Gunderson and Holling, 2002).

3.3 Resistant problems

Each new natural resource policy was promoted with the promise of a 'solution' to the situation that was identified as the 'problem'. Nonetheless natural resource problems persisted and in many cases intensified. A clear conclusion was that natural resource management policy failure was a systemic widespread problem in Australia (Syme *et al.*, 1994) and elsewhere (Gunderson and Holling, 2002). The reasons cited for policy failure are many and varied, and exist at a number of hierarchical levels from global to the individual land user. Equally concerning as the rates and extent of degradation is the fact that natural resource problems tend to recur following serial policy interventions designed to 'fix the problem'. Yaffee (1997) proposed that environmental policy problems recur as a result of bias in the way decisions are made. Drawing from a range of case studies, Yaffee (1997) identified five types of behavioural biases that influence individual, organisational and institutional decision-making and the problems that they generate (Table 3.5). A review of the literature identifying the causes of natural resource degradation reveals these biases in natural resource management policy in Western Australia (Section 4.7). The reasons given in the literature for natural resource degradation are as wide as the perspectives taken and the worldviews of the researchers, from a focus on the biophysical issues to economic to social issues, and from policy analysis to organisational theory.

In the Australian context one reaction to the recognition of policy failure was an increase in policy research, analysis and evaluation (Mobbs and Dovers, 1999; Bellamy and Johnson, 2000; Dovers, 2000a; Kington, 2000). Some of the main reasons cited for policy failure were methodological failure of policy (Patterson and Williams, 1998; Wallace, 2003), makeshift policy development and amnesia (Dovers, 2000a), the requirement for industry restructuring, the problems of rural sociology, and the differential rates of change in communities (Barr and Cary, 2000). For example, agriculture is made up of many small businesses, some of which are economically viable and environmentally sound, but agricultural structural adjustment and costs in assistance have contributed to unsustainable land management practices. In 1996–7, an average year climatically, 80% of the profits at full equity

Table 3.5. *The behavioural biases that generate environmental policy*
problems

Behavioural bias	Policy problem created
Short-term rationality outcompetes long-term rationality	Poor long-term direction
Competition supplants cooperation	Impasses and inferior solutions
Fragmentation of interests and values	Impasses and inferior solutions
Fragmentation of responsibilities and authorities	Slow and inconclusive decision-making, diminished accountability, and piecemeal solutions
Fragmentation of information and knowledge	Inferior solutions

Source: Yaffee (1997)

from Australian agriculture came from just 1% of farmland (National Land and Water Resources Audit, 2002). In the same year the cost of assistance to industry was over $2.2 billion AUD (Hickman and Andrews, 2003). Rural adjustment policy is a good example of incremental policy development in which lessons are not learnt along the way, highlighting one of its limitations (Botterill and Chapman, 2002). Rural adjustment policies applied without the consideration of sustainable land management policies have contributed to resistant natural resource degradation (Hickman and Andrews, 2003). Others examined more fundamental systemic reasons such as lack of understanding of the social context.

There has been a consistent use of metaphor that portrays how people think about and conceptualise their relationship with the environment and one can trace changes of thought through the changes in metaphor. The most common metaphor in Australia until the 1990s was the military metaphor that construed people's battle against an enemy. This metaphor was extant in 1996 when the 'The War on Salt' was being waged (Government of Western Australia, 1996b). Also this policy incorporated the words 'Restoring Nature's Balance', signifying that it was believed that we understood and could overcome and control nature. Within a four-year period when, from both scientific research and the evidence across the landscape, it was clear that the war was being lost, the metaphor changed to 'Living with Salt' (Murray–Darling Basin Ministerial Council, 2000b) and shortly thereafter to 'Worth their Salt' (Peeters, 2001). The latter metaphor was used for those who were contributing to 'Winning the War'.

Although the natural resource policies of the 1990s have increased the understanding by farmers of the issues in the environmental system, the complexities of the interactions of the environmental system and the social and economic systems may not be well understood. Other important factors in the domains of willingness and capacity as to how land mangers will respond to policy initiatives also require further investigation (Bekle, 2002). If metaphors are truly used in a figurative sense and not just the literary sense (refer to discussion in Section 4.4.3), it would appear we are still fighting the war and perhaps in general little has changed in how the human/nature relationship is understood. For in the general context of natural resource management it has been proposed that the failure of past policies has lead to 'a pathology of less resilient and more vulnerable ecosystems' (Holling, 2003).

Agricultural policy has been dominated by regulatory, advisory and voluntary measures to address pollution and land degradation from an agriculture perspective, for example, codes of practice, continuous improvement and extension services for technology development and transfer. These advisory and institutional measures do not guarantee outcomes with greater environmental or social benefits. The identification and analysis of social factors that contributed to land degradation are particularly important, as human intervention, through effecting land use change, will be required to mitigate the effects of past land management practices. In recent decades these social factors associated with land degradation have been identified, and include poor land management, inadequate technology, poverty, decisions of social and political structures (Chisholm and Dumsday, 1987; Sala and Conacher, 1998), and institutional structures (Cortner *et al.*, 1998). However, there remains a lack of recognition of the supremacy of social and human capital, particularly in local groups (Pretty and Howard, 2001).

The lack of efficacy of past natural resource management policy led some institutional leaders in Australia to consider the consequences of past policy and management of natural resources and posed new challenges. For example, hypothetically from the year 2025, Cullen (2000) reflected on the past 25 years of research and policy, and compared it with that of the twentieth century. In this satirical piece he concluded, 'Clearly the failures of our knowledge generation and knowledge delivery activities of the last century are obvious to us all now'. Cullen continued by challenging those responsible for the future direction of natural resource management, asking whether they will be part of the problem (business as usual) or part of the solution. Cullen (2000) and Harris (2002) proposed that both research and development were being called on to produce systems solutions. Harris (2002) described this change as a need for 'solutions that link science to innovation and global economic policy to global environmental concerns and to regional development', highlighting the hierarchical nature of the problem.

3.4 Concluding remarks

If we are to apply Bradsen's 'acid test' for policy effectiveness (Bradsen, 1988), then past policies have failed to resolve natural resource problems. The long-term degradation caused by unsustainable land management practices is of national significance. The translation of policy into practice and the delivery of integrated or holistic policy over the past 20 years remains an elusive objective. Natural resource problems have been, and continue to be, treated reactively, commonly with a reliance on technology-driven mechanisms to deal with the adverse impacts, often from the need to employ a 'quick fix' to problems that have reached or are reaching a critical level. The estimates of the costs of lost production and costs to mitigate degradation and to prevent further damage have continued to rise. It is now appreciated that some degrading processes, for example the hydrological processes and the related issue of soil salinity, are intractable. Natural resource degradation is a more challenging and costly task than it once seemed, and the ways that are being used to solve these problems are not working.

Conceptually, how we understand the world is based on a particular way of understanding – a paradigm of how we think the world works, based on assumptions, theories and models. The paradigm on which natural resource management was based in the twentieth century is examined in Chapter 4.

4

The epistemology of natural resource management of the twentieth century

> One main aspect of the evolution of human systems is that
> paradigms – sets of ideas and practices – wear out.
> *Kenyon B. De Greene, 2000*

4.1 Introduction

Over the past 116 years, natural resource policy and management in the WA agricultural region have failed to resolve some of the most pressing large-scale natural resource management problems. Despite specific policies designed to manage and control the problem it would appear that they have had little effect in changing human behaviour to adopt more sustainable land management practices. Consequently it is proposed that where problems persist in complex social systems, for example the interaction of people and nature in agriculture, it indicates areas in which our mental models consistently fail (Meadows and Robinson, 1985; Jayaratna, 1994; Senge *et al.*, 1994).

The conventional wisdom of the latter part of the twentieth century has operated as if scientific decision-making is objective, neutral and divorced from the social and political domains (Ludwig *et al.*, 2001). Normal disciplinary science was adopted as the dominant intellectual influence on environmental and natural resource management policy (Howlett and Ramesh, 1998; Lubchenco, 1998). However, a growing body of scholarship, supported by social movements for a more democratic science, has contended persuasively that in reality there can be no neat separation of technical facts and social values (Checkland, 1984; Meadows and Robinson, 1985; De Greene, 1993; Blann and Light, 2000a). What we consider to be facts depends ultimately on an accepted paradigm based on social premises. Science is a social activity and scientific knowledge is to a certain extent negotiated and moulded by people's values. Consequently contending paradigms will define 'the problem' in different ways. Each generates its own assessment of 'the problem' in terms of its own definition of what that problem is, resulting in competing and mutually exclusive descriptions and boundaries around the problem.

When one acknowledges that any problem can be conceptualised in multiple ways, and the way it is conceptualised differs depending on the perspectives and worldviews of those involved (for example, the multiple views of stakeholders), it implies the need to expand, integrate and triangulate from multiple problem-solving paradigms, approaches, theory and tools (K. Blann, personal communication July 2003). For these reasons there is a critical need for a broader and deeper debate about:

1. the paradigms that have historically shaped natural resource management and policy (historical context);
2. the paradigms that currently underpin natural resource management and policy (current context); and
3. alternative paradigms (to create plausible futures).

Our mental models help us to understand how the 'real world' works; in essence, the subject of philosophy. Philosophy is a system of theories, a construction by people, on the nature of things (epistemology) or of rules for the conduct of life (Allen, 2000).

In this chapter, we consider the epistemology that has underpinned natural resource management during the twentieth century. Following a brief examination of the characteristics of paradigms, we examine alternative frameworks for explicating how we understand and portray reality. Secondly, we identify and describe the normal science problem-solving paradigm that underpinned the philosophy and practice of command and control policy (CCP) related to natural resource management. Thirdly, we examine the literature on organisational analysis and change, to draw comparisons and identify areas of convergence in frameworks for analysis of organisational change.

Organisational analysis is important in natural resource management for at least two reasons. Firstly, natural resource problems are set within an organisational context, because forms of social organisation are used by people to solve problems (Vayda and McCay, 1975). Secondly, such an analysis helps us to understand how organisational dimensions from the individual to the group level (regional, state, national) might be involved in achieving outcomes, for example, effectiveness of a strategy, productivity of a system, sustainability or resilience of a system. Three spatial frameworks for organisational analysis (Burrell and Morgan, 1979; Quinn and Rohrbaugh, 1983; Blann and Light, 2000a) that map competing paradigms, values and worldviews are examined because of their importance in the evolution and construction of new conceptual models for understanding natural resource management problems. Of central importance to each of the models are the 'means', or the processes, as well as the 'ends', or goals. For example, the constructs of effectiveness, sustainability and resilience have been conceived as the 'ends'.

Also we examine whether, in the past, management has really adopted the prevailing scientific viewpoints. Until quite recently the arguments were that management was taking up the latest scientific understandings. A paradigm-based examination of command and control policy (CCP) and integrated natural resource management policy is made in order to understand the social reality of the two policy approaches. The analysis of the epistemology of natural resource management of the twentieth century provides the foundation for moving forward to Chapter 5 in which we analyse the new and emerging theories proposed for new ways to conceptualise and to increase our understanding of the dynamics of natural resource management.

4.2 The conflict between the perception and the reality of nature

Scientific (nomothetic) methodologies have dominated natural resource management in the twentieth century and have constrained how reality is understood and how it is investigated (Hayles, 1995). However, one of the most important developments over the last two decades has been the recognition of the limits of the philosophy of normal science (Fletcher and Davis, 2003), that is, the limitations of how reality is conceptualised and the limitations of the traditional scientific method to address certain types of problems. The limitations of the normal scientific method are particularly obvious when social issues are an integral part of the problem situation when the context is important and often complex.

The call for new paradigms in natural resource management struggles with defining a role for social science from two perspectives; firstly, from the problem of communication across the culture gap of practitioners in different disciplines including the language barrier between the sciences, and secondly, from the more comprehensive stance of social sciences being perceived as reinventing nature (Soulé, 1995). While social scientists explicitly acknowledge that our paradigms have a powerful effect on how we interpret the world around us, natural resource scientists, when confronted with alternative paradigms, sometimes fail to appreciate the degree to which their own concepts of nature are culturally and academically determined (Hull *et al.*, 2002). The paradigm is implicit rather than explicit.

We argue that greater clarity in relation to the fundamental or systemic causes as well as the direct causes of natural resource problems will be gained through a plurality of approaches that examine multiple ways of understanding and viewing these problems. We argue that a pluralistic approach, integrating diverse philosophies from normal science and social science within a post-normal science paradigm (see Section 5.5), will aid in the conception and modelling of the fundamental causes of natural resource problems.

Problems of natural resource degradation in landscapes highly modified for commodity production have their roots in social action. Therefore social action will be required to effect changes in land management practices to halt and reverse the degrading processes. The obstacles to changing land management practices lie in three areas: firstly in decisions and choices the individual makes, secondly in the organisations created to manage land, and thirdly in the collective decisions and choices that society makes based on their values. Decision-making processes are complex and struggle with issues within the domains of willingness, capacity and understanding (Gallopin, 2002), founded on changing human values and social paradigms (Doyle and Kellow, 1995).

This is not an exhaustive discussion on the philosophy of science; rather it is an examination of the alternative ways that science has informed and directed natural resource management and policy. It also provides a context from which to explore emerging philosophies, paradigms and theories being promoted in the literature to help understand potential transformations in human and natural systems (examined in Chapters 5 to 7).

4.3 Paradigms

Conceptually, the way that we understand the world (reality) is based on a particular paradigm. Kuhn (1970) popularised the term 'paradigm', which he described as sets of linked assumptions, concepts and common language about the way the world works. The notion of a paradigm contains elements that provide the means to examine problems, to understand situations and, under certain circumstances, to propose solutions. However, the use of the term paradigm has been expanded to a wide variety of interpretations and is often used loosely, even by Kuhn (1970) as well as others (Guba, 1990). Once a paradigm is chosen, the philosophy of that paradigm will dictate its assumptions and practice. These are components of the mental models of the intended problem-solver, all of which are simpler representations of the real world, constructions to help make sense of complicated and complex situations. The way in which we comprehend the world around us is an ongoing and contentious debate in the philosophy of science and is often framed in terms of dichotomies, for example, between constructivism and positivism, or holistic and reductionist. In this chapter we explore three frameworks for representing the tension between alternative ways in which reality is represented.

The analysis of alternative assumptions of how we understand reality and portray that reality was once more commonly the subject matter of the social sciences (Burrell and Morgan, 1979; Guba, 1990). It is not normally felt to be necessary for advocates of the traditional or normal scientific approach to analyse the theoretical presuppositions of paradigms because the ontology, epistemology and methodology (see Section 4.3.1) is assumed to be positivist, although this once strongly held position is changing. The literature warns of going beyond the normal scientific paradigm (Soulé, 1995). In an interdisciplinary synthesis of the 'nature of nature', radical forms of 'post-modern deconstructivism' were critically analysed and it was proposed that such a dialogue could be just as destructive as chainsaws and bulldozers in the process of nature conservation (Soulé, 1995). Soulé (1995) challenged theorists who engaged in constructivist dialogue to do so with the aim of protecting nature. Increasingly, natural resource problems are seen as having a social component requiring better understanding of social science paradigms and theory. So it is with the ethos of helping to understand the complex relationships between people and nature and to protect nature that we undertake this analysis.

4.3.1 Ontology, epistemology, human nature and methodology

Paradigms may be considered as models for understanding reality and are described using the following categories: ontology, epistemology, human nature and methodology (Burrell and Morgan, 1979) (Figure 4.1).

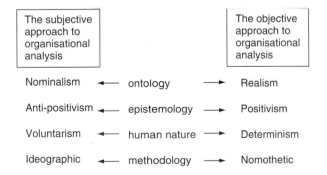

Fig. 4.1. The subjective–objective dichotomy for analysing assumptions about the nature of social science. *Source:* Burrell and Morgan (1979)

Table 4.1. *Ontology, epistemology, human nature and methodology*

Ontology	Epistemology	Human nature	Methodology
Relates to the nature of existence	Relates to the nature and understanding of knowledge, the theory of how knowledge is constructed	Relates to the relationship between human beings and their environment	Relates to the process of understanding
What is the nature of the knowable, or what is the nature of reality?	What is the nature of the relationship between the knower (the inquirer) and the known (or knowledge)?	What is the nature of the relationship between the knower and their environment?	How should the enquirer go about developing new knowledge?

In this figure the extreme dichotomies are identified between the subjective–objective approaches to organisational analysis. Methodologies are guided by ontological, epistemological positions and human nature, and will in turn guide the choices of method and recording techniques employed, and how results are interpreted and reported (Table 4.1). The recording technique or the way information is captured is a sub-component of the methodology. Any discussion of these concepts necessarily overlaps and one cannot discuss one without the other or necessarily separate them.

4.3.2 Normal science paradigm

Normal science is that body of research which has as its basis a body of accepted theory and methods, concepts, definitions and procedures and is often referred to as a paradigm. During the twentieth century, until the mid 1970s normal science was the dominant orthodoxy of inquiry for the physical and natural sciences. However, from the mid 1970s, the normal science paradigm became contested even while still widely practised (Ziman, 2000; Gauch, 2003). It was proposed that normal science was practised and justified under certain conditions according to this line of reasoning because of the lack of worthy theoretical and methodological alternatives (Norgaard, 1989).

The normal science paradigm has a number of assumptions (Table 4.2). For example, it assumes that there is certainty in decisions and that

Table 4.2. *Assumptions and characteristics of the normal science paradigm*

problem solving	one 'truth' or best answer	averages always dominate
assumed predictability	context not very relevant	reversibility
certainty	observer status objective	externalities not important
control	focusses on parts	equilibrium
determinism	analysis reduction	asymptotic stability
single linear causality	structural constancy	rationality

Sources: Bawden *et al.* (1985); Funtowicz and Ravetz (1990); Tognetti (1999); Rosenberg (2000); Holling *et al.* (2002b)

decision-makers can predict, manage and control outcomes in the environment (Bawden *et al.*, 1985; Funtowicz and Ravetz, 1990; Tognetti, 1999; Rosenberg, 2000; Holling *et al.*, 2002b). In addition the paradigm assumes a mechanistic world ruled by deductive logic and mathematics in which equilibrium-centred thinking dominates (De Greene, 1993). It is assumed that natural resources can be controlled through the process of acquiring enough information, which combined with computer power results in the ability to predict the spatial and temporal environmental outcomes with certainty (Tognetti, 1999). The normal science paradigm is a problem-solving paradigm, which in the Hawkesbury Hierarchy of approaches to problem-solving and situation improvement (Bawden *et al.*, 1985) is most suited to problems classified as basic research (Table 4.3).

The foremost methodology within the normal science paradigm was empirical experimentalism (the hypothetico-deductive method (Romesburg, 1981) also known as the scientific or nomothetic method) (Figure 4.1). This method is usually identified by four steps (Stokes, 1998):

1. observation and description of a phenomenon or problem;
2. formulation of a hypothesis to explain the phenomenon: in physics, the hypothesis often takes the form of a causal mechanism or a mathematical relationship;
3. use of the hypothesis to predict the existence of other phenomena, or to predict quantitatively the results of new observations; and
4. performance of experimental tests of the predictions by several independent experimenters and properly performed experiments.

Table 4.3. *The Hawkesbury Hierarchy of approaches to problem-solving and situation improvement*

Problem focus	Classification	Outcomes
Given this complex problem situation, how can I improve the situation?	Soft systems research	Client satisfaction
Given this system, how can I optimise its performance?	Hard systems research	Performance optimisation
Given this component, how can I improve its effectiveness?	Applied research	Problem resolution
Given the phenomenon, why is it so?	Basic research	Puzzle resolution

Source: Bawden *et al.* (1985)

This method relies on the use of standard scientific techniques and procedures for gathering, sorting, processing and applying information. It also involves a peer review process for ensuring the standard quality and validity of results. This process also serves to maintain the survival of the paradigm. These techniques are appropriate for situations with high levels of certainty and low levels of risk, characteristics not often found in social and biological systems.

4.4 Organisational analysis

The study of organisation is central to the fields of science and social science and covers most aspects of human endeavour; therefore, in order to understand problems with social aspects a knowledge of organisation theory is required (Jayaratna, 1994). Organisation theory literature is extremely wide and its boundaries are cutting across many other intellectual approaches. Accordingly the literature has produced such theoretical areas as economic organisational theory and ecological organisational theory (Ruef, 2002), because it was suggested that human organisations as much as plants and animals have an ecology (Ausubel, 1993). Ruef (2002) examined 25 years of research in organisational ecology that gave rise to a proliferation of mechanisms that sought to explain processes of decline and resurgence in mature industries. He concluded that the complex cycles of industrial evolution could be largely explained through the same theoretical principles of ecological mechanisms in population growth models without being supplemented with additional assumptions.

A number of theoretical frameworks for organisational analysis appear in the literature (for example, Runciman, 1963; Robertson, 1974; Quinn and Rohrbaugh, 1983), and for disciplined inquiry in general (Guba, 1990). Other theoretical perspectives under the rubric of postmodernism were developed in the 1980s and 1990s in the social sciences for understanding organisational perspectives (Calas and Smircich, 1999). In addition to the three organisational frameworks examined in detail below, other frameworks have contributed to the overall understanding of organisation theory, specifically the viable systems model (Beer, 1959, 1979, 1981), the conceptualisation of organisations as metaphors (Morgan, 1986), and the concept of human activity systems (Checkland, 1984; Checkland and Scholes, 1990).

In the following sections we focus on those areas of organisational analysis that are relevant to some of the fundamental problems of organisation across disciplines, that is, the dynamics of organisational change, the management of uncertainty and the tensions arising out of competing values and perspectives. Using three well-known frameworks (Burrell and Morgan, 1979; Quinn and Rohrbaugh, 1983; Blann and Light, 2000a) (Sections 4.4.1 to 4.4.3), we demonstrate that the effectiveness literature and resilience literature can be considered as analogues of one another within the general area of organisational theory. For example, much of the debate about resilience theory revolves around attempts to clarify the elusive construct of resilience and robustness (Resilience Alliance, 2002; Gunderson and Holling, 2002) and may be compared with that of organisational theory, which attempts to clarify the similarly elusive construct of effectiveness of an organisation or system (Senge *et al.*, 1994; Ackoff, 1999). This section addresses the debate that surrounds the apparent contradictions in the criteria selected for measuring the means and the ends for the effectiveness of organisations or systems. The debates on what constitutes the criteria for these constructs in the resilience and organisation literatures depends on the mental constructs and worldviews of the proponents. Hence composite definitions have become broad, compromising their success, particularly for effectiveness and sustainability. For example, in a review of the effectiveness literature, imprecise definitions and conceptual overlap were found among 30 criteria used (Quinn and Rohrbaugh, 1983).

4.4.1 The framework of Burrell and Morgan for sociological paradigms of organisation

The classic framework of Burrell and Morgan (1979) for understanding the sociological paradigms and theories of organisation has proven to be useful and has been adopted by several authors to explore the implications of social theory in systems methodologies. For example, this framework has been used effectively in the fields of soft systems methodology, information systems, systems thinking and system dynamics to examine social theories implicit in each of the methodologies (Checkland, 1984; Jackson, 1991, 1993; Waring, 1996; Lane, 1999).

Various dichotomies in social theory exist that have tended to treat theories as separate, often in opposition, and worldviews as types that cannot be reconciled, the position taken by Burrell and Morgan (1979). This notion is now rejected (Guba, 1990; Waring, 1996; Lane, 1999) and replaced with one that views the various paradigms as commensurable. The acceptance of the view that paradigms are commensurable allows the practitioner to adopt a methodology or a suite of methodologies from more than one paradigm. Without this ability one would be constrained to practise methodologies that fitted within only one worldview. However, although commensurable, there still existed the paradox that all values or worldviews were required for a system or organisation to be effective or resilient, while still being seen as in opposition.

In the social sciences Burrell and Morgan (1979) proposed that all theories of organisation can be categorised into four worldviews or sociological paradigms, Radical Humanism, Radical Structuralism, Interpretive Sociology and Functional Sociology, based on four sets of meta-theoretical assumptions. The framework of Burrell and Morgan (1979), shown in a simplified form in Figure 4.2, has proven to be a useful heuristic device for debating the underlying assumptions of social reality, while still being based on straightforward definitions.

The framework is generated by two intersecting dimensions, the philosophy of science along one axis (the subjective–objective dimension) and a theory of society along a second axis (the sociology of radical change and the sociology of regulation). These dichotomies, although useful, artificially separate the categories along a continuum, as is the case with all the static frameworks.

The subjective–objective axis

Normal scientific method in the natural sciences strongly influenced positivist sociology (Figure 4.2). Consequently, natural science methods and models were adopted as the principal means of enquiry in a range of sociological disciplines (Burrell and Morgan, 1979; Norgaard, 1989). One consequence was that the social world was treated as if it were the natural world. In the human sciences, at the subjective extreme, an individual interprets the world as having multiple realities that are compared and contrasted interpretively. At the other extreme an individual interprets the world as a single reality with

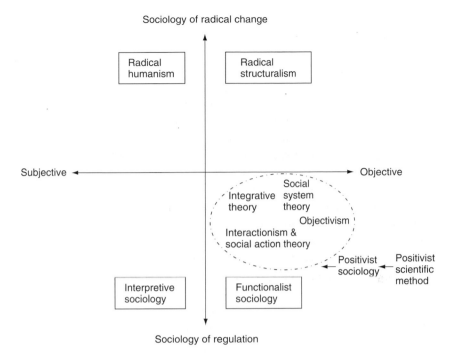

Fig. 4.2. Framework proposing four paradigms for the analysis of social theory created by the juxtaposition of two axes, subjective vs. objective and the sociology of regulation vs. radical change. The social theory of natural resource management policy lies in the Functionalist Sociology quadrant identified by the dashed line. *Source:* modified from Burrell and Morgan (1979)

certainty of knowledge that can be predicted and controlled. However, there is a continuum between the two.

The regulation–radical change axis

The regulation–radical change axis covers the range of worldviews about social order. Burrell and Morgan (1979) considered that the previous typologies of order versus conflict were problematic and replaced them with the notions of regulation and radical change. The sociology of regulation refers to the writings of theorists who are concerned to provide explanations of society that emphasise its underlying unity and cohesiveness and the regulation of human affairs. It attempts to explain why society holds together rather than splits apart. The sociology of radical change at the other extreme refers to schools of thought concerned with crisis, radical change and structural conflict that are characteristics of modern society (Burrell and Morgan, 1979; Norgaard, 1989).

4.4.2 Quinn and Rohrbaugh's competing values approach for organisational analysis

An alternative approach that brings an awareness of the conceptual biases that each person may bring to any management, problem-solving or decision-making situation is the competing values approach (CVA) (Quinn and Rohrbaugh, 1983). The CVA was developed initially from research conducted on the major indicators of effective organisations. Since then this framework has been applied successfully in situations in which effectiveness is value-dependent, for example, for examining the tension between people's values in group model building (Zagonel, 2002), public education (Barath, 1998) and organisational leadership (Quinn, 1996). These examples represent situations all of which exhibit characteristics of complexity and uncertainty and where values are either in dispute or there are multiple values expressed. We have included the CVA in this examination of three frameworks because of the parallel that can be drawn between the effectiveness of an organisation as a system and the effectiveness or resilience of any other system including social-ecological systems (discussed in Chapter 5). The framework serves a number of important functions. It organises the organisational effectiveness literature, indicates which concepts are most central to the construct of organisational effectiveness, makes clear the values in which the concepts are embedded, and demonstrates that the effectiveness literature and the general literature on organisational analysis are analogues of one another. This framework then provides a basis to examine subsequent efforts at organisational assessment in Blann and Light's framework (Blann and Light, 2000b) and from there an examination of the dynamic adaptive cycle (Holling and Gunderson, 2002) in Chapter 5.

Quinn and Rohrbaugh (1983) discovered empirically two major dimensions underlying people's conceptions of effectiveness. These value dimensions are represented in a two-dimensional spatial framework (Figure 4.3). Together the two dimensions form four quadrants, each representing a distinct set of organisational (or it could equally be system) effectiveness indicators. The first value dimension, represented on the horizontal axis, is related to organisational focus, either from an internal or an external emphasis on the wellbeing and development of people in the organisation itself. The second value dimension, represented on the vertical axis, differentiates between dichotomies in structure within an organisation, identifying either a preference

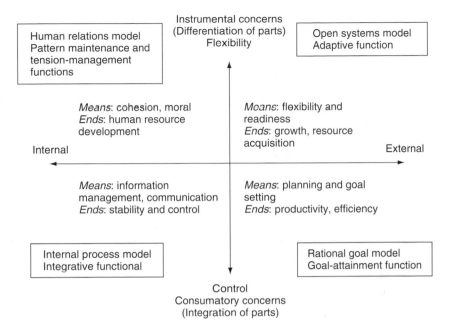

Fig. 4.3. Quinn and Rohrbaugh's effectiveness framework. *Source:* Quinn and Rohrbaugh (1983)

for stability and control, or a preference for flexibility and change. Each quadrant of the framework represents one of four major models of organisation and management theory: (1) the human relations model, (2) the open systems model, (3) the internal process model, and (4) the rational goal model. These four models represent paradoxes in trying to explain organisational effectiveness as they are represented as opposites. Each requires different means to achieve different ends. However, the paradox is that not one model of and by itself will achieve an effective outcome.

The human relations model places an emphasis on flexibility and internal focus, and stresses cohesion, morale and human resources development as criteria for effectiveness. The open systems model emphasises flexibility and external focus, and stresses readiness, growth, resource acquisition and external support. The rational goal model emphasises control and an external focus, and views planning, goal setting, productivity and efficiency as effective. The internal process model emphasizes control and an internal focus, and stresses the role of information management, communication, stability and control. These paradoxes identified in organisations are analogous with the characteristics of the adaptive cycle discussed in detail in Chapter 5. The adaptive cycle is a heuristic model that represents the dynamics in complex systems that demonstrated evolution through stages of exploitation, growth, collapse and renewal (Holling and Gunderson, 2002). The characteristics that confer resilience on a system are the juxtaposition between phases that are adaptable and flexible, and stable and controlled.

4.4.3 Blann and Light's 'root metaphor' framework

The history of metaphor revolves around the literal/figurative debate, which addresses the core questions, 'How central is metaphor to language? (is it necessary for linguistic expression?)' and 'How central is metaphor to cognition? (is it necessary for thought?)' respectively (Ross, 1993). Those that adopt the literal viewpoint propose that metaphor is a rhetorical, linguistic phenomenon rather than an issue of conceptual representation (world knowledge). Thus, metaphor affects how we talk about the world, but not how we see the world. Alternatively, those that adopt the figurative viewpoint believe that metaphors are derived from our role as 'situated agents' in the real world, and reflect sensory experience of reality. In this sense, metaphor bridges the divide between the sensory and the symbolic. More significantly, metaphor has the power to alter our conceptual systems and change the ways in which we see the world, and is at the root of our creative powers, serving an important function in the way we *understand* things that is irreducible and irreplaceable. It is now clear from a review of the recent literature on complex systems that the use of metaphor is deliberately being employed in the figurative sense (also adopted in this book) in areas of science investigating 'messy' or 'wicked' problems, when people's values can 'cloud' the issues under discussion (Funtowicz and Ravetz, 1990; Krugman, 1996; Lissack, 1997; Blann and Light, 2000a; Gunderson and Holling, 2002). Therefore, cognition of a problem is improved through the use of conceptual figurative metaphor, which is particularly important for gaining understanding of problems and processes of change in complex systems, and is further developed in Chapter 5.

It is possible to have two dichotomous conceptions about models and metaphors that represent reality. The first conception is based on the assumptions of normal science, that scientific methods can predict the future and control it. The second alternative conception embraces uncertainty and possible alternative ways of understanding in an interpretive approach and dialectical style. A dialectical style assumes that there are many different interpretations based on different scientific paradigms, experiences and value systems that cannot easily be reconciled (Guba, 1990). No one interpretation may be complete, and as a result many realities are possible. Therefore, change almost always involves both harmony and conflict, attraction and repulsion and change cannot occur in an entirely harmonious group. If this second conception is acknowledged and accepted, there can be no single truth or goal (Ravetz, 2002). Although an interpretive approach is very different from the normal science approach to knowledge acquisition, it is proving useful in helping scientists adapt to some new functions in understanding uncertainty and complexity in integrated natural resource management (Ausubel, 1993; Attwater, 2000; Gunderson *et al.*, 2002a).

In a static dichotomous framework composed of two value sets, Blann and Light (2000a) showed the types of problems best addressed by normal science (Figure 4.4). They are deterministic, short-term problems normally of small scale and with a focus on a single objective. The appropriate method tends to be composed of controlled replicated experiments that search for direct cause and effect. The two circles show that unintended consequences may result when this approach is applied to complex problems that are extracted

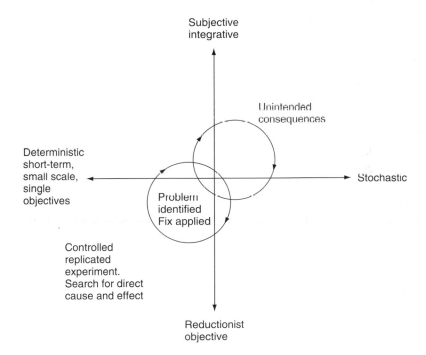

Fig. 4.4. Consequence of applying the normal science paradigm to complex problems. Normal science is located in the bottom left-hand quadrant. *Source:* redrawn from Blann and Light (2000a)

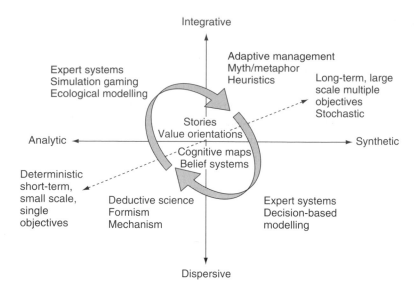

Fig. 4.5. Blann and Light's framework for analysing alternative worldviews. *Source:* redrawn from Blann and Light (2000a)

from their context and fixes are applied exogenously; that is, the method is inappropriate for the type of problem. Blann and Light (2000a) recognised the need for multiple modes of enquiry in the process of adaptive management for natural resources and consequently they developed a three-dimensional framework characterising the 'decision problem-world' that combined metaphors, knowledge, tool and methods (Figure 4.5). In this framework the 'decision problem-world' can be organised into varying matrices characterised by the type and complexity of the problem. This framework incorporates axes that recognise the need for multiple modes of enquiry and illustrates how the way one chooses to conceptualise a problem stems from one's worldview or 'root metaphors', and in turn influences the choice and selection of tools appropriate for understanding the world and/or finding answers to 'the problem' either in an ontological or epistemological sense.

In the comprehensive framework of Blann and Light (2000b) there are three dichotomies: (1) integrative:dispersive, (2) analytic:synthetic, and (3) deterministic:stochastic. The adaptive management approach to natural resource management has been placed in the top right-hand model of the framework. This position acknowledges the integrative nature of adaptive management (on the first axis), the need for synthesis (on the second axis) and the need for long-term, large-scale studies with multiple objectives (on the third axis). The arrows encircling the crossing point of all three axes and all four quadrants represent the requirement for a dialectical approach. A dialectical approach, which may involve participation with a wide range of stakeholders (and therefore potentially opposing perspectives) is used as a tool for challenging assumptions, forcing learning and building constituencies and advocacy for the process. Also, the circling arrows demonstrate that values play a part in the application of all knowledge tools and methods from all dichoto-mous viewpoints represented in the framework. By adopting multiple methods characterised in this framework, Blann and Light (2000b) suggested that it may lead to surprisingly sophisticated depictions of causal relationships and interpretations of the existence of alternative explanations. This position is consistent with the use of triangulation as a method proposed for policy analysis in situations of complexity and uncertainty (Roe, 1998).

In appraising these static spatial frameworks, one of the major objec-tions and enduring debates surrounds the apparent incommensurability of the competing paradigms in the framework of Burrell and Morgan (1979), which has arisen because the concepts are placed at opposite poles of the spatial model in a type of oxymoron or a combination of seemingly contradictory concepts. The competing values in the framework of Quinn and Rohrbaugh (1983) and the competing 'root metaphors' in the framework of Blann and Light (2000b) provide a more effective means to examine in a systematic way the various social models. Modern social theories seek to dissolve the barriers between the dichotomies such that they are not mutually exclusive, but rather are all required to produce effective organisations. The models within the frameworks are described as simultaneous complementary opposites, and all models are required to produce the 'end', whether the 'ends' are effectiveness of organisations or resilience of social-ecological systems.

4.5 Underlying paradigm of command and control policy

Command and control policy (CCP) was based on the normal science paradigm (that is, a problem-solving paradigm) with an accepted nomothetic methodology described in Section 4.3.2. CCP is the common term for the prescriptive and interventionist approach generally applied to natural resource management prior to the inception of integrated natural resource management. CCP was the model of choice and was often applied in a reactive manner in response to the negative symptoms of natural resource management on the agricultural landscape. Holling and Meffe (1996) proposed that 'The command-and-control approach, when extended uncritically to treatment of natural resources, often results in unforeseen and undesirable consequences. A frequent, perhaps universal result of command and control as applied to natural resource management is reduction of the range of natural variation of systems their structure, function, or both in an attempt to increase their predictability or stability.' The negative effect or symptoms of agricultural land management were perceived as 'the problem' in the tradition of the normal scientific problem-solving paradigm (Holling and Meffe, 1996).

4.5.1 Multidisciplinary methodology

Biophysical scientists addressed natural resource management as independent fragmented problems from disciplines such as botany, zoology and hydrology in multiple independent ways for science to inform the policy process. The translation into policy followed the 'single issue–single solution' approach often with linear thinking of the type that implies that if the problem increases then more of the same solution is required to fix the problem. This approach is consistent with the assumptions and characteristics of the normal science paradigm (Table 4.2). Consequently, the policy process was assumed to be based on a rational objective decision-making process. For example, periodic changes in the levels of land degradation were responded to by incremental amendments to legislation that expanded the scope and powers as a means to control the problem. The normal science influence was implicit in natural resource management policy, dominating and influencing the command and control and integrated approaches (Norgaard, 1989; van den Bergh *et al.*, 2000).

4.5.2 Normal science methodology in relation to command and control policy

One purpose for monitoring natural resources is to generate adequate information for policy intervention. Here, too, the normal scientific method was influential in the type and way information was collected and how it was interpreted through the identification of indicators, criteria and the choice of measurement techniques for various natural resource problems, for example, individual measurements on soil and water factors, and plants and animals. From the review of natural resource degradation in Chapter 3 it is clear that existing natural resource policies, both CCP and integrated natural resource management, have failed to manifest sustainable land management practices that will mitigate natural resource degradation. Critics of CCP sought alternative approaches to address the problem of natural resource management, resulting in a proliferation of new methodologies (Harris, 2002). However, rather than these new approaches being fundamentally different in philosophical approach they were alternative methodologies within one paradigm. Patterson and Williams (1998) proposed that this was based on the misguided assumption, from the epistemological perspective of the rational normal science paradigm, that science equals methodology. Meppem and Bourke (1999) also took this view, arguing that the conventional conceptualisation of environmental problems remained a largely disciplinary-based exercise that relied on abstracting the environmental issues from their real-world complexity. Moreover, these were based on assumptions of instrumental rationalism, that is, the sort of mathematical logic that allows us to solve technical problems such as designing and building bridges with an objective rationale. The above findings suggest that the practitioners shared an implicit philosophical and theoretical mental construct founded on normal science. Therefore, natural resource degradation was seen as a biophysical methodological problem that required the addition of new techniques to be incorporated into scientific tool kits (Sexton, 1998). Together the two dimensions form four quadrants, each representing a distinct set of organisational (or it could equally be system) effectiveness indicators. The challenge of developing sustainable natural resource management in agricultural systems is not primarily technical or scientific, for example, in developing new technologies or disease-resistant or ecologically friendly crop varieties (Meadows and Robinson, 1985; Röling and Wagemakers, 1998), nor is it an analytical challenge of developing appropriate policy and economic instruments. Agriculture is placed within the category of complex systems, where multiple perspectives, values, and ecological complexity defy reductionism (Röling and Wagemakers, 1998; Meadows and Robinson, 1985; Gunderson and Holling, 2002; Pretty *et al.*, 2001).

4.6 Underlying paradigm for integrated natural resources management

Here we examine the proposition that integrated natural resource management has a philosophy that is post-normal (see Section 5.5) but as yet either (1) lacks the methods to put into effect the prescribed philosophy, or (2) practitioners retain and adopt a generally normal scientific approach. Therefore, methodological alternatives that have evolved have the characteristics of the normal science paradigm that are not designed to solve problems in complex systems and consequently, as observed by practitioners of integrated natural resource management, it is difficult to translate the rhetoric of the philosophy into practice (Gunderson *et al.*, 1995; Bellamy and Johnson, 2000; Blann and Light, 2000a). It is hypothesised that CCP and the alternative integrated natural resource management and policy form a cluster solely within the Functionalist Sociology Paradigm as was discussed for the influence of normal science on the social sciences (Figure 4.2).

In a transition away from CCP approaches for natural resource management the primary focus was directed away from outcomes (the ends), and the process (the means) became of primary importance. All types of approaches under the umbrella of integrated natural resource management bear the same theoretical hallmark with a trend towards a more holistic systems-based approach with increasing community involvement in decision-making and an emphasis on community participation in the process and planning. This approach recognised the need to apply theories and practice from domains other than agriculture, such as ecology, policy science and social science (Bellamy and Johnson, 2000). Two of the major responses to the failure of CCP come under the rubric of integrated natural resources management; these are adaptive management (AM) and integrated catchment management (ICM). Adaptive management and ICM were often combined in a complementary fashion and included social, institutional and structural issues, acknowledging the interaction between people and their impact on natural resources.

Integrated natural resource management also encompasses more than one discipline and hence the terms inter-, multi- and transdisciplinary are often found in this literature. The most commonly used term in natural resource management has been interdisciplinary and in the context used here, it refers to the use of an integrating theory or framework to link two or more disciplines such that experts in each field work together to address a problem, or such that a single researcher draws on the different disciplines to address a problem (Mobbs and Dovers, 1999), whether at the methodological level within the normal science paradigm or across alternative paradigms.

The rhetoric of these integrated resource management approaches included the objectives of the integration of community involvement, technical knowledge, organisational structure and policy objectives. Also these changes reflected more fundamental issues in relation to policy, for example, about the role of law, the role of government, and the type of relationships between elements of government and the elements of community. These can be set out in a dichotomy of views (Clark, 1993): obligations vs. opportunities; stick vs. carrots; command vs. consensus; prescriptive vs. facilitative; and rights vs. responsibilities. Integrated natural resource management has become divorced from CCP and is largely in the arena of non-statutory policy, with an emphasis on facilitation, education and learning. However, Bellamy *et al.* (2001) made two conclusions in regard to current integrated natural resource management: firstly, there was a lack of a common theoretical base upon which such approaches were developed and implemented and secondly, no clear evaluating framework existed to guide improvements in the way that adaptive approaches actually contributed towards achieving sustainable and equitable resource use and management.

4.6.1 Adaptive management

Adaptive management has its origins in the Adaptive Environmental Assessment and Management (AEAM) process developed in the late 1970s as an alternative method to traditional principles and procedures for environmental management (Holling, 1978). Holling (1973) contended that certain ideas in ecology had led us astray and developed a new approach that had as its basis the need to understand new concepts in ecology such as uncertainty and the possibility of surprise in ecological and social systems, dynamic equilibrium, multiple stable states and the resilience of systems. Based on these different principles, theory and concepts, adaptive management was formulated as a dynamic adaptive process of policy design involving learning, a contrast to static CCP. Proponents of the adaptive management approach argued that it increased knowledge acquisition rates, enhanced information flow among policy actors, and provided opportunities for creating shared understandings (epistemology). Instead of making isolated decisions on the basis of a fixed body of knowledge, adaptive management regards each decision as part of an ongoing series in a dynamic process set within the wider context.

Cumming (2000) proposed that the context for adaptive management consisted of at least six sets of factors or drivers that influenced resource management practices. These are ecological, social, economic, technical, legal and political. Each has its own set of values, goals and criteria on which to judge the outcomes. From an institutional point of view the process is one of influencing individual or group behaviour to manage natural resources. Holling (1978) recommended that within an adaptive management context environmental dimensions should be introduced at the very beginning of the development or policy design process and should be integrated as equal partners with economic and social considerations. In support of the adaptive management approach, Lessard (1998) developed a framework for management calling on the principles described by Holling (1978). Following the early work of Holling (1978), Walters (1986) identified three phases of adaptive management:

1. preadaptive, in which there is a lack of information;
2. adaptive, in which hypotheses and alternative models are formed as information grows, and in which surprise is seen as unexceptional; and
3. certainty equivalent, in which there is no further advantage in experimentation and managers should act according to the best model of the system as if based on certainty.

Although adaptive management is commonly stated as a goal of management, it is widely misunderstood from a number of perspectives. Firstly, and of greatest importance, from the underlying philosophical basis, its epistemological foundations are post-normal, not traditional normal science. Secondly, it is not trial and error. Thirdly, it is not a planning tool and fourthly, it is not a conflict resolution process (Blann and Light, 2000a; Light, 2000; Ludwig *et al.*, 2001). In an appraisal of the progress, or lack thereof, made by adaptive management, Lee (1999) made three conclusions:

1. adaptive management had been more influential as an idea than as a practical means of gaining insight into the behaviour of social-ecological systems (SESs);
2. adaptive management should be used only after disputing parties have agreed to an agenda of questions to be answered using the adaptive approach, noting that this was not how the approach had been used; and
3. efficient, effective social learning, of the kind facilitated by adaptive management, is likely to be of strategic importance in governing ecosystems as humanity searches for a sustainable economy, with the proviso that it is practised as prescribed.

Light (2000) reported that it was relatively easy to prove the value of adaptive approaches but it was difficult to implement the approach.

Sayer and Campbell (2001) proposed that the more recent and more successful examples were those that had drawn upon and had integrated tools and concepts from different disciplines and scientific fields in comparison with earlier attempts. Light (2000) concluded that despite the efforts of a few who pioneered this work, the knowledge and understanding of resource management accumulated in comprehensive and systemic ways has not been imparted to current generations of natural resource managers who may not fully understand the alternative problem-solving paradigm. This was shown to be equally true in Western Australia, as discussed in the history and policy of the WA agricultural region in Chapter 2.

Much of the understanding of adaptive management is tacit and unexpressed, residing with those few who have done the work. The application of the method once out of their hands relies on the mental models of the practitioners who practise it. We suggest that the adaptive management approach has become a stepwise instrumental application of the approach in those cases in which it has been least effective. The approach has become applied as a 'tool' in the sense that it was applied in an inappropriate 'recipe-style stepwise' manner because of the failure to examine the assumptions and philosophy of the approach (Bateson, 1979; Patterson and Williams, 1998). If practised without an understanding of the underlying philosophy it will not allow the old models and beliefs to be challenged. It is also proposed that it may not be feasible to implement adaptive management without simultaneously attending to the institutional, organisational and political arenas in which management must be conducted (Blann and Light, 2000a). An early Western Australian example of the adaptive management process was in the context for decision support for natural resource planning in the Blackwood River Basin (Ewing and Argent, 2000).

4.6.2 Integrated catchment management

Integrated catchment management (ICM) is described as being composed of a philosophy, a process and an outcome or product (Mitchell, 1991; Syme *et al.*, 1994). Mitchell (1990) recognised three levels of increasing integration using the management of water as an example. Firstly, it could imply the systematic consideration of the various dimensions of water quantity and quality (for example, surface and groundwater) composing an ecosystem formed by a number of interdependent components. While considered to be systematic, conceptually this is akin to a reductionist closed system approach. Secondly, it could imply that while water is itself a system, it is also a component of a wider system that includes land and the wider environment. The important point is that changes in one system will have consequences in the others. The third and even broader interpretation is with reference to the interrelationships between water and the broader environment as an ecosystem, and the social system including economic development. This third interpretation requires not only the integration of methodology but also an examination of the possible range of paradigms that facilitate understanding of the interactions among the ecological, social and economic sciences.

One typology of problem-solving was constructed by Bawden *et al.* (1985) and is shown in the Hawkesbury Hierarchy in Table 4.3. The trend in this typology is from taking the phenomenon as a given in an ontological sense to understanding the complex problem situation in an epistemological sense. The distinction between these extremes of the typology is based on the construction and definition of the problem. For example, in the ontological sense the problem is taken as a given without other possible interpretations, whereas in an epistemological sense there may be multiple ways of understanding 'the problem' based on the alternative worldviews of those involved. The mental construct and adopted paradigm of the problem solvers are important factors that serve to define the context of 'the problem' and determine what information is collected and the methods of examination.

4.7 Policy evaluation

4.7.1 Command and control policy

Top down command and control policy (CCP) approaches in natural resource management failed to resolve the problems in natural resources in many different national contexts (Holling and Meffe, 1996; Bardsley *et al.*, 2001; Clausen and McAllister, 2001; Lal *et al.*, 2001). In the 1970s when many of these landmark policies were established, issues were considered to be largely local, reversible and direct, whereas today impacts are changing rapidly, are considered to be irreversible, and geographically are at a global scale (Daily, 2000). Although objectives were set, they were without context and often in the absence of a regional planning and process framework. Across the whole of Australia this deficiency is now being addressed through a national policy aimed at developing regional natural resource management strategies and plans. However, these are not part of the statutory planning framework perhaps because land use planning and land management planning are considered to be two different processes.

These early policies were criticised on the basis that they neglected the intrinsic cycles of natural and social systems, were inefficient or even worse than doing nothing, and were based on static rather than dynamic models (Holling and Meffe, 1996). Furthermore, CCP approaches have also been described as ineffectual or unsatisfactory, often achieving undesired management outcomes (Lal *et al.*, 2001). Mullner *et al.* (2001) more disparagingly described similar policies in the USA as 'autocratic natural-science-based management of renewable resources' institutionalised in the early twentieth century following the principle of management based on science with administrative decisions by professional agency employees. Consider, for example, the conclusion about failure in forestry planning in the USA in which the technical and systematic processes that were designed to reach the 'right' answer were inadequate (Patterson and Williams, 1998).

Bardsley *et al.* (2001) proposed that natural resource policy was based on political expediency and identified four characteristics of natural resource policy that contributed to its failure.

1. Environmental policy treated each segment of the environment separately as individual concerns. Each separate policy was judged on its merits within a particular context. Unless the chain of contextual factors is identified and the decision-making rules changed, there will be little change in actions and outcomes (Edwards and Steins, 1999). Change will require a divergence from normal science methodology and the adoption of an alternative philosophy and methodology that identifies the contextual factors.
2. Policy has not taken account of how incentives change behaviour.
3. Policy formulation and implementation have not been dealt with together.
4. There has been little or no monitoring and auditing of environmental outcomes resulting in lack of accountability of public money.

In general, natural resource issues were a secondary consideration to the primary productive purpose of a region and consequently the former were dealt with in a reactive manner rather than a proactive preventative manner (Clausen and McAllister, 2001). For example, on private land in the WA agricultural region the primary objective was agriculture, and issues of natural resource management, other than for productivity, were add-ons when and if agricultural profit permitted.

Following the Rural Boom, concern over the alleged failure of public policy led to a resurgence of policy analysis studies in the 1980s. Under the general heading of policy research, there are many ways in which an examination of the problem of policy failure might be approached. Accordingly, the intent can vary greatly, depending on the aim, the methods and the affiliation of the researcher (Hogwood and Gunn, 1992). Mobbs and Dovers (1999) made a broad distinction between descriptive and analytical policy research, consistent with the categories of Hogwood and Gunn (1992) who distinguished between policy studies and policy analysis respectively, although these typologies are by no means definitive or exhaustive. Mobbs and Dovers (1999) also identified some common methodological approaches that might be applied to natural resource management: for example, political science approaches; psychological/sociological approaches; policy/program evaluation; public choice approaches; legal policy research; institutional analysis; policy cycle analysis; and decision process approaches. There is no agreed approach to applied policy analysis and policy evaluation has been criticised as too often coming from a single disciplinary perspective (Syme and Sadler, 1994).

In public policy there are two overarching schools of thought. The dominant of these is the positivist, rational and empirical school in which there are five commonly used methods: surveys, experimentation, interview, use of data and the use of case studies. Post-positivist or subjective research methods include history, naturalistic inquiry, and stories. Post-positivists such as Sabatier and Jenkins-Smith (1993) and Fox (1990) argued that the analysis of policy implementation had become too complex for the rational positivist approach and suggested that a more intuitive or participatory approach of the post-positivist or subjective school was required.

Whether or not specific actors have been attributed with a role in the policy, the nature of policy implementation studies depends on the fundamental epistemological or ontological premises of the researcher (Howlett and Ramesh, 1998). In a review of policy change, Howlett and Ramesh (1998) proposed that most early positivist policy analysis studies argued that actors and their behaviour made very little difference to policy outcomes. These studies would occupy a position within the functionalist paradigm in the Burrell and Morgan framework shown in Figure 4.2. In contrast the more recent post-positivist approaches to the study of policy making focus on the way in which the language of politics 'constructs' public policy. In particular, the language of politics is predisposed with interpretations of what the policy 'problem' is, in an ontological sense.

Recent policy analysis models have made greater attempts to integrate the broader suite of important factors that link policy to performance or effectiveness. To achieve better integration the models were designed to take a macro-level perspective focussing on the tractability of 'the problem' with reference to the social and political context rather than becoming immersed in the detail (Sabatier and Mazmanian, 1980). The changes between the macro- and the micro-level analysis frameworks highlighted the perennial problem of the tension between theory and practice in policy studies. Lester and Goggin (1998) argued for the need for reform in policy implementation studies, suggesting that fundamental changes were required that moved the orientation away from the reductionist positivist tradition of normal science towards a 'post-positivist epistemology'.

Dissatisfaction with the outcomes of implementation research led to the development of the Advocacy Coalition Framework, evolved from an earlier implementation analysis framework (Sabatier and Mazmanian, 1980). The new approach emphasised the need for new conceptual approaches that included policy dynamics and learning over time within a systems framework (Sabatier and Jenkins-Smith, 1993). The approach focussed on the establishment and maintenance of competing 'coalitions' of interest groups, government institutions/agencies, and key individuals, each attempting to realise their preferred policy options in a subsystem of political pressure, strategy, and information sharing called the 'policy subsystem'. Sabatier and Jenkins-Smith (1993) proposed that values underpin the guiding instruments or strategies that influence decision making and provide the causal theory upon which policy positions are constructed. Shared values can be used to map the relationship between various organisations within the subsystem. This latter policy analysis method is appropriate for the evaluation of the integrated and adaptive management approaches that have dynamic characteristics, involve coalitions of groups at the local, regional, state and national levels, and involve knowledge acquisition, since the Advocacy Coalition Framework predicts that policy core beliefs hold coalitions together. Coalition survival during policy implementation, especially in the face of unanticipated complexity and uncertainty, requires learning and the ability to adapt to changing policy conditions. This approach is also consistent with the theoretical changes taking place in natural resource management described in Chapter 6.

We suggest that the epistemology of CCP of natural resource management of the twentieth century was based on the normal science paradigm (positivist orientation) and is concerned with the direct cause and effect level of understanding within the concept of single-loop learning in which information feedback is interpreted by existing mental models and assumptions. In single-loop learning, feedback operates in the context of existing decision rules, strategies, culture and institutions, which in turn are derived from our mental models. In contrast double-loop learning is concerned with feedback from the 'real world' in which it can stimulate changes in mental models. Such learning involves new goals and new decision rules, not just new decisions (Sterman, 2000) (Figure 4.6).

In the United Kingdom some of the key lessons of the Economic and Social Research Council's (ESRC) Global Environmental Change Programme (ESRC Global Environmental Change Programme, 2000) are:

1. that all policy domains need to incorporate environmental and social aspirations and hence involve human values;
2. decisions have to deal with conflicting opinions about environmental problems;
3. the risks environmental problems pose to different groups in society; and
4. the need to build trust and engage citizens in solutions.

Although the programme originally focussed on global issues, it increasingly turned its attention to the implementation of sustainable development and in doing so research investigated smaller-scale measures and processes – at

(a)   (b)

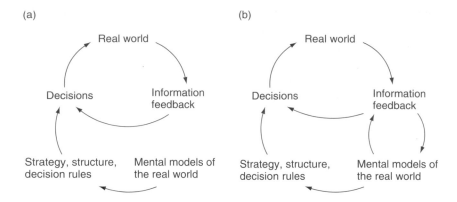

Fig. 4.6. Single- and double-loop learning. Single-loop learning (a) occurs when information feedback is interpreted by existing mental models. The learning feedback operates in the context of existing decision rules, strategies, culture and institutions, which in turn are derived from our mental models. In contrast, double-loop learning (b) is concerned with feedback from the real world in which it can stimulate changes in mental models. Such learning involves new goals and new decision rules, not just new decisions. *Source:* Sterman (2000)

local, national and regional levels – which contribute to the achievement of sustainability at the global scale.

In addition to policy failure as a cause for natural resource degradation there is now an extensive literature proposing that natural resource management problems stem from the interdependencies of natural, political and social systems, and technology, often being described as 'messy' or 'wicked problems' (Mason and Mitroff, 1981; Bellamy *et al.*, 1999; Bellamy and Johnson, 2000), and will require very different ways in which to conceptualise and understand them (discussed in Chapter 5).

4.7.2 Integrated natural resource management

Although the rhetoric of integrated and adaptive approaches to natural resource management is embracing general theoretical developments in systems theory, ecology and the participative and adaptive management philosophies (Gunderson *et al.*, 1995; Patterson and Williams, 1998; Bellamy *et al.*, 2001), there are few methodologies to evaluate policy implementation based on the same foundations. Bellamy *et al.* (2001) believed this limitation contributed to the failure of policy initiatives to address sustainable and equitable resource use. Bellamy *et al.* (2001) identified a lack of evaluating frameworks to help guide continuous program development in the way natural resource management initiatives contribute to ongoing improvements in resource use, sustainability and social wellbeing of communities concerned. Bellamy *et al.* (2001) reviewed previous evaluation techniques and found conventional economic methodologies to be inadequate to meet the multiple objectives of natural resources management. In addition, two specific models of policy implementation evaluation, the Mazmanian–Sabatier model (Sabatier and Mazmanian, 1980) and the Planning, Research, Implementation, Monitoring and Evaluation Framework (PRIME) (Syme *et al.*, 1994) for the development, implementation and evaluation of whole catchment management plans, were criticised for deficiencies in addressing instrumental assumptions (that is, causal theory in terms of the model) and deficiencies in problem context or formulation and structures, respectively. The more recent Advocacy Coalition Framework of Sabatier and Jenkins-Smith (1993) may have been a more appropriate framework to use to evaluate these approaches but was not included in Bellamy's research.

In order to fill the gap of lack of comprehensive evaluating frameworks for policy implementation, Bellamy *et al.* (2001) devised an integrated systems-based framework for the evaluation of natural resource management policy initiatives with three objectives to provide:

1. a basis for an integrated evaluation of the different perspectives (for example, social, economic, environmental, institutional and technical) on the performance of the natural resource management initiative;
2. a framework for guiding implementation; and
3. a rigorous basis for synthesising findings.

We suggest that a fourth objective might be realised in the construction of an evaluation framework. It may also act as a tool to help understand 'the problem' in the epistemological sense.

The framework of Bellamy *et al.* (2001) comprises the identification of seven components:

1. the context, which is composed of environmental, economic, social, institutional and technological factors;
2. the issue characterisation;
3. the object or intent;
4. instrumental assumptions;
5. process of implementation;
6. products; and
7. outcomes in an iterative process that includes review.

It marks a major shift towards incorporating the theory of systems into natural resource management. It does so by emphasising the importance of the context or 'problem situation' and by providing for two important steps in the process, the implementation stage and a rigorous basis for synthesising the findings. However, this framework omitted one important component. Although Bellamy *et al.* (2001) identified in the text a range of factors that reflect the worldviews or mental constructs of the evaluation team (for example, the values, priorities, experiences and organisational culture) which will influence the formulation of the problem and the analytical models used, it was not incorporated explicitly as a step in the framework. Consequently this framework suppresses the importance of mental constructs to the process and the potential impacts that this may have on the outcomes of the evaluation. Because of this the mental constructs including assumptions of the researcher are not made explicit. Hull *et al.* (2002) showed empirically that assumptions about nature were embedded in people's preferences for environmental policy and management and constrained people's vision of what environmental conditions could and should exist, thereby constraining the future that could be negotiated, further emphasising the need for the practitioner's assumptions to be made explicit.

In this book a general systemic framework for understanding problem-solving (Jayaratna, 1994) is used and described in Section 5.2. There are three contexts in which any method is used and their identification is important in understanding how they are used and whether or not they are effective (Jayaratna, 1994). The three contexts are creation, selection/interpretation and action. The constructed method reflects the mental constructs of the creators, whereas the people who select the method to solve their perceived problem may try to interpret the method through their own mental constructs. Those who ultimately have to use the method may apply it according to their mental constructs; consequently the context in which the method users interpret the method may change its nature, form, structure and content, and therefore its effectiveness (Jayaratna, 1994). A fuller examination is given in Chapter 6.

4.8 Concluding remarks

In this chapter we have examined a number of the theoretical factors that underpinned policy and natural resource management, emphasising the importance of paradigms and conceptual metaphors. CCP and integrated natural resource management policy are components of a policy mix which has been inadequate as the driver of behavioural change in agriculture towards sustainable land management outcomes. Not only were the policies based on disciplinary science, but also the policy-makers and managers were products of the same system, trained mostly in narrowly focussed disciplinary research, which shaped their mental constructs. Although integrated approaches had an alternative epistemology to that of CCP, this was not adopted and the approaches were practised with the epistemology of normal science. That is to say, those who selected and used the method may have interpreted the method through their own mental constructs. Therefore, the policy models, whether they were CCP or one of the integrated methodological alternatives, were shown to be practised within the normal scientific paradigm. Out of this paradigm came such axioms as the integrity and stability of nature and the view that people were outside the system in an objective approach. Consequently changes in natural resource management policy from CCP to integrated approaches operated only at the level of tools, techniques and methods and were not marked by a paradigm shift. However, the ecology of the 1990s and 2000s has replaced these notions with concepts of resilience, non-linearity and multiple-stable states, and the dynamics of systems of linked people and nature (Wallington *et al.*, 2001). Science, society and nature are interlinked into a whole system, and a new epistemology, theory and praxis are required to meet the challenges of producing resilient sustainable systems.

From the review of natural resource degradation in Chapter 3, it is clear that existing natural resource policies have failed to manifest sustainable land management practices that will mitigate natural resource degradation. The current integrated resource management policies, which support adaptive management, are the latest attempt to address the issues of natural resource degradation. The audit of natural resource management since 1997 (National Land and Water Resources Audit, 1997) has shown no improvement in natural resources despite the amount of public funding directed at these issues.

It has been suggested that the failure of science to resolve certain problems may be due to uncertainty about whether the appropriate questions are being asked, and whether problems are addressed with appropriate theoretical and methodological tools and within an appropriate paradigm (Wynne, 1974). It is time to rethink the questions when decisions result in persistent problems. Science, society and nature are interlinked, and a new epistemology, theory and praxis are required to meet the challenges with a greater emphasis on the way that we understand, define and formulate the problem. In Chapter 5, we review the literature for the emerging theories of understanding the dynamics of natural resource management in complex systems and construct a framework from which to examine the dynamics of the WA agricultural region.

5

A contemporary epistemology and framework for natural resource management of the twenty-first century

> Separations of disciplines and politics are artefacts of the human mind,
> not characteristics of the real world.
>
> *Donella Meadows and Jennifer Robinson, 1985*

5.1 Introduction

In Chapter 4, we examined the epistemology of natural resource management of the twentieth century and we made the case that natural resource management was based on the normal science paradigm and that there was a need to change towards a pluralistic and holistic approach. At the time when many natural resource policies were established, issues were considered to be largely local, reversible and direct, whereas today impacts are changing rapidly, are considered to be irreversible, and geographically and economically interactions occur at a global scale (Daily, 2000; Lambin *et al.*, 2001). Conceptual development has not kept pace with the speed of changes that alter and control the processes in large-scale systems (Gunderson and Pritchard, 2002). Poor conceptual development of these systems has hindered our understanding of their dynamic behaviour and weakened our ability to respond to increasingly uncertain behaviour, with neither appropriate policy nor management.

The way we perceive problems and how we go about problem solving and decision making depends on human interpretation of information (Meadows and Robinson, 1985). Information from the past and present is required to make decisions and to take action, and that requires knowledge of the future and the consequences of those decisions. Models, that is, any set of generalisations or assumptions about reality, are the means that humans use to help in problem solving, prediction and decision making. Models take many forms although the most common are mental models, which make up part

83

of a person's mental construct (discussed in Section 5.2.2). They can also take the form of conceptual models, physical analogue models, mathematical models or visual models. Key features common to the development of any model include: simplifying assumptions must be made; boundary conditions or initial conditions must be identified; and the range of applicability of the model should be understood. We present a general framework that serves as a way of understanding the area of problem solving involving the 'problem situation', the intended problem solver and the problem-solving process that leads into an examination of an alternative epistemology for understanding natural resource problems.

We examine the general systems literature to provide a critical review of the evolution of a paradigm proposed as a potential alternative for understanding and investigating natural resource management issues and problems as they are coming to be understood in the twenty-first century. The central issue is that we need to develop novel conceptual models that incorporate notions of complexity, uncertainty and resilience. From this review we construct a framework that we hope makes a substantial contribution to an improved understanding of natural resource problems and the nature of decision making. This is composed of a paradigm, an overarching approach; four bodies of theory; two methods that may be applied to make a strategic analysis; and a perspective that links the socio-economic and ecological systems in a combined complex system – the social-ecological system (SES). Complex social systems for the purposes of this approach are those societies that come under the commonly understood definition of 'developed', have undergone industrialisation, have created multiple institutions and have interactions across temporal and spatial scales (Meadows and Robinson, 1985). In addition this chapter serves several functions; firstly, to articulate the epistemological underpinnings for the framework; secondly, to identify and describe the key concepts of the framework; and thirdly, to define the terminology used in the forthcoming chapters. Terms are also defined in the Glossary. The framework is then applied to the case study of the WA agricultural region in Chapters 6 and 7.

5.2 A framework for understanding problem-solving processes

Problems are defined here as a mismatch between the perceived 'current state' of a situation and the perceived 'desired state' for that situation (Jayaratna, 1994). The context in which problems are solved may be viewed from a narrow disciplinary context through to an interdisciplinary or transdisciplinary context, and consequently the questions raised about the elements of the situation to be taken into consideration can vary accordingly. Since the 1970s in natural resource research and environmental management there has been a trend towards increased emphasis on a wider context that includes social-environmental interaction. In order to take account of these changes it is necessary to view the problem-solving process in a different way and to examine the implications that arise from this new approach. A generic framework that can be used to understand the area of problem solving and to evaluate the appropriateness of particular methods is the Normative Information Model-based Analysis and Design (NIMSAD) framework (Jayaratna, 1994). This framework uses nomenclature conventions consistent with soft systems methodology (Checkland, 1984) and includes a particular way of thinking about and describing the world. The real world is taken to consist of both the 'thinking world' and the 'action world' of the intended problem solver. The 'thinking world' is the methodology user's conceptualisation about the intended actions and the 'action world' is the situation in which methodologies are used for bringing about transformations.

The framework consists of the evaluation of three elements, namely the 'problem situation' (the methodological context), the intended problem solver (the methodological user), the problem-solving process (methodology) (Figure 5.1) (Jayaratna, 1994).

The framework has three aims:

1. to serve as a way of understanding the area of problem solving, in general;
2. to help evaluate methodologies, their structure, steps, form and nature; and
3. to help to draw conclusions.

It is a systemic framework because the process of problem formulation uses the epistemological notion of 'systems'. The problem formulation phase activities involve the critical examination of the rationale for the 'current' and 'desired' states, formulation of problem statements and hence the identification of relevant notional system(s) which if put into effect in the action world will result in transformation of the system. In soft systems there are three conceptual worlds: 'the real world', 'the thinking world' and 'the action world'.

It is important to discriminate between the use of the term 'systems analysis' and 'systemic analysis'. The notion of breaking down to understand (for example, separating something into its constituent parts) originates from the normal scientific method. Because the method is to break things down into

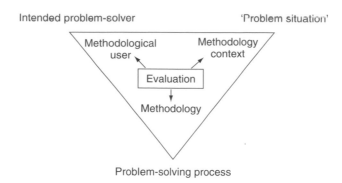

Problem-solving process

Elements	Phases	Stages
1. The 'problem situation'		
2. The problem solver		
3. The problem-solving process	1. Problem formulation	1. Understanding the 'situation of concern'
		2. Performing the diagnosis (where are we now?)
		3. Defining the prognosis outline (where do we want to be and why?)
		4. Defining problems
		5. Deriving notional systems
	2. Solution design	6. Performing conceptual/logical design
		7. Performing physical design
	3. Design implementation	8. Implementing the design

Fig. 5.1. The essential elements of the systemic evaluation framework. *Source:* redrawn from Jayaratna (1994)

parts the term 'system' is largely ignored; rather the focus is on the scientific meaning of the term 'analysis'. The properties that are unique to the level of the 'whole' are defined as its emergent properties. Thus systems analysis as it is currently defined could be left to mean the study of an existing system in the ontological sense, while systemic analysis could be considered as a process of

Table 5.1. *Systemic analysis vs. systemic design*

Criteria	Systemic analysis	Systemic design
Role	Problem formulation using systems notions	Solution design using systems notions
Function	To identify relevant notional system(s) to the desired state	To identify relevant elements of the notional system(s)
Primary concern	To define the context relevance of systems	To define the relevance content of systems
Addresses questions	What? and Why?	How? and Whom?
Measures of performance	Contribution of notional system's performance to the desired state	Contribution of the integrated elements to the notional system's performance
Primary skills required	Critical thinking	Creative thinking

Source: Jayaratna (1994)

critical enquiry into situations with the use of the notion of 'systems'. Because of this confused understanding of the activity of problem formulation, this stage of evaluation has remained outside the domain of many methodologies of normal science.

Systemic analysis is essentially the process of deriving notional systems and understanding their relevance to the situation in which 'problems' are perceived. Systemic design is the process of deriving models (using the notion of 'systems') that are expected to bring about the behaviour of the notional systems (see Table 5.1).

5.2.1 Element 1: problem situation (methodological context)

This section discusses the first of the elements of the framework, namely the 'problem situation'. It is generally recognised that natural resources have at least three broad factors that influence the characterisation or formulation of the problem. These three factors are the social, economic and environmental dimensions. These, however, may be expanded and at least seven sets of factors or drivers have been recognised: ecological, social, economic, technical, legal, institutional and political (Cumming, 2000; Bellamy *et al.*, 2001). Each has its own set of values, goals and criteria on which to judge the outcomes.

5.2.2 Element 2: intended problem solver (methodological user)

This section focuses on the role of the intended problem solver. In normal science this component of the framework would not be considered as important because the assumptions in normal science are that the problem is external to the problem solver and that the right answer may be achieved by any problem solver. However, numerous factors are influenced by the intended problem solver either implicitly or explicitly. They may be selected on gut feelings, hunches and assumptions, or at other times the selection is prompted by the explicit concepts, models and methodologies that are employed (Jayaratna, 1994). In a systems approach to natural resource management, Bellamy *et al.* (2001) identified this point, as discussed above, but did not incorporate it explicitly in the framework. Thus however powerful, useful and effective a methodology may be, the success of effective and efficient methodology depends, among other things, on the personal characteristics or the mental construct of the intended problem solver (Jayaratna, 1994). The mental construct is illustrated in Figure 5.2.

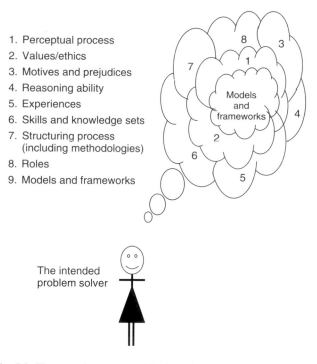

1. Perceptual process
2. Values/ethics
3. Motives and prejudices
4. Reasoning ability
5. Experiences
6. Skills and knowledge sets
7. Structuring process (including methodologies)
8. Roles
9. Models and frameworks

The intended problem solver

Fig. 5.2. The mental construct of the intended problem solver. *Source:* Jayaratna (1994)

The mental construct is composed of nine elements: the perceptual process, values/ethics, motives and prejudices, reasoning ability, experiences, skills and knowledge sets, structuring process (including methodologies), roles and models and frameworks.

5.2.3 Element 3: the problem-solving process (methodology)

If a methodology is to be considered as a way of problem solving, it needs to show that it can help to perform three phases, which are problem formulation, solution design and design implementation. These three phases have been expanded to form eight detailed stages, which are applicable to any problem-solving process (Figure 5.1).

In summary, in any problem-solving context there are three essential elements, namely, the problem situation, the problem solver, and the problem-solving process on which the evaluation is based to assess the performance on any methodology. I propose that applying this framework, within the post-normal science paradigm, will provide a new understanding and conceptualisation of natural resource management problems. These three elements are interrelated and essentially provide the underlying assumptions about how things are and also a commitment to how they will be in the future. There is also an emotional investment in these underlying assumptions because they define one's world and oneself, they define one's paradigm (Meadows, 1991). Proposing that there are alternative ways of defining a problem will challenge how many people think about natural resources and how we currently manage them. We require these new methods to help us to think differently about 'messy' problems in natural resource management, to have the opportunity for their improvement.

5.3 Messy problems in natural resource management

Applying normal scientific method to natural resource problems has met with frustration for practitioners and policy makers. Because of the difficulty of dealing with these problems and the inability of current analytical methods to propose solutions to them, these problems have been labelled as 'messy', 'wicked' and 'ill-structured' (Wynne, 1974; Waldrop, 1992; Bellamy and Johnson, 2000). Bellamy and Johnson suggested that because of these 'wicked' problems there was a trend away from the traditional rational planning approach, to an adaptive learning approach in the Australian agricultural environment. The term 'wicked' problems was originally applied to group decision support systems in planning (Rittel and Webber, 1973) and then received further development when it was linked with complexity theory (Karacapilidis, 2000). Application of the term followed in natural resource management when the inherent characteristics of natural resource problems were perceived to be consistent with those of 'wicked' problems in other disciplines (Bellamy and Johnson, 2000) and are mirrored by 'messy' problems in the discipline of systems thinking (Waldrop, 1992; Vennix, 1999). Through the process of review of regional case studies it was identified that many institutional frameworks had become outdated because they could not adapt to changes in the communities with the required speed (Bellamy and Johnson, 2000). This supports the proposition that the barriers and their solutions to complex problems may be more socio-economic or institutional than scientific in nature (Szaro *et al.*, 1998). To facilitate improved management decisions it was suggested that the interface between social, economic, physical/biological and ecological models must be improved (Szaro *et al.*, 1998).

5.4 Complexity

Complexity is an umbrella concept that incorporates the new insights of hierarchy theory, catastrophe theory, self-organising theory (including non-equilibrium thermodynamics) and chaos theory and the associated issues of uncertainty, surprise and emergence across scales (Kay and Schneider, 1994). Waldrop (1992) reviewed the development of the concept of complexity which arose from an interdisciplinary group of scientists in the Santa Fe Institute in the mid 1980s, in various fields including cybernetics, economics, nuclear science, physics and biology. The convergence of disciplines that have contributed to the different aspects of systems science is shown in the genealogy of systems science in Figure 5.3.

The theory of complexity (Waldrop, 1992) and its ancillary theories of complex adaptive systems (Holland, 1992), adaptive management (Holling, 1978; Walters, 1986), resilience (Gunderson and Holling, 2002), consilience (Wilson, 1999) and post-normal science (Funtowicz and Ravetz, 1990; Kay and Schneider, 1994) are being proposed to meet the real world challenges of policy development and management strategies for natural resources management, including agro-ecosystems (Gill, 2001) and rangelands (Walker and Abel, 2002) in Australia. Initially these approaches developed novel ways in which to conceptualise and understand how complex systems function.

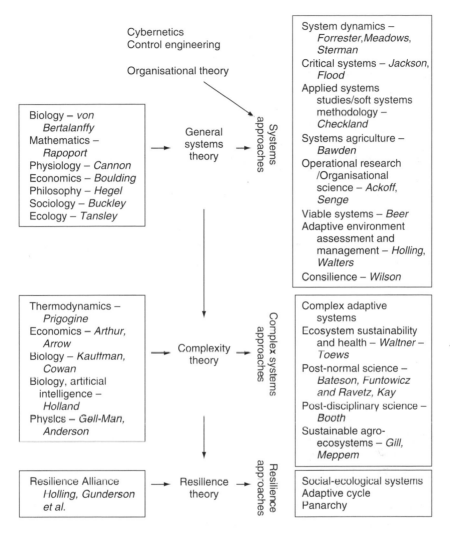

Fig. 5.3. A genealogy of systems science, identifying some key researchers associated with each tradition. The most relevant are cited in the text.

Lee (1993) proposed that the key factor that influenced the functioning of complex systems is the mismatch of scale between human responsibility and ecosystem interactions. The dynamics of the whole system may become particularly unpredictable when the dynamics of fast variables (social and economic variables) and of slow variables (for example, ecosystem processes) become synchronous. In this arena of uncertainty in problem solving the gap between hard quantitative tools of the normal science paradigm and the resolution of uncertain issues can lead to what have become known as soft disasters (ESRC Global Environmental Change Programme, 2000). Soft disasters are described as environmental and political crises that are perceived to emerge only slowly but at high costs to society, not least due to the erosion of public confidence and legitimacy, that is to say, when science and policy no longer are credible or accepted by key stakeholders (or other powerful individuals or institutions).

In keeping with Kuhn's two characteristics for the acceptance of a new paradigm (discussed in Chapter 4) Waltner-Toews (1996) proposed that, at least within the field of complex ecosystem health, a large enough body of scientists believe that:

1. the old way of doing things is seen to be inadequate to the task;
2. a new way has been proposed and seen to be a possible better alternative; and
3. the new way must now be demonstrated to be a better way.

The third point is consistent with Kuhn's second point that the new paradigm is sufficiently open-ended to allow for further refinement.

5.5 Post-normal science paradigm

Whatever we do is based in some way on an underlying set of beliefs or assumptions about the world around us. Often these assumptions are internalised and implicit in the way we think and act and may unconsciously introduce biases into our research. The ability to think about potential alternative paradigms means being conscious and critical about the fundamental assumptions and philosophies that shape the way we approach problems. Therefore, one way to show explicitly the paradigm that shapes our actions is to identify the assumptions that underpin it. Table 5.2 identifies the assumptions and features of two paradigms. The first is that commonly displayed in the twentieth century, as was described in Chapter 4, and the second is an alternative post-normal science paradigm proposed for the twenty-first century (Checkland, 1984; Milbrath, 1989; Jayaratna, 1994; Dore *et al.*, 2000; Sterman, 2000; Gunderson and Holling, 2002).

Key factors that shape the alternative paradigm are the requirement for a fundamental understanding of the 'problem situation' within its context and recognition that knowledge of the future is made difficult because of the emergent system properties that produce unpredictable and uncertain future dynamics.

Table 5.2. *Contrasting paradigms between the normal science dominant in the biophysical sciences of the twentieth century and an alternative paradigm emerging in the twenty-first century*

A commonly displayed twentieth century paradigm	An alternative paradigm for the twenty-first century
Problem solving and goal seeking orientation	Learning orientation
Priority on economic growth and development	Focus on sustainability and the long-term
Focus on short-term or immediate prosperity	Focus on long-term or future prosperity
Assumed predictability and certainty	Unpredictability and uncertainty
Control	Adaptive management
Single linear causality	Recognition of need for holistic/integrative thinking
One 'truth' or best answer	Does not produce final answers
Context not very relevant	Context is important
Observer status objective	Observer status is constructed or interpreted
Focusses on parts	Focus on holism and integration
Analysis/reduction	Synthesis
Structural constancy	Structure changes affect function
Reversibility	Recognition of hysteresis and irreversibility
Asymptotic stability	Multiple stable states
Reliance on simple cause and effect	Recognition of emergent properties of systems
Assumes systems models to be models of the world (ontologies)	Assumes systems models to be intellectual constructs (epistemologies)
Science and technology have the answers	Scepticism and critical evaluation of science and technology
Talks the language of problems and solutions	Talks the language of 'situation of concern' and accommodations

Sources: Checkland (1984), Milbrath (1989), Jayaratna (1994), Dore *et al.* (2000), Sterman (2000), Gunderson and Holling (2002).

Post-normal science owes its origins to the research of Gregory Bateson (Bateson, 1979) who was originally an anthropologist and ethnographer in the discipline of second-order cybernetics (that is to say, the science of communication and complex control processes through which self-organising biological and social systems regulate themselves and maintain homeostasis or stability within a given environment). This area of research developed into the theory of knowledge and in 1958 was identified as a new kind of science for which there was no satisfactory name (Bateson, 1979). Through this process Bateson developed a number of principles to underpin this new science which later became known as post-normal science (Funtowicz and Ravetz, 1990).

There were two major principles that underpinned Bateson's approach. The first principle was an emphasis on the need for a process that assists the inclusion of diverse perspectives, that is one that facilitated an understanding of relationships among different aspects of a problem. The second principle was the need for social learning that included an adaptive approach to valuation. This social learning approach enquired into the process by which values are constructed, thus incorporating a reflexive approach to decision making.

Normal science is unable to deal effectively with either the need to accommodate diverse perspectives (and values) or the uncertainty of future system behaviour. Under conditions of uncertainty, standard decision-making tools that rely on quantifiable and objective facts often fail. Uncertainty arises from complex, value-laden and subjective situations that do not conform to set assessment criteria. This deficiency led to debate on new and adequate ways of dealing with and managing uncertainty. Expectations of certainty and stability about the future are being replaced with expectations of uncertainty and surprise. Therefore, the management of uncertainty is central to the management of messy or complex problems. Uncertainty has been organised by either category or level. For example, it has been proposed that uncertainty can be ascribed to five categories as shown in Table 5.3 (Fletcher and Davis, unpublished).

Alternatively, rather than defining uncertainty into separate categories, attempts have been made to identify different levels of uncertainty in relation to decision making in which some types of uncertainty are considered more seriously than others. Four levels of increasing uncertainty have been reported as risk, lack of understanding, ignorance and indetermination (Wynne, 1992; Yearly, 2000; Robertson and Hull, 2003). The first level of risk is involved with issues of statistical accuracy, precision and reliability. Level two uncertainty is identified in relation to level of knowledge or ignorance of the system, only the key factors of which are known. The third level of uncertainty is identified by increasing ignorance about the parameters in the system; that is, we don't know what we don't know. At the extreme end of uncertainty there is indetermination in which future system behaviour cannot be known because of the emergent properties of the system that arise through social action within the system.

At the most extreme level of uncertainty, Funtowicz and Ravetz (1992) identified situations in which facts are uncertain, values are in dispute, stakes are high and decisions are urgent. They postulated that such circumstances

Table 5.3. *Categories of uncertainty*

Category	Description
Randomness	Lack of a specific pattern of data
Vagueness	Imprecision of definition
Conflict	Equivocation, ambiguity, anomaly or inconsistence in the combination of data or evidence
Incompleteness	That which we do not know, know we do not know, and do not know we do not know. Includes what is too complicated and/or what is too expensive to model
Relevance	Issues and information that may or may not impact on the proposition being addressed

Source: Fletcher and Davis (unpublished)

required very different practices from normal science, proposing ideas of post-normal science as a worthy alternative. The difference between normal and post-normal science is conceptualised in Figure 5.4 in a typology of approaches to science. As system uncertainties and decision stakes rise, the need increases for a new or post normal science. Proponents of a post-normal science challenged that value-free science cannot exist, argued that values matter, that these must be stated explicitly and consequently that the mental constructs of those involved are important (Funtowicz and Ravetz, 1992; Vennix, 1999; Hull *et al.*, 2002). This is opposed to normal science that takes the position of an objective science. Although Funtowicz and Ravetz (1992) identified important differences between normal science and post-normal science, they also stressed that the two sciences were complementary. The type of science applied is necessarily dependent upon the type of problem to be addressed (as shown in the Hawkesbury Hierarchy of approaches to problem solving and situation improvement (Table 4.3)).

Traditional disciplinary science that underpinned natural resource policy has given the expectation that there is certainty in decisions and that decision makers can control and manage changes in the environment. It is now acknowledged that the science of ecology, one of the keystone sciences on which natural resource management is based, is an uncertain science and was not well handled by policy or management (Dovers, 2000b). Until recently, a major gulf has existed between so-called pure research and applied research. Theory was developed with little reference to 'real' systems, and much ecological research has had little apparent relevance to environmental problems (Hobbs, 1998) and hence may have been a contributing factor to natural

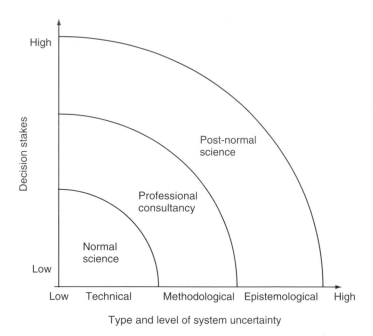

Fig. 5.4. A typology of approaches to science. *Source:* Funtowicz and Ravetz (1992); Ravetz and Funtowicz (1999)

resource degradation. Not only is ecological theory changing but also many assumptions of traditional disciplinary science are being challenged in the way they relate to natural and social systems. Complexity and uncertainty are key components of contemporary environmental theory and therefore are redefining the sciences of nature and human society, and changing the role of science in decision making (Robertson and Hull, 2003) and improving the public's trust in environmental politics (Wynne, 1992; ESRC Global Environmental Change Programme, 2000).

5.6 Systems approach

In this section we examine the theoretical constructs and evolving processes for policy and management for natural resources, which have their foundations in general systems theory: ecology theory, resilience theory and system dynamics. The development of systems theory is based on the understanding of the inter-relatedness and interdependence of the components or parts that make up a whole. Systems exhibit a phenomenon known as emergence, defined as having properties that the system's components by themselves do not have and cannot be explained by the properties of the subcomponents (Clayton and Radcliffe, 1996). The properties of the whole are destroyed when a system is dissected, physically or theoretically, into its isolated subcomponents (Capra, 1996). The consequence of this understanding is that issues that are viewed from a systems perspective are examined in terms of relationships, integration and with an emphasis on the principles of organisation, rather than concentrating on the individual parts.

Systems science includes a diverse group of sciences and in its current form its origins can be traced to the convergence of ideas from the individual disciplines of biology, mathematics, physiology, economics, philosophy, sociology and ecology (Figure 5.3). Consequently, it is proposed that systems thinking is a meta-discipline that can be used to talk about other disciplines (Checkland, 1984). Figure 5.3 shows the genealogy of systems science and some of the key researchers associated with each tradition and those that are relevant to this book are described in the following sections in this chapter.

Tainter (1988, 1996) and Dorner (1997) presented arguments for the differences that exist between a governance that is based on the 'problem-solving' paradigm and one that is based on the 'systems thinking' paradigm. The thrust of the argument is that sustainable societies will never be achieved unless the policy-making processes and institutions of government are remodelled on the basis of the 'systems thinking' paradigm. Theories of collective action, organisation and processes for citizen and stakeholder participation play crucial roles, since it is they who, collectively, 'know' the whole system in its current state, and it is they who will have to implement the new system in order to achieve sustainability. Sayer and Campbell (2001) suggested that systems modelling is a fundamental tool in integrated approaches to natural resource management and appropriate at many points in the adaptive management cycle. The issues of natural resource protection and management span all the spatial and temporal hierarchical levels, for example, at the global scale (Daily, 1997; Rosser, 2001) and at the landscape/regional/catchment scales (Bellamy *et al.*, 1999). It is being argued that systems perspectives are able to fill the gap in natural resource management by serving either as explanations of phenomena or as metaphors that provide insight into complexity and complex systems (Gill, 1996; Ison *et al.*, 1997; Bellamy *et al.*, 2001).

5.6.1 General systems theory

Von Bertalanffy's general systems theory, which was developed in the 1930s to 1940s, was one of the first schools of thought that provided alternative models and modes of inquiry to the reductionist methods of disciplinary science (von Bertalanffy, 1968). It was designed to overcome the problems of the ever increasing specialisation of modern science and was generally applicable to systems in economics, biology and society. To quote from von Bertalanffy (1968), it was '... necessitated by the enormous amount of data, the complexity of techniques and of theoretical structures within every field. Thus science is split into innumerable disciplines continually generating new sub-disciplines. In consequence, the physicist, the biologist, the psychologist and the social scientist are, so to speak, encapsulated in their private universes, and it is difficult to get word from one cocoon to the other.' Also he proposed that 'There appear to exist general system laws which apply to any system of a particular type, irrespective of the particular properties of the systems and the elements involved. Compared to the analytical procedure of classical science with resolution into component elements and one-way or linear causality as basic category, the investigation of organized wholes of many variables requires new categories of interaction, transaction, organization, teleology...'.

Not surprisingly, the concepts arising from an interdisciplinary general systems approach have been applied to a variety of areas, the genealogy of which is shown in Figure 5.3. These include soft systems methodology (Checkland, 1984), hard systems thinking (Forrester, 1989), learning and cognition (Forrester, 1992), biology, control and artificial intelligence (Holland, 1992), human geographical enquiry (Walmsley, 1972), business architecture (Gharajedaghi, 1999), sustainable agro-ecosystems (Gill, 2001), agricultural production systems (Keating and McCown, 2001; Meadows and Robinson, 1985), linking science and policy (De Greene, 1993), post-normal science (Funtowicz and Ravetz, 1992), adaptive environmental management (Holling, 1978), ecological economic systems and policy (Rosser, 2001), integration of social, economic and ecological science and policy in order to discover foundations for sustainability (Walker, 2000), and scenario development in socio-economic political systems (Berkhout *et al.*, 2001).

5.6.2 Ecology theory

Ecology has as its basis the study of systems. The British ecologist Tansley (1935) first introduced the term 'ecosystem', which he defined as a system resulting from the interaction of all the living and non-living factors of the environment. Odum (1959) suggested that the ecosystem can be regarded as the fundamental unit of study. However, consistent with systemic process of enquiry, the boundary of the system is dependent on the area of interest to the investigator and early attempts to develop a theoretical framework in ecology proved difficult (McIntosh, 1980). The science of ecology was considered to

Table 5.4. *Ecology: a theoretical framework*

Organisational level	Key concepts and processes	Corresponding management level
Individual	Energy balance, physiological and behavioural responses	Species reintroduction
Population	Population growth and regulation, density dependence/independence, species interaction, co-evolution, population genetics	Species orientated management
Community	Environmental gradients and ecotones, niche theory, diversity, food webs, stability and resilience, succession	Reserve management
Ecosystem	Energy flow, trophic levels, biogeochemical cycles	Reserve management
Landscape/region	Geomorphological processes, hydrologic cycles, connectivity Island biogeography, climate patterns	Catchment, regional, multi-authority management
Global	Biomes, greenhouse effect, acid rain, global climate	National/international

Source: Hobbs (1988)

be so complex that any attempt to develop ecological theory could not account for environmental variability (Hobbs, 1988). However, a broad theoretical framework has been developed for ecology (Hobbs, 1988). This framework links the smallest level, the individual, to the greatest level, the global level, through a series of hierarchical levels (Table 5.4). The development of theory necessarily involves the generation of general principles. However, attempts to implement natural resource management based on these generalities failed to provide guidance in specific cases (Hobbs and Yates, 1997).

In the late 1970s, Holling (1978) considered that some ideas about ecology and ecosystems and their methods of characterisation had led us astray because they had not been based on sound understanding of the behaviour of systems. Holling (1978) was concerned with how an ecological understanding could be used to improve management and guide development in a variety of ecological systems; for example, forest management, salmon management, high mountains regional development and a wildlife impact information system. There is now considerable evidence in the literature that demonstrates that the behaviour of the ecological system was only one side of the equation and that resource management has paid too little attention to the influence of institutions (Holling, 1978; Dovers and Wild-River, 2003) and how social and human capital affects environmental outcomes (Pretty and Howard, 2001). Essentially the interconnections between the two dominant systems, ecosystems and social systems, have been dealt with as though those interactions were absent or weakly linked.

The key properties of ecosystems that were identified as being particularly important with respect to management practices are the organisation of ecological systems and their spatial and temporal behaviour (Holling, 1978). Although there are many structural variables in an ecosystem, everything is not strongly connected to everything else and, therefore, there are implications for what should be measured and managed, to be effective in changing the system's behaviour (Holling and Gunderson, 2002). There is also spatial heterogeneity of the variables within the ecosystem and impacts are not uniform or gradually diluted over space, and this has implications for how intense potential impacts will be and where they may occur. System organisation, and spatial and temporal behaviour are responsible for the three major characteristics of ecosystems; stability, resilience and dynamic variability. The consequence of having these characteristics for management is that we have to expect the unexpected and that sharp shifts in behaviour are natural for many ecosystems. Therefore, it was proposed that traditional ecology theory and methods of monitoring and assessment may have misinterpreted these dynamic characteristics as unexpected or perverse as opposed to normal system behaviour dictated by system structure (Holling *et al.*, 2002b). On this basis, the new theory of ecosystems proposes that environmental quality is not achieved by eliminating change, and that variability, not constancy, is a feature of ecological systems that contributes to their persistence and to their self-monitoring and self-correcting capacities (Gunderson and Holling, 2002; Fey, 2002; Berkes *et al.*, 2003). Hence, systems that conform with these properties and characteristics require a management philosophy and practice that can accommodate decision making under uncertainty.

The concept of adaptive management arose to fill the gap between the new theory and practice of management of 'wicked' problems in natural resources. Adaptive management was first applied as an explicit policy at the ecosystem scale in 1984 in the Columbia Basin and became the guiding premise of the systems planning approach adopted by Holling (1978). General understanding of this new body of theory is not widespread in the natural resource institutional, policy and management environment in Western Australia, and this is considered to have been a contributing factor to the lack of effectiveness in the

Table 5.5. *Forrester's seven properties of complex adaptive systems*

1. They are counterintuitive
2. Complex systems are remarkably insensitive to changes in many system parameters
3. Complex systems counteract and compensate for externally applied corrective efforts
4. Complex systems resist most policy changes
5. Complex systems contain influential pressure points often in unexpected places from which forces will radiate to alter system balance
6. Complex systems often react to policy change in the long run in a way opposite to how they react in the short run. Worse before better makes beneficial policies hard to implement and maintain to the point where they bear fruit. Better-before-worse makes policies that are detrimental in the long run hard to abandon.
7. Complex social systems tend towards a condition of poor performance.

Source: Forrester (1961)

practice of adaptive management in the 1990s in the WA agricultural region (C. Keating, personal communication August 2003), as discussed in Chapter 4.

There is a special class of complex systems that are termed adaptive which have been described by seven properties (Table 5.5) (Forrester, 1961). The unique feature that distinguishes these from other kinds of complex systems is that adaptive systems in some way interact with their environment and change in response to environmental change. This potential for systems to be adaptive and self-organising is responsible for many natural resource problems and policy resistance, which are discussed below and exemplified in the case study in Chapters 2, 6 and 7.

5.6.3 Resilience theory

The origins of the construct of resilience, although not identified as such, can be traced to the ecological anthropology literature in an examination of people's responses to hazards in which it was noted that responding adaptively involved responding to the imminent hazard and maintaining the capacity to respond in the future (Vayda and McCay, 1975). As a result the literature in the interdisciplinary field of ecological anthropology holds a significant contribution to the concept of resilience (Hansson and Helgesson, 2003). The construct of resilience is increasingly being used within the natural sciences (particularly ecology) (Holling, 1973; Davidson-Hunt and Berkes, 2003), the social sciences (particularly economics) (Hansson and Helgesson, 2003;

Davidson-Hunt and Berkes, 2003) and the health sciences (particularly mental health) (Bonanno *et al.*, 2001; Olsson *et al.*, 2003) literatures. Resilience and the related construct of robustness are widely used in the natural and social literatures, in association with the central construct of stability (or constancy) (Hansson and Helgesson, 2003).

There are two basic types of stability that draw attention to the tension created between efficiency on the one hand and persistence on the other, or between constancy and change, or between predictability and unpredictability (Holling, 1973; Hansson and Helgesson, 2003), a tension also noted in the organisational analysis debate (discussed in Section 4.4). The first definition refers to actual absence of change (or constancy) with a focus on the objective or 'ends' of optimal performance. The second definition refers to how a system copes with disturbances focussing on persistence, variability and unpredictability, covered by the notions of resilience and its limiting case robustness (Holling, 1973; Hansson and Helgesson, 2003). The use of the terms resilience and robustness by Hansson and Helgesson (2003) equates to the constructs of engineering resilience and ecological resilience identified by Holling (1973). In the literatures of natural science, social science, engineering and health science some terms have been used interchangeably with resilience, for example, 'robustness', 'stability', 'reliability', 'persistence', 'survivability'. Examples of these uses are being collated and clarified in a joint project of the Resilience Alliance and the Santa Fe Institute's Robustness Program (Resilience Alliance, 2002). The use of the term resilience in this book is consistent with Holling's 'ecological resilience', which is taken to mean the way to understand how ecosystems maintain themselves, or adapt, following perturbation or rapid change (Gunderson and Holling, 2002).

In recent years resilience theory has received considerable development in addressing two paradoxes identified by Holling *et al.* (2002b). In an attempt to resolve the paradoxes, four provisional propositions, six assumptions and twelve conclusions have been reported. In the quest for a theory of adaptive change, Holling *et al.* (2002b) examined many case studies and identified two paradoxes (Table 5.6) that prevented any quick and easy predictions about the potential for a system to collapse. The first was the Paradox of the Pathology of Regional Resources and Ecosystem Management and the second was the Trap of the Expert. In addition Gunderson *et al.* (2002b) made four provisional propositions about the behaviour of large-scale systems, based on a review of ecological processes, with the proviso that they may not be appropriate for other disciplines (Table 5.7). Walker *et al.* (2002) proposed six assumptions about systems made up of humans and nature (Table 5.8) and Holling (2000) made twelve conclusions from empirical examples, models and

Table 5.6. *Two paradoxes of regional resource management*

Paradox 1. The pathology of regional resource and ecosystem management

Observation: New policies and development usually succeed initially, but they lead to agencies that gradually become rigid and myopic, economic sectors that become slavishly dependent, ecosystems that are more fragile and a public that loses trust in governance.

The paradox: If that is as common as it appears, why are we still here? Why has there not been a profound collapse of exploited renewable resources and the ecological services upon which human survival and development depend?

Paradox 2. The trap of the expert

Observation: In every example of crisis and regional development we have studied, both the natural system and the economic components can be explained by a small set of variables and critical processes. The great complexity, diversity, and opportunity in complex regional systems emerge from a handful of critical variables and processes that operate over distinctly different scales in space and time.

The paradox: If that is the case, why does expert advice so often create crisis and contribute to political gridlock? Why, in so many places, does science have a bad name?

Source: Holling *et al.* (2002b)

Table 5.7. *Four provisional propositions about large-scale systems*

1. **The organisation of regional resource systems emerges from the interaction of a few variables**. The essential structure and dynamics of complex systems are produced by the interactions of at least three, but no more than six, variables that operate at spatial and temporal scales that differ by approximately an order of magnitude.
2. **Complex systems have multiple stable states. Complex systems can exhibit alternative stable organizations**. Transitions between different organisations are due to changes in the interaction of structuring variables. Change often occurs when gradual change in a slow variable alters the interactions among fast variables.
3. **Resilience derives from functional reinforcement across scales and functional overlap within scales**. Resilience derives from both a duplication of function across a range of spatial and temporal scales and a diversity of different functions operating at each scale.
4. **Vulnerability increases as sources of novelty are eliminated and as functional diversity and cross-scale functional replication are reduced**. Diminished sources of novelty reduce the ability of a system to recover from disturbances. The elimination of structuring species or processes can cause an ecosystem to reorganise. A reduction in functional diversity and duplication of functions reduces the ability of a system to persist.

Source: Gunderson *et al.* (2002b)

Table 5.8. *Assumptions of systems under resilience theory*

Resilience assumptions
1. The existence of thresholds and hysteretic effects should be assumed.
2. Assumes dynamic and unknown probabilities.
3. It is based on imperfect knowledge, and utility depends on social context.
4. Market imperfections are the norm and market-based evaluations are the norm.
5. Agents hold preferences over outcomes, social, economic and political processes.
6. Expert solutions do not maximise legitimacy.

Source: Walker *et al.* (2002).
Walker *et al.* (2002) used the term 'social-ecological systems' (SESs) for large-scale regional systems made up of humans and nature.

tests (Table 5.9). These paradoxes, propositions, assumptions and conclusions are tested in Chapters 6 and 7 for their applicability to the WA agricultural region.

In its current form resilience theory aims to understand three fundamental themes (Gunderson *et al.*, 2002a). The first considers the characteristics of stability, resilience and change from one state to another in systems with multiple stable states. The second considers cross-scale interactions, and the third is one of adaptive change and learning using the heuristic model or metaphor of the adaptive cycle (Section 5.6.4). The two aims of resilience management are (1) to prevent the system from moving to unintended system configurations in the face of external stresses and disturbance; and (2) to nurture and preserve the elements that enable the system to renew and reorganise itself following a massive change (Walker *et al.*, 2002). Resilience theory also gives us a new language and concepts to describe and help understand phenomena in the process of dynamic change in linked SESs.

5.6.4 The adaptive cycle

Holling's four-phase adaptive cycle (Figure 5.5) is a three-dimensional heuristic model for understanding the process of change in complex adaptive systems and can be used to identify structure, patterns and causality (Holling, 1995). The fundamental conceptual model describes in theoretical terms, perpetual and ever-changing time periods of the flow of events through four phases in an ecosystem. These four phases are exploitation, conservation, release and reorganisation (represented by r, K, Ω and α respectively).

Table 5.9. *Twelve conclusions of resilience theory*

Summary statement	Conclusion
1. Multiple states are common in many systems.	Abrupt shifts among a multiplicity of very different stable domains are plausible in regional ecosystems, in some economic systems, and some political systems. The likelihood of such shifts is determined by the resilience of these domains as measured by their size. The costs of such shifts depend on the degree and duration of reversibility from one domain to another.
2. The adaptive cycle is the fundamental unit of dynamic change.	An adaptive cycle that aggregates resources and periodically restructures to create opportunities for innovation is proposed as a fundamental unit for understanding complex systems from cells to ecosystems to societies.
3. Not all adaptive cycles are the same and some are maladaptive.	Variants to the adaptive cycle are present in different systems. These include physical systems with no internal storage, ecosystems strongly influenced by external pulses, and human systems with foresight and adaptive methods to stabilise variability. Some are maladaptive and trigger poverty and rigidity traps.
4. Sustainability requires both change and persistence.	Sustainability is maintained by relationships among a nested set of adaptive cycles arranged as a dynamic hierarchy in space and time – the panarchy.
5. Self-organisation provides the arena for change.	Self-organising by ecological systems establishes an arena for evolutionary change. Self-organisation of human institutional patterns establishes the arena for future sustainable opportunity.
6. Three types of learning can be identified	Panarchies identify three types of change – incremental, lurching and transforming – each of which can generate a correspondingly different kind of learning.
7. The world is lumpy.	Attributes of biological and human entities form clumped structures that reflect partial organisation, create diversity and contribute to resilience and sustainability.
8. Functional diversity builds resilience.	Functional groups across size classes of organisms maintain ecosystem resilience.

(*cont.*)

Table 5.9. (*cont.*)

Summary statement	Conclusion
9. Tractability comes from the 'Rule of Hand'.	Being as simple as possible, but no simpler than necessary, leads to the 'Rule of Hand'. Understanding a panarchy and its adaptive cycle requires a model of at least three to five key interacting components, three qualitatively different speeds, and non-linear causation. Vulnerability and resilience of the system change with the slow variables. Spatial contagion and biotic legacies generate self-organisation patterns over scales in space and time.
10. Systems of humans and nature can behave differently than their parts demonstrating emergent behaviour within integrated systems.	Linked ecological, economic and social systems exhibit emergent behaviour. The behaviour is a result of strong connectivity between the human and ecological components and the presence of non-linearity and complexity, as suggested in the 'Rule of Hand'.
11. Management must cope with surprise and unpredictability.	Managing complex systems requires confronting multiple uncertainties. These can arise from technical considerations, such as model structure or analytic framework. The examples suggest that as much complexity exists in the social dimensions as in the ecological ones, and that managers must juggle shifting objectives.
12. Adaptive management outperforms other management approaches.	Slow variables, multi-stable behaviours and stochasticity cause active adaptive management to outperform optimisation approaches that seek stable targets.

Source: Holling *et al.* (2002a)

The cycle describes the slow accumulation of capital, for example, natural or social capital, interspersed with rapid phases of reorganisation where for transient moments novelty can emerge to become subsequently incorporated into another cycle. This was originally a two-dimensional model expressed by two properties (1) the potential for change and (2) connectedness or the structure of the component parts. This model was subsequently modified into a three-dimensional model (Figure 5.5) by including a third property, resilience (Holling and Gunderson, 2002). The levels of each of these three properties ebb and flow between phases (Table 5.10). If each property is given a relative level of either high or low then the characterisation of each phase is given by the combination of the three properties.

The adaptive cycle is often described in terms of two loops, the frontloop, consisting of the exploitation (r) and the conservation (K) phases and the backloop consisting of the release (Ω) and the reorganisation (α) phases. Structural changes occur among system variables as the cycle moves through the four phases. These changes are inherent features of evolving systems driven by instability, and therefore a critical question to ask in these systems is (in terms of the adaptive cycle), 'What are the factors that produce instability in the cycle to cause it to go from the conservation phase to the release phase and from the reorganisation phase to the exploitation phase?' Alternatively,

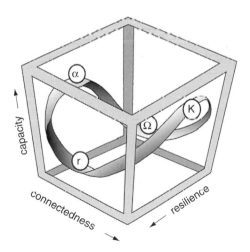

Fig. 5.5. Heuristic model of the adaptive cycle. The adaptive cycle is a three-dimensional heuristic model. The resilience of the system expands and contracts throughout the cycle in relation to the potential and connectedness among the variables. r, exploitation phase; K, conservation phase; Ω, release phase; α, reorganisation phase. *Source:* Gunderson and Holling (2002)

Table 5.10. *The level of each of the three variables that characterise the four phases of the adaptive cycle*

Phase	Potential	Connectedness	Resilience
α Reorganisation	high	low	high
K Conservation	high	high	low
r Exploitation	low	low	high
Ω Release	low	high	low

Source: Gunderson and Holling (2002)

in systems thinking the same question could be, 'What are the factors that control or limit exponential growth?' Resilience theory uses the changes in the levels in the three properties (potential, connectedness and resilience) to help explain the dynamics among the four potential phases in the adapting system.

The original concept of the adaptive cycle emerged from case studies of ecosystems in temperate regions of the world. However, since then it has been applied to a variety of case studies from different climatic regions, for example, arid rangelands in Australia (Walker and Abel, 2002), temperate agro-ecosystems (Walker *et al.*, 2002), tropical coral reefs and wet and dry tropical forests (Gunderson and Pritchard, 2002). Also the adaptive cycle has been used to explain and interpret system behaviour not only in SESs but also in other disciplines, such as in the history of business and economics, and is claimed to have universal applicability (Gunderson *et al.*, 2002a).

The metaphor of the adaptive cycle captures very elegantly and dynamically the epistemology of the organisation of form and change put forward by Bateson (1979) in which he proposed that humans' ability to survive depends on their ability to cope and adapt to change. Bateson (1979) proposed that the balance for change lies somewhere between complete stability and utter chaos, which are qualities that also may be used to describe any system. For example, a well integrated and smoothly functioning system is rigid and prone to resist change. Reciprocally, a poorly integrated system is inefficient, but easily adaptable to change. System level change can occur only if the system as a whole can relax and allow for inner contradictions. It is only after the change has entered the system, affecting all of its components and affecting the self-organising properties of the system, that the system can both retain the change and increase its efficiency and effectiveness.

The adaptive cycle is appropriate for structures within a specific range of scales. For those dynamics that occur at multiple scales, for example across the local, regional, national and global levels, a model of cross-scale ecological organisation was developed. Multiple levels of smaller adaptive cycles together make up a panarchy, which describes the dynamic nature of interacting hierarchies of complex adaptive systems, either spatial or temporally one inside the other, and is used to explain complex system behaviour (Gunderson and Holling, 2002).

5.6.5 Synthesis of organisational analysis and the adaptive cycle metaphor

Three frameworks of organisational theory were described in Chapter 4. All three were static spatial frameworks using axes describing dimensions reflecting dichotomies of organisational preference. Organisational analysis frameworks were predisposed towards concepts of equilibrium, had a static bias, and were critiqued for their failure to deal adequately with contradictions such as change and uncertainty (Quinn and Rohrbaugh, 1983). They were constructed as static spatial frameworks formed by axes of dichotomies of competing factors or values. Prior to the development of adaptive cycle and resilience theory, theories of organisational analysis have not dealt well with these contradictions, particularly the paradoxes for the need for change and stability, and growth and decay. Resilience theory and the adaptive cycle metaphor have bridged this theoretical gap, making a significant contribution to the constructs of effectiveness and resilience. Rather than identifying the phases as competing in an either/or dichotomy, with one having greater value than the other, the adaptive cycle model infers that all four phases are essential to maintaining the resilience of the system. This can be compared with the concept of effectiveness in the competing values framework of Quinn and Rohrbaugh (1983) in which three sets of competing values were recognised as dilemmas in the organisational literature. The emergence of one pair of competing values, flexibility versus stability, reflected the basic dilemma of organisational life. The differing viewpoints in considering order and control versus innovation and change are at the heart of the most heated debates in the philosophy of sociology, political science and psychology (Hayles, 1995; Habermas et al., 1996) and so it appears to be in resilience theory.

Notably, the dynamic model of the adaptive cycle overcomes the key failure of the static spatial frameworks in the selection of criteria for resilience. Resilience cannot be measured by addressing any one of the criteria from one of the four phases, but can only be measured by the integration of criteria from all four phases. This is because measuring resilience by criteria of the conservation phase ignores the criteria from the other three phases. In practice this is what has happened in many systems including agro-ecological systems in which measures of success such as effectiveness were based on criteria such as growth and productivity, ignoring all other criteria of resilience. Stability, growth and productivity are factors that characterise the frontloop of the adaptive cycle and it is posited that most policy was developed to perform under these conditions (Gunderson and Holling, 2002). It is now becoming apparent that the key phases in the adaptive cycle are those of the backloop, and therefore policies will be required that are designed to maintain the factors that allow for reorganisation, novelty and renewal.

5.6.6 System dynamics

System dynamics is based on causal interrelationships that are observed, deduced or presumed to be true, and not on any particular management, economic or social theory, and is thus intrinsically neutral between these theories. In many applications it therefore offers the opportunity to support open debate and serve as an 'honest broker' of ideas. Hence system dynamics is an appropriate philosophy and methodology to use in an integrative and interdisciplinary paradigm such as post-normal science.

System dynamics was developed during the 1950s primarily by Forrester (1961) and did not evolve from the general theory of systems discussed above (see Figure 5.3). Rather it combined ideas from three fields: (1) control engineering (the concepts of feedback and system self-regulation), (2) cybernetics (the nature of information and its role in control systems), and (3) organisational theory (the structure of human organisations and the mechanisms of human decision making). From these basic ideas Forrester (1961) developed a guiding philosophy and a methodology comprising a set of representational techniques for understanding, specifying quantitative models and simulating system behaviour over time, specifically for complex systems composed of multiple-loop feedback loops, which were originally applied to the management of industrial firms.

System dynamics theory and practice is intended to help understand and solve dynamic problems in complex systems (Sterman, 2000) using the concept of feedback control theory (Fey, 2002). The primary assumption of system dynamics theory is that persistent tendencies of any complex social system arise from its internal causal structure – from the pattern of physical constraints and social goals, rewards, and pressures that cause people to behave the way they do and to generate cumulatively the dominant dynamic tendencies of the total system (Meadows and Robinson, 1985). Theoretically, system dynamics assumes that the world is composed of multiloop feedback-dominated, non-linear, time-delayed systems (Meadows and Robinson, 1985), which makes this method appropriate for the investigation of the WA agricultural region because it is an example of a complex large-scale system that has persistent dynamic patterns with long time horizons and broad interdisciplinary boundaries. System dynamics is used here because it is well suited to understanding general trends and includes a set of concepts, representation techniques and beliefs that can integrate concepts from the physical, biological and social sciences (Meadows and Robinson, 1985).

The literature on system dynamics is extensive, and includes the early work on the underlying philosophy (Forrester, 1961); mathematical models of world systems in a highly aggregate form (Meadows, 1972); feedback concepts, systems theory and human system analysis (Richardson, 1991); dynamics of organisational change (Senge *et al.*, 1994); counterintuitive behaviour of social systems (Forrester, 1995); a computer aided approach to policy analysis and design (Richardson, 1996); policy analysis in complex systems (Sterman, 2000) and feedback control in human systems (Fey, 2002). The span of applications has grown extensively and now encompasses work in many diverse fields including the environment (Ford, 1999), natural resource management (Grant *et al.*, 1997), trade relations in the global economy (Saeed, 1998), sustainable agriculture (Gill, 1999), social systems (Meadows, 1972), commodity systems (Sawin *et al.*, 2003), business (Sterman, 2000), health systems (Cavana *et al.*, 1999) and change and uncertainty (Maani and Cavana, 2000). These are excellent texts on the philosophy and application of system dynamics, the central concepts of which are described briefly below. System dynamics is often viewed as a 'hard' systems thinking approach, as it is often applied to natural systems or designed physical systems. However, system dynamics has developed into a method for studying dynamic complex social systems because it is grounded in the theory of non-linear dynamics and feedback control (Meadows and Robinson, 1985). System dynamics is reported to draw on cognitive and social psychology, economics and other social sciences in order to apply the method to human systems as well as physical and technical systems (Sterman, 2000) and is intended to solve dynamic problems in existing living systems by achieving improved future time patterns for problematic variables (Fey, 2002). System dynamics was shown to increase organisational learning, increase understanding of the processes involved in the problems of concern, and help to change individual's mental models in the sense of double-loop learning in group model building (Barnabé and Fischer, 2002).

System dynamics is concerned with the dynamic tendencies of complex systems, for example, what kinds of behaviour patterns they generate over time. The notion of dynamic tendencies includes such things as under what

Table 5.11. *The system dynamics modelling process*

Step	Description
1	**Problem articulation – boundary selection.** This includes theme selection, key variable selection, time horizon selection and the definition of the dynamic problem or reference modes. In this step it is important to identify the historical behaviour of the key concepts and variables and what their behaviour might be in the future.
2	**Formulation of the dynamic hypothesis.** This includes initial hypothesis generation with an endogenous focus and developing maps of causal structure using tools such as model boundary diagrams, subsystem diagrams and causal loop diagrams.
3	**Formulation of a simulation model.**
4	**Simulation model testing.**
5	**Policy design and evaluation.** This includes scenario specification, policy design, 'what if …' analysis, sensitivity analysis and analysis of potential interactions of policies.

Source: Sterman (2000)

conditions the system as a whole is stable, unstable, oscillating, growing, declining, self-correcting or in equilibrium. There are five steps in the system dynamics modelling process, which are conducted in an iterative fashion (Table 5.11). Here we adopt a qualitative system dynamics approach in which Steps 3 and 4 are not undertaken.

Understanding and interpreting these dynamics is the basis of resilience analysis and of the resilience management framework proposed by Walker *et al.* (2002) (described in Section 5.6.3), which is treated as a complementary method to system dynamics in this book. The system dynamics approach requires a shift in thinking. In particular, it requires a move away from emphasising the influence of isolated events and their causes towards the examination of 'the problem' made up of interacting parts. For example, we explore natural resource processes and thus the focus is on problems generated by the interactions among people and ecosystems. All behaviour is assumed to be part of one or more systems. Consequently, with a systems approach, the internal structure of the system is often more important than external events in generating the behaviour. Therefore, in order to change the behaviour of a system, higher leverage comes from a change in the structure rather than from changing individual events.

In the identification of a problem and then its formulation it is important to identify events, patterns and structures. This is because to start to consider system structure you must first generalise from specific events associated with 'the problem' to considering patterns of behaviour that characterise the situation. This task involves the induction of a model from observation, which usually requires the investigation of how one or more variables of interest change over time. Graphs or time horizons of change over time are known as reference modes and are discussed in greater detail in Chapter 6 with examples from the WA agricultural region.

The dynamics arises from the pattern of physical constraints and social goals, rewards and pressures that cause people to behave the way they do and to generate cumulatively the dominant dynamic tendencies of the total system (Meadows and Robinson, 1985). Explanations of dynamic behaviour of long-term social problems are considered to arise within the internal structure rather than from external disturbances. In the complex system the cause of a problem situation may lie far back in time (a delay) from the symptoms, or in a completely different and remote part of the system. In fact, causes are usually found not in prior events but in the structure and policies of the system.

To avoid policy resistance and to find high leverage policies requires us to expand the boundaries of our mental models so that we become aware of and understand the implications of the feedbacks created by the decisions we make. That is, we must learn about the structure and the dynamics of the increasingly complex system in which the problem situation is embedded. This requires altering the boundary of the system to include factors considered to be part of the structure of the whole system and not just the subsystem in which 'the problem' is located. The important concepts and tools employed in system dynamics are boundaries, feedback, inertia or delay, single-loop learning, double-loop learning, influence diagrams and causal loop diagrams (described in the following sections). System dynamic models are usually intended for use at the general understanding or policy design stages of decision making. Therefore, they tend to be process-orientated, fairly small and aggregated, although there are notable exceptions to this generalisation, such as the world model (Forrester, 1971).

Model boundaries and boundary diagrams

The issue of delineation of model boundary is a difficult task. In system dynamics it is guided as much as possible by a dynamic hypothesis and by parsimony. In the real world a boundary does not exist but it is conceived as a concept, which helps us to make sense of reality and will have a major influence on the model design and subsequent outcome. Whenever a boundary is chosen the modeller makes choices about what to include in the model and whether the variables chosen are to be treated as endogenous, exogenous or as environmental variables. This process increases the transparency of the model.

Environmental variables have a specific definition in system dynamics and are identified as those that are not included in the model but are used to indicate the assumptions on which the model is built and which may be influential and may be included in future iterations of model building. Implicit in these assumptions is a particular epistemology and, therefore, it is indicative of the choice of the decision-making methodology and technology used, and hence the model of reality represented (Carrier and Wallace, 1994). In disciplinary science the bounding of the problem will normally be constrained by the specific assumptions of the discipline. Thus competing and mutually exclusive descriptions may arise from separate disciplinary perspectives. Alternatively in post-normal science (discussed in Section 5.5) the boundary of the model will include a more wide ranging or different set of assumptions arrived at through the accommodation of multiple worldviews.

Boundary diagrams (Figure 5.6) (Meadows and Robinson, 1985), also known as bull's-eye diagrams (Ford, 1999), are a concise way to portray the system boundary of the model and help to make explicit the assumptions of the modeller. The environmental variables could, of course, include many variables, but the list is restricted to those that are closely related to the endogenous and exogenous variables to draw attention to the assumptions that

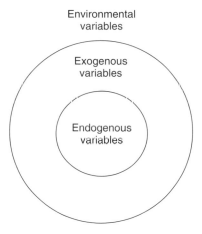

Fig. 5.6. Structure of a boundary diagram. The diagram distinguishes among three sets of variables. Endogenous variables are determined within the model (contained within feedback loops) and are placed in the inner circle. Exogenous variables affect the state of the model system but are not affected by it and are placed in the outer circle. Those variables that are not included in the model, known as environmental variables, are placed outside the outer circle. *Source:* Meadows and Robinson (1985)

define the model's boundary and to indicate the most useful areas for possible model expansion. Closed boundary and nested structure of feedback loops in a system dynamics model satisfy the requirements for the characteristics of the construct of a 'panarchy' for the structure of SES, discussed in Section 5.6.4.

Feedback and causal loop diagrams

Richardson (1991) traced the development of the concept of feedback in social science and systems theory in the literature over the past two hundred years and proposed that feedback is a natural and crucial property of social systems and argued for the importance of incorporating the concept into social science, systems theory and social policy. Two kinds of feedback loops are distinguished that account for all the dynamics that arise in a system; these are reinforcing (or positive) loops and balancing (or negative) loops (Figure 5.7).

Causal loop diagrams are a technique to represent the information feedback at work in the system. The word 'causal' refers to cause and effect relationships and the word 'loop' refers to a closed chain of cause and effect (Figure 5.7). Causal loop diagrams are designed to communicate the central feedback structure and are not detailed descriptions of the model (Maani and Cavana, 2000). Causal loop diagrams, also known as influence diagrams, are drawn using arrows that link related concepts, with the arrowhead showing the direction of the influence. A causal loop diagram is one tool to help identify the key issues within a 'problem situation' such as 'messy' problems in natural resource management. Causal loop diagrams are part of the second step in system dynamics modelling process, model conceptualisation and they aid in envisioning the causal feedback structures capable of reproducing the problematic behaviour.

Coyle (2000) identified the following uses of causal loop diagrams:

1. they put a very complex problem which may require many pages of narrative explanation onto one piece of paper;
2. identifying feedback loops may help to explain behaviour or to generate insights; and
3. identifying feedback loops may identify the wider contexts of a modelling task.

The method of developing causal loop diagrams is well documented elsewhere (Coyle and Alexander, 1997; Maani, 2001; Sterman, 2002). The models in this book were constructed in Vensim PLE.

The logistic function, also described as the s-shaped growth curve is a common method of interpreting change in systems sciences (De Greene, 1993). All the dynamics in a system arise from the interaction of just two

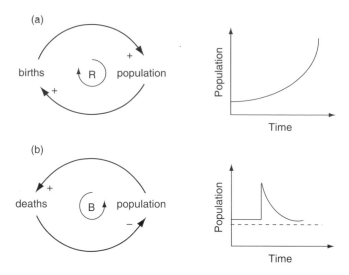

Fig. 5.7. Feedback loops and causal loop diagram construction. The arrows in causal loop diagrams are labelled + or − depending on whether the causal influence is positive or negative. The + sign is used to represent a cause and effect relationship in which the two variables change in the same direction. Hence in (a) above an increase in births causes an increase in the population. It could also mean that a decrease in births causes a decrease in population. Compare this with (b). The − sign beside the arrowhead is used to represent a cause and effect relationship in which the two variables change in the opposite direction. Hence in (b) above an increase in deaths causes a decrease in the population. It could also mean a decrease in deaths causes an increase in population. A tendency for a system to return to its original state after a disturbance indicates the presence of at least one strong negative feedback loop. The loops are described as being either reinforcing (R) or balancing (B). The feedback loop involved with births in (a) above is typical of a reinforcing feedback loop and is identified with an R sign in the centre of the loop. Conversely in (b) above the feedback loop involved with deaths is typical of a balancing feedback loop and is identified with B sign in the centre of the loop. *Source:* Sterman (2000)

types of feedback loops, reinforcing and balancing feedback loops (Sterman, 2000). The s-shaped growth curve is produced from behaviour dominated by positive feedback loops, but as the system grows, there is a non-linear shift to dominance by negative feedback that counteracts the growth and often exhibits an inflexion point (Figure 5.8). The s-shaped growth curve describes resource limited exponential growth.

The adaptive cycle metaphor incorporates the concept of feedback and is concerned with the properties of the system (potential, connectivity and resilience) that are responsible for growth in a system and what slows down

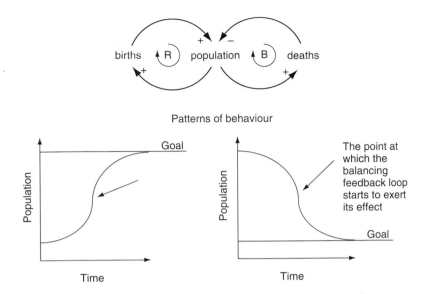

Fig. 5.8. Combination of positive and negative loops producing s-shaped growth in the context of population dynamics. When positive and negative feedback loops are combined a variety of patterns are possible. This example shows a situation where a positive feedback loop leads to early exponential growth, but then a negative feedback loop comes to dominate the behaviour of the system. The negative feedback loop produces the goal-seeking behaviour. *Source:* Sterman (2002)

that growth (almost always s-shaped) and may cause the system to collapse. The feedback concept is the foundation of system dynamics and is used to examine the dynamics of the WA agricultural system in Chapter 7. In Chapter 7, we integrate qualitative system dynamics analysis with resilience analysis (conducted in Chapter 6).

Qualitative *vs.* quantitative system dynamics modelling

Although considered by some to require fully quantified computer simulation (Sterman, 2000; Homer and Oliva, 2001), others argue for the utility of qualitative methods for helping to understand the system (Wolstenholme, 1983; Coyle, 2000) and use them to identify the factors that interact to drive the system (Cavana *et al.*, 1999). Those who believe that qualitative modelling is a useful thing to do argue that it may lead to a better understanding of the system in public health policy (Cavana *et al.*, 1999) and strategic public decisions (Kljajic *et al.*, 2002) and the process of constructing these models is much more important than the model itself. The debate of which form to use, qualitative or quantitative, is intrinsically linked to the philosophy of the researcher and the types of questions being asked. Qualitative knowledge is most appropriate to situations with unstructured problems in which the definition of 'the problem' and the designation of the objectives are problematic. These situations are best addressed by soft systems approaches and are often the most difficult to resolve because systems in which humans are involved are always multi-valued (Checkland, 1984). There are aspects of organisation that do not easily lend themselves to quantitative interpretation, for example, values of ecological capacity and social capacity (discussed in Chapter 7). Under these circumstances qualitative arguments such as 'explanations in principle' may lead to interesting consequences and interpretations (von Bertalanffy, 1968). The questions may be of an ontological or an epistemological nature. In the former there is a desire to 'define' the right system from within a positivist philosophy, and hence the researcher may choose to use a quantitative model. From the epistemological perspective there is a desire to 'understand' the system, in which case the researcher may choose the qualitative form. Wolstenholme (1990) claimed the primary role of models in system dynamics is to aid thinking rather than as representations of the real world. In this role qualitative system dynamics helps to link the behaviour of the system with the structure of the system including the strategies, policies and decision rules. The approach taken here is qualitative model conceptualisation, combined with the building of scenarios developed in Chapter 6. We propose that this method will help decision makers in their selection of the strategies and policies under conditions of uncertainty.

5.7 The social-ecological system perspective

For much of modern history and the science of natural resources management, people were treated as if they were outwith the natural system and as if humans dominated ecosystem behaviour (Vitousek *et al.*, 1997). This position has been slowly changing, initiated in the international policy arena by the United Nations Conference on the Human Environment in Stockholm in 1972. For the first time nations of the world came together to discuss environmental issues that were impinging upon the human environment. Since then, the strategies that come under the umbrella of sustainability have continued to document the feedback loops between humans and their environment.

However, within the theoretical context it has been the construct of resilience that has made a major contribution to the development of an understanding of a humans-in-ecosystem perspective (Davidson-Hunt and

Berkes, 2003). Systems composed of humans and nature are more than just a collection of people and nature; they make up linked social-ecological complex systems which have been described as social-ecological systems (SESs) (Waltner-Toews, 1996; Kay *et al.*, 1999; Walker, 2000; Berkes *et al.*, 2003). The theory and principles that apply to systems, complex systems and complex adaptive systems apply also to SESs (Gunderson and Holling, 2002).

Integral to the impact of human interactions on ecosystems is the existence of interactions across multiple scales from the local to the global levels as well as cumulatively across temporal scales. In resilience theory the manner in which the elements of complex adaptive systems are organised, either spatially or temporally one inside the other, is termed a 'panarchy' and is used to explain complex system behaviour (Gunderson and Holling, 2002). Hence one cannot 'know the system of interest' outside of its history and without placing it into context by expanding the spatial boundary of the system.

5.8 A framework for a new approach

The preceding discussion examined the systems literature to identify the key components from which a framework for a novel approach to natural resource management issues (Figure 5.9) could be constructed.

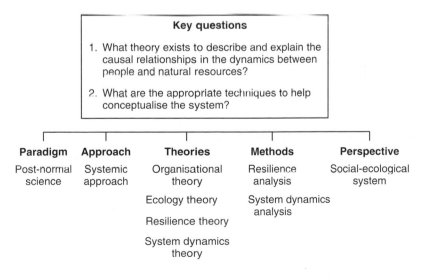

Fig. 5.9. A framework for a new approach comprising the paradigm, approach, theories, perspective and methods.

This framework defines the overarching structure, major components and key content areas required to provide a novel way in which to gain a greater understanding of the fundamental or root causes of natural resource problems. It is composed of five parts and defines the paradigm, the approach, the body of theory, the methods and the perspective. The framework provides a means to analyse the dynamics of the WA agricultural region using resilience analysis in Chapter 6 and system dynamics analysis in Chapter 7.

6

Model conceptualisation of the Western Australian agricultural region. Part 1: resilience analysis

... our purpose is to develop an integrative theory to help us understand the changes occurring globally. We seek to understand the source and role of change in systems – particularly the kinds of changes that are transforming, in systems that are adaptive. Such changes are economic, ecological, social and evolutionary. They concern rapidly unfolding processes and slowly changing ones – gradual change and episodic change, local and global changes.

C. S. (Buzz) Holling, Lance H. Gunderson and Donald Ludwig, 2002

6.1 Introduction

A new paradigm, post-normal science based on systems thinking, has been developed and continues to evolve. It is being promoted and adopted as a means to understand decision-making processes under conditions of uncertainty and counterintuitive behaviour of complex linked social, ecological and economic systems (Funtowicz and Ravetz, 1992; Jasanoff *et al.*, 1997; Kinzig *et al.*; Gunderson and Holling, 2002). The principles, theory concepts and language of this paradigm are contributing to the considerable effort now being directed towards meeting the real world challenges of policy development and management for sustainable natural resources management from the perspective of social-ecological systems (SESs).

The WA agricultural region is an example of a SES with a history of agriculture of over 116 years described in Chapter 2. The region has successively been changed from a highly biologically diverse system dominated by perennial native vegetation to one dominated by annual cropping systems contributing to the regional, state and national economies. However, this has come at a cost. The negative environmental impacts of the dominant land management practices are now well documented (Chapter 3). The resilience of the system is constantly being tested by local and regional as well as global forces.

The agricultural industry is composed of many individual enterprises directly and indirectly associated with one another. This system consists of millions of individual decisions, the aggregate effects of which are linked through behavioural relationships that may shift over time. This book does not examine the behavioural relationships by looking at the psychology and motivation for those individual decisions, but rather by observing what their aggregate effects have been in the past, concentrating on the gross scale.

Under the umbrella of post-normal science we identified four sets of theories and two methods of analysis that have been influential in illuminating the dynamics and understanding the characteristics of resilience in SESs at the regional scale. The post-normal science paradigm and its composite elements described in Chapter 5 are constructed into a framework and are used in this chapter and Chapter 7 to build a conceptual model of the WA agricultural region. Two complementary methods are used to examine the resilience and dynamics of the WA agricultural region as a SES. Firstly, resilience analysis is used in this chapter to conceptualise the SES at the regional scale. The paradoxes, propositions, assumptions and conclusions of resilience theory (Tables 5.6 to 5.9) and the adaptive cycle metaphor (Figure 5.5) are used to interpret the dynamics and to identify factors of importance to the resilience of the SES. Secondly, in Chapter 7 system dynamics analysis is used to examine potential cross-scale interactions among local, regional and global levels.

6.2 Integration of resilience analysis and system dynamics

Any intervention in a system is inherently a dynamic problem, as the purpose is to change the behaviour, over time, from what it would have been towards a more desirable state. Therefore, a method that incorporates a dynamic analysis and includes systemic assumptions is clearly required, identifying both resilience analysis and system dynamics as potential candidates. In problem articulation, system dynamics modelling seeks to define or characterise a problem dynamically, that is as patterns (trends and oscillations) of behaviour of state variables over time. State variables as the name suggests characterize the state of the system. State variables are also known as stocks and are points of accumulation. These reference modes or sets of graphs show the development of the behaviour of state variables (Sterman, 2000) and hence are a useful supporting tool to interpret the adaptive cycle. The minimum number of variables should be chosen to identify the structural reasons for the system's behaviour and to identify the potential causal relationships among the variables. This belief in building models as simple as possible has been expressed in the principle 'Rule of Hand' (Holling *et al.*, 2000) (that is just sufficient parsimony) and is consistent with the system dynamics methodology (Sterman, 2000), suggesting that the behaviour of complex systems can be explained by five or less driving variables.

The purpose of the two methods in this book is to develop a conceptual model to increase the understanding of the dynamics of the WA agricultural region; resilience analysis using the adaptive cycle and panarchy metaphors and a qualitative system dynamics model using causal loop diagrams. The first step in both analyses is the development of reference modes of behaviour.

Resilience analysis has the advantage of being largely metaphorical and provides a novel conceptual framework for problem formulation in linked systems of people and nature. Rather than being solution orientated it provides ways to characterise a system and interpret its dynamic behaviour, which may be either adaptive or maladaptive. Resilience analysis captures the essence of 'the problem' in terms of its internal structure and cross-scale interactions. Consequently it can act as a precursor to the more formal qualitative system dynamics. Qualitative system dynamics has the advantage of focussing attention on the multiple feedback loops and the cross-scale interactions between the regional and global forces, in a more structured format.

We use a double methodological aspect in that it combines two of the systems methodologies in analysing one problem. The benefit of using both the resilience analysis and system dynamics methods is that they are complementary, each with its own strengths and weaknesses for analysing complex problems. The context of this approach and the interaction of these two methods is novel, as is the application of qualitative system dynamics modelling of a SES. Resilience analysis is in its infancy and Walker *et al.* (2002) proposed a provisional four-step framework for resilience analysis and management, with an emphasis on stakeholder involvement in a participatory approach (Table 6.1).

The method used by Walker *et al.* (2002) is consistent with the general system dynamics modelling process shown in Table 5.11, with group model building with stakeholders (Wolfenden, 1999; Zagonel, 2002) and adopted here. In this book resilience analysis is considered as the whole framework of Walker *et al.* (2002), not only Step 3, and in our analysis did not involve stakeholders. Also, rather than discuss the scenarios early, we do this as part of the synthesis in Chapter 8.

Table 6.1. *A four step framework proposed by Walker et al. (2002) for the analysis of resilience in social-ecological systems*

Step	Description
1	**Resilience of what?** The development of a conceptual model of the SES, based strongly on stakeholder inputs. It bounds 'the problem' and elicits information on the important issues in the SES and the major drivers. It includes the historical profile of the system at three scales – local, regional and multi-regional.
2	**Resilience to what? Visions and scenarios**. The aim of this step is to develop a limited set of possible future scenarios that includes the outcome of uncontrollable and ambiguous drivers. Scenarios are used as a means of confronting stakeholders with possible surprises.
3	**Resilience analysis**. The aim of this step is to identify possible driving variables – the crucial slow variable – and processes in the system that govern the dynamics of those variables that stakeholders deem to be important – the ecosystem goods and services – looking especially for threshold effects and other non-linear dynamics. Steps 1 and 2 generate two sets of information: major issues about future states of the system that are of concern to stakeholders; and major uncertainties about how the system will respond to drivers of change.
4	**Resilience management – evaluation and implications**. The final step involves a stakeholder evaluation of the whole process and the implications of the emerging understanding for policy and management actions. A successful resilience analysis identifies the processes that determine critical levels of the system's important control variables. This set of processes leads to a corresponding set of actions that can enhance or reduce resilience and that, therefore, form the basis for resilience management and policy.

Source: Walker *et al.* (2002)

6.3 Conceptual model

Conceptual models or descriptions of the 'problem situation' are representations of our present understanding of the overall system of interest and are an important first step in resilience analysis (Walker *et al.*, 2002) and system dynamics (Sterman, 2000). In this chapter the conceptual model was constructed at the regional scale from the historical data of the WA agricultural region provided in Chapters 2 to 4 and with specific data on ecological, economic and social variables to understand the situation of concern.

6.3.1 Understanding the situation of concern

Resilience theory (examined in Chapter 5) provides some direction to the choice of system boundary, and the number and characteristics of variables that potentially may be important in producing the behaviour of the system and that are used to create a dynamic hypothesis. The WA agricultural region was defined in Figure 1.1. Conceptually the WA agricultural region is composed of three interlinked subsystems, the ecological, social and economic subsystems, which together make up a SES (described in detail in Chapters 2 and 3) and provide a qualitative description of system behaviour and the salient system features from which the important variables were identified. The important variables that changed over time and are considered to produce the behaviour of the WA agricultural region, based on the previous strategic analysis, are:

1. land use change;
2. the number of agricultural establishments;
3. farmer age;
4. farmer terms of trade; and
5. the wheat yield.

6.3.2 Ecological reference modes of system behaviour: the dynamics of land use

A general conceptual model of the dynamics of land use change is used to show the land use system in the WA agricultural region (Figure 6.1). Land use is classified into six major types.

1. Primary native vegetation: natural native vegetation regenerating by natural stages of succession.
2. Secondary native vegetation or regrowth: land cleared in large areas (often former crop or pasture land) left to natural succession, usually sufficiently degraded not to return to primary native vegetation. In the WA agricultural region the rates of return to secondary native vegetation are unknown and are currently under investigation.
3. Cropland: cultivated and planted annually with food crops.
4. Pastureland: covered with grasses, legumes or herbaceous species for grazing livestock.
5. Commercial plantation: land deliberately planted and maintained in tree monoculture and often in exotic species.
6. Unproductive land: land that has been so degraded that it produces virtually no useful species. Usually supports very little growth and will not return naturally to categories 1 or 2.

The predominant progression of land use change in the WA agricultural region is from primary native vegetation to a productive broadacre agricultural

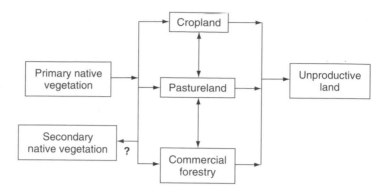

Fig. 6.1. A conceptual model of land use change patterns in the WA agricultural region.? indicates that the return of land to secondary native vegetation in Western Australia is currently under investigation.

system. Although the WA agricultural region has been persistent as an intensive agricultural system for more than 100 years, the land use has been dynamic. The history of the dynamics of land use is illustrated by classifying and identifying the temporal patterns of land use change between 1900 and 2000 and predicted changes to 2050, shown in Figure 6.2. This figure shows a reduction in primary native vegetation from a landscape of approximately 100%

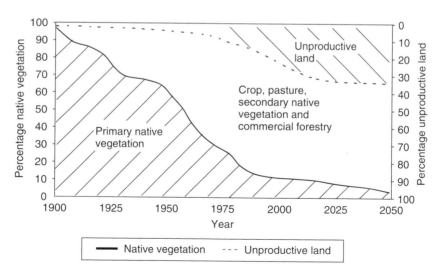

Fig. 6.2. Changes in land use in WA agricultural region between 1900 and 2050. *Sources:* 1900–94 – Beeston *et al.* (1994), Burvill (1979); predicted 2000–50 – Government of Western Australia (1996a).

native vegetation in 1900 to become only 10% of the land use in 2000 (as described in detail in Chapter 2). It is suggested that tree health may continue to decline due to other effects including soil salinity, grazing and pest invasions, and many more trees will eventually be lost from the landscape, which will exacerbate the hydrological imbalance (Saunders *et al.*, 2003). To place this rate of change in the global context, one estimate of the total conversion of primary native vegetation to cropland worldwide is 10.7 million square kilometres, of which 20% was subsequently abandoned (Lambin *et al.*, 2001).

In our example of the WA agricultural region the percentage of land use which is unproductive is based on values of land that is already saline and on the predictions of the future extent of salinity to 2050 based on groundwater trends and 'best guess' future land use (Hatton *et al.*, 2003). In the WA agricultural region areas of unproductive land due to inundation and soil salinity appeared in the early 1900s within a few years of land clearing for agriculture. By 2000 16% of land in the WA agricultural region had developed soil salinity and was largely unproductive for commercial agriculture (National Land and Water Resources Audit, 2001a). A new hydrological equilibrium affecting 33% of the WA agricultural region is predicted to be reached between 2030 to 2050 in some areas on the western edge of the WA agricultural region, while in the eastern parts of the region equilibrium may potentially take as long as 300 years (Hodgson *et al.*, 2004). The prediction of the amount of land that will become unproductive (33%) is based solely on the effects of salinity and does not include any other forms of land degrading processes that may partially reduce soil fertility, such as acidification, sodicity and erosion (National Land and Water Resources Audit, 2002).

There is a time delay between the direct cause and the effect, that is, land clearing causing inundation and soil salinity. Temporal separation between cause and effect has been reported to contribute to the intractable nature of many natural resource problems (Meadows and Robinson, 1985). Recently some land use change from cropland to commercial forestry has occurred in part to combat the hydrological imbalance, although this represents a very small proportion of the total land area and is mostly in areas with rainfall greater than 600 mm to the western and southern edges of the WA agricultural region, and will have no positive effects for large areas that are or will become salt affected.

6.3.3 Socio-economic reference modes of system behaviour

The socio-economic variables used in this conceptual model of the WA agricultural region were wheat yield, farmer terms of trade, the number of farms between 1900 and 2000 (Figure 6.3 (a), (b), and (c) respectively), and farmer age, as discussed below.

Wheat yield (economic production target)

The gross value of agricultural commodities produced in Western Australia in 1998–9 was $4.3 billion with a significant proportion, $1.6 billion (37%), of the gross value of production obtained from wheat (Australian Bureau of Statistics, 2003). The productivity of Australia's grain farms has been rising by an average of 3.2% a year for several decades. This high sustained rate has kept the farms financially viable despite concomitant falls in farmer terms of trade (Passioura, 2002), substantial extension of cropping into more marginal lands, and increasing areas of soil salinity as discussed in Chapter 2. The trends for wheat yield for Australia and Western Australia between 1900 and 2000 (Hamblin and Kyneur, 1993; Passioura, 2002) are shown in Figure 6.3 (a). For agronomic reasons wheat productivity has increased at different rates and increased rapidly from the early 1980s (Hamblin and Kyneur, 1993). The rates for Australia have not been steady but came largely during three well separated decades; the 1900s, 1950s and 1990s (Figure 6.3 (a)) (Passioura, 2002). In the last decade the rates have reached their highest through a set of complex factors in agronomy and genetic improvement. However, despite these increases Australia had the lowest rate of increase in wheat yield between 1950 and 1990 compared with its competitors on the world market (Hamblin and Kyneur, 1993).

Farmer terms of trade

The farmer terms of trade (prices of agricultural commodities in comparison to the price of farm inputs) for Australia are shown Figure 6.3 (b) (National Land and Water Resources Audit, 2002). These national figures are taken as representative of the Western Australian position because most of the wheat produced is an example of a standardised undifferentiated raw material, discussed further in Chapter 7. Since the 1960s there has been a declining trend although punctuated with years with better terms of trades caused by combinations of good climatic seasons and high wheat prices. Because of the declining terms of trade, large numbers of farmers in broadacre agriculture in Australia had a zero or negative profit at full equity on the basis of a five-year average to 1996–7 (National Land and Water Resources Audit, 2002). This declining trend has made it increasingly difficult for small and marginal agricultural enterprises to maintain their livelihoods solely by engaging in agricultural activities (Barr and Cary, 2000; Cary *et al.*, 2002; Tonts and Black, 2002). With low or zero profit there is little opportunity to adopt sustainable

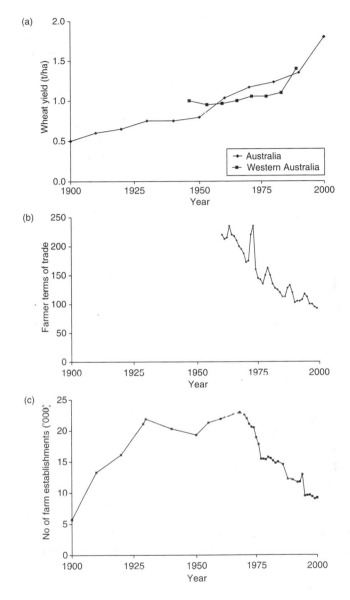

Fig. 6.3. Socio-economic reference modes. (a) Trends in wheat yields in Australia and Western Australia between 1900 and 1994. Source: Hamblin and Kyneur (1993); Passioura (2002). (b) Trend in Australian farmer terms of trade between 1960 and 2000. Farmer terms of trade: the ratio of the index of prices received by farmers to the index of prices paid by farmers. Reference year 1997/1998 = 100. Source: National Land and Water Resources Audit (2002). (c) Trend in the numbers of farms in the agricultural region of Western Australia between 1900 and 2000. *Sources:* 1900–76 – Burvill (1979), 1977–94 – Australian Bureau of Statistics, 1995 and 2000 – ABARE (2002).

land practices that may involve land use change and would be costly to adopt in the short term. The declining terms of trade have also influenced the economic need to clear more land for production to gain economies of scale.

The number of broadacre farms

The definition of a farm is a matter of interpretation. In this book the definition was taken from the primary data source, which was the Australian Bureau of Agriculture and Resource Economics (ABARE) surveys designed on the basis of a framework drawn from the Business Register maintained by the Australian Bureau of Statistics (ABS). A farm establishment is defined as an agricultural operation with an Estimated Value of Agricultural Output (EVAO) above a certain threshold. The EVAO varies over time and for the 1999–2000 survey was $22 500.

The number of farm establishments in the WA agricultural region rose to a maximum of approximately 23 000 in 1968. Since then the number of establishments declined sharply to approximately 9000 in 2000 shown in Figure 6.3 (c). In 2003 there were just over 8000 farming enterprises with an annual decline of around 7%. In recent times a lack of large areas of native vegetation available for conversion to cropland has prevented continuous growth by way of clearing more land. Consequently the need for efficiencies of scale has come from farm consolidation (Mackenzie, 2004). Some of the large corporate family farms in Western Australia now cover areas of as much as 80 000 acres. Although the lifestyle of some farmers with small enterprises became less economically viable, farm adjustments and restructuring did not always follow the neoclassical course of farm exits and property amalgamation (Barr, 2000), and the decisions are classed as being boundedly rational (Walker *et al.*, 2002), that is, made with imperfect knowledge and context specific in which emotions are involved with the decision-making process. The extent to which emotions are involved with problem solving is considered to be a non-trivial component and this may take on particular significance with decisions involving family farms (Barr, 2000).

Farmer median age

On many family-run farms the main adjustment was the abandonment of expectations of intergenerational transfer. Coupled with this was a deferral of farm exit in response to lack of perceived alternatives available to broadacre operators. Consequently the number of older farmers has increased. In Western Australia the mean age of farmers increased from 48 to 52 years between 1990 and 2000 (ABARE, 2001). A similar trend was also recorded for changes in farmer age throughout Australia (Barr, 2000). Barr (2000) suggested that this trend cannot continue and anticipated there will be a major restructure in farming enterprises when older farmers exit the industry.

6.4 Resilience analysis

6.4.1 Model diagnosis

The model diagnosis uses resilience theory and the adaptive cycle metaphor to understand and propose causal relationships to explain the trends and dynamics just described. The history of the management of the region between 1889 and 2005 (described in Chapters 2 to 4) was analysed to identify major events that may be used to identify the phases of potential adaptive cycles that occurred over this period of time (Table 6.2).

First adaptive cycle

For the first 60 years of the Western Australian colony's history, pastoral activities were developed ahead of agriculture and only 28 000 hectares were developed for cropping by the 1880s. In the period labelled The Move Forward, Western Australian government policy significantly influenced land development. By the late 1920s, 30% of the area identified now as the WA agricultural region was cleared of native vegetation and prices for wool and sheep were high. The features of this period are characteristic of the forward loop (r to K) of the adaptive cycle (Table 6.2). In the adaptive cycle this is explained by an increase in the capacity or potential of the system, an increase in the degree of connectedness among the agents in the system and a loss of resilience (Table 5.10). As the agents become overconnected, the resilience is further reduced causing the system to move into the backloop of the adaptive cycle.

The 16-year period between the Great Depression of the 1930s and the Second World War, the start of the backloop, the release phase of the adaptive cycle, was marked by hardship in agriculture with low potential for change, high connectedness, particularly in institutions and low resilience. Record low prices for wool and wheat, and dry climatic conditions caused farms to be abandoned, producing conditions in which institutional change could occur and produce novel structures as the cycle entered the reorganisation phase (α). The reorganisation phase is characterised by high potential, low connectedness and high resilience (Table 5.10). Multiple factors were instrumental to this reorganisation phase in a short period between 1945 and 1949 leading

Table 6.2. *Historical profile of major events in natural resource management in the WA agricultural region between 1889 and 2003. The phases and duration of two potential adaptive cycles are shown that occurred over this time period*

Date	Historical period	Cycle	Duration (Years)	Adaptive cycle phase	Event or practices that characterise the phases
1889–1929	The Forward Move	1	40	Exploitation (r) Conservation (K)	Land settlement and expansion of agricultural areas, high wheat and wool prices.
1929–45	Depression and the War	1	16	Release (Ω)	Low wheat and wool prices, farms abandoned, drought.
1945–9	Recovery	1	4	Reorganisation (α)	Farm amalgamation, technological and scientific innovation.
Years per cycle	**60**				
1949–69	The Rural Boom	2	20	Exploitation (r) Conservation (K)	Expansion of agricultural lands, favourable climatic conditions, cheap and abundant fuel, over/production.
1969–79	A Troubled Decade	2	10	Release (Ω)	Market regulation (wheat quota introduced), widespread land degradation including salinity, drought.
1980–90	Environmental Awareness	2	10	Reorganisation (α)	Habitat protection (Conservation through Reserves), Australian Conservation Foundation and National Farmers Federation alliance.
1990–2000	Decade of Landcare	2	10	Reorganisation (α)	Institutional reorganisation through partnership programs at national, state and regional level for natural resource management.
2000–3	Turn of the Century	2	3+	Reorganisation (α)	Industrial agriculture.
Years per cycle	**54+**				

to economic recovery beginning in 1949, such as advances in technology, scientific innovation and institutional change including farm amalgamation to make farm sizes more viable. At this time of change the agents in the system were weakly connected allowing the potential for change to increase. The resilience to external disturbance was also greater at this time. This completed one iteration of the adaptive cycle (Table 6.2).

Second adaptive cycle
The second iteration of the adaptive cycle began with The Rural Boom. Cheap and abundant fuel and abundant labour, which when combined with favourable climatic conditions and a development orientated Government produced a rapid expansion of agricultural lands, characteristic of the frontloop of the adaptive cycle. The rate of clearing increased from 36 000 hectares a year for 1930–49 to 364 000 hectares a year for 1949–69 (Figure 2.2), which increased the area of agricultural land from 33% to approximately 90% of the region. The major commodities (grains, wool and meat) experienced high prices in the 1960s (Hamblin and Kyneur, 1993) resulting in overproduction in the industry worldwide in a typical commodity system pattern of behaviour (described further in Chapter 7). This period is represented by the exploitation (r) to conservation phases (K) of the adaptive cycle.

Then followed A Troubled Decade, marking the beginning of the backloop of the adaptive cycle with the release phase, in which the Australian Government introduced quotas to regulate the production of wheat and at the same time prices fell. Land degradation began to be perceived as a greater problem and there was a drier than average climatic period. From 1980 onwards there was massive change and reorganisation in institutions marking the beginning of the reorganisation phase and continuing the backloop through to the present. Two specific examples of institutional change are the unprecedented alliance of the Australian Conservation Foundation and the National Farmers Foundation who joined together in an attempt to try to combat the growing problems of salinity. The need to allocate lands for conservation was also recognised at this time and was implemented through the Conservation Through Reserves program by the WA Department of Conservation (now the WA Department of Environment). In the 1990s further institutional reorganisation occurred through the construction of partnerships across scales in government from regional natural resource groups to state and national organisations.

In 2003 these relationships among the tiers of government were becoming increasingly formalised (increasing their degree of connectedness and potentially their rigidity). Institution restructure continues, including the development of policy that incorporates economic solutions for natural resource management. Increasingly market-based mechanisms and creation of property rights for ecosystem services are being promoted for natural resource management policy (National Land and Water Resources Audit, 2001b).

6.4.2 Long-wave economic Kondratiev Cycles

Evolutionary cycles are ubiquitous in nature and have been identified in systems created by human society including the economy (De Greene, 1993; Carry, 1996). Cyclicity in the economy has been identified at four temporal scales at least (Table 6.3), ranging from the short-wave Kitchin Cycle of between three and seven years, through the Juglar and Kuznets Cycles, to the long-wave Kondratiev Cycles of between 45 and 60 years (De Greene, 1993).

There is controversy regarding the existence of Kondratiev Cycles (De Greene, 1993) and their methodology of construction (Carry, 1996). However, Carry (1996) critically analysed the nature of the debate surrounding the deterministic or probabilistic determination of the Kondratiev Cycles and concluded that Kondratiev's treatment of uncertainty in the conception of the long-wave economic cycle is consistent with modern authors and provides the evidence for the existence of such cycles. In addition, Berry (1991) made an extensive analysis of economic data and found new evidence for the reliability of long-wave economic theory. The Kondratiev Cycles show the behaviour over time of the evolution of modern industrial societies, a phenomenon that shows patterns of boom and bust, characterised by four phases, prosperity, recession, depression and recovery shown in Figure 6.4. The Kondratiev upwave consists of the phases of recovery and prosperity and the Kondratiev downwave consists of the recession and the depression phases. Table 6.4 summarizes the four Kondratiev cycles that have been described between 1785 and 2000, each of between 41 and 63+ years. Kondratiev's work was extended in the 1930s by the prominent economist Joseph Schumpeter (Schumpeter, 1950). Schumpeter emphasised the role of technical innovation in producing the dynamics of the cycles particularly with reference to the bunching of innovation in the phase of depression equivalent to the release (Ω) to reorganisation (α) in the adaptive cycle. This bunching of innovation produced 'gales of creative destruction' (Schumpeter, 1950), whereby an ensemble of technologies both creates new opportunities for economic growth and paves the way for the slowdown of growth and replacement by newer technologies. In relation to cycles of dominance in cultures, this sequence of events has been described with these words, 'Things will be undone by the myth that created them' (Sewell, 2003).

Table 6.3. *Four temporal cycles identified in the economy*

Cycle name	Approximate cycle duration (years)
Kitchin or business Cycle	3 to 7
Juglar Cycle	8 to 10
Kuznets Cycle	15 to 25
Kondratiev Cycle	45 to 60

Source: De Greene (1993)

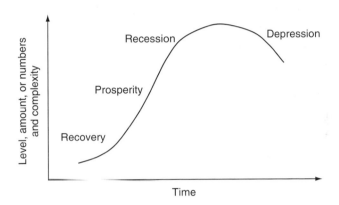

Fig. 6.4. The Kondratiev Cycle shows the behaviour over time of the evolution of modern industrial societies, a phenomenon that shows patterns of boom and bust, characterised by four phases: prosperity, recession, depression and recovery. *Source:* De Greene (1993)

Holling and Gunderson (2002) made use of Schumpeter's theories in the development of the adaptive cycle for describing the changes from the conservation phase (K) to the release phase (Ω) and adopted the use of the term 'gales of creative destruction'. Of the three commonly identified classes of social theories of change (life-cycle representation, gradualist life-cycle and revolutionary change models) Schumpeter adhered most closely to the revolutionary change model, recognising the four-phase properties of complex evolving systems and the tensions they generated to produce stages of growth and transformation. For example, Schumpeter (1950) saw socio-economic transformations proceeding such that market forces stimulated innovation in the exploitation or r phase; institutional hierarchies, monopolism and social rigidity controlled the K phase of consolidation; forces of 'creative destruction' triggered the release or Ω phase; and technological invention determined the source for a phase transformation to the reorganisation α phase.

Table 6.4. *The four Kondratiev Cycles described for the period 1785 to 2000*

| Phase | Kondratiev Cycles | | | |
	1	2	3	4
Recovery		1840–1860	1896–1905	1937–1948
Prosperity	1785–1815	1860–1873	1905–1920	1948–1970
Recession	1815–1825	1873–1886	1920–1929	1970–1990?
Depression	1825–1840	1886–1896	1929–1937	1990?–2000?
Dominant new technologies or industries in each cycle	steampower, textiles	coal, steel, railroads	oil, electricity, chemicals, automobiles	aircraft, electronics, computers, control systems, rockets and missiles
Cycle length	55+ years	56 years	41 years	63+ years

Adapted from De Greene (1993)

Such complementary theories of revolutionary change in social and biological systems provided insight for the adaptive cycle (Gunderson *et al.*, 2002a). Conceptually the phases of the Kondratiev Cycle and the adaptive cycle may be compared (see Table 6.5).

The durations of each of the two adaptive cycles are synchronous with the third and the fourth long-wave economic Kondratiev Cycles. The upwaves of the Kondratiev Cycles shown in Table 6.4 are in the order of 50% to 60% of the total duration of the Kondratiev Cycle. The durations of the frontloops in the two adaptive cycles that describe the behaviour of the WA agricultural region constitute approximately 66% and 57% of the duration of the cycle. This is considerably less than the 75% of time suggested for the frontloop of the adaptive cycle described by Holling and Gunderson (2002). The adaptive cycle heuristic model was developed from empirical data on biological systems in which the characteristics of biological processes were described by means of a slow build up of resources or capital in the frontloop, occupying 75% of the total duration of an adaptive cycle, which was released in one rapid catastrophic event in the backloop occupying only 25% of the duration of the adaptive cycle (Holling and Gunderson, 2002). However, the WA agricultural region does not conform to the model of long slow accumulation of capital. The duration of the frontloop occupied between 57% and 66% of the total duration of the cycle, less than the 75% described by the adaptive cycle model. An alternative proposition based on the Kondratiev

Table 6.5. *Relationship between the phases of the*
Kondratiev Cycle and the adaptive cycle

Kondratiev Cycle	Adaptive cycle
Recovery	α–r
Prosperity	r–K
Recession	K–Ω
Depression	$\Omega - \alpha$

The Kondratiev upwave consists of the Recovery and
Prosperity phases
The Kondratiev downwave consists of the Recession and
Depression phases

Cycles may be used to explain the behaviour of the WA agricultural system.
The economic/technical factors at the global scale, which are responsible for
the dynamics of the Kondratiev Cycle have entrained a similar cycle in the
WA agricultural region. That is to say, the dynamics of the WA agricultural
system were strongly influenced by exogenous factors at the global scale
with little controlling influence from natural resource policy or by other
endogenous balancing feedback to change the behaviour of the system.

6.4.3 Pathological states

If each of the three properties (potential, connectedness and resilience) in
the adaptive cycle is given two nominal levels, either low or high, then the
adaptive cycle model uses only four of the possible eight combinations (2^3)
of the three properties. Two of the other four combinations are suggested as
pathological states labelled the Poverty Trap and the Rigidity Trap by Holling
et al. (2002c) and shown in Figure 6.5. These are departures from the adaptive
cycle and may occur if the adaptive cycle collapses. The levels of the three
properties of the Poverty Trap and the Rigidity Trap are given in Table 6.6.

For example, the Poverty Trap is characterised by all three properties
having low values creating an impoverished system. The Poverty Trap is most
likely to occur by changes in the release (Ω) or exploitation (r) phases of the
adaptive cycle shown by the arrows in Figure 6.5. From the release phase
(Ω) a change from high to low connectedness will result in a combination of
the three properties characteristic of a Poverty Trap and in the exploitation
phase (r) a change in resilience from high to low will effectively achieve the
same configuration of low levels of all three properties. It would be more
difficult to enter the Poverty Trap from the other two phases (conservation

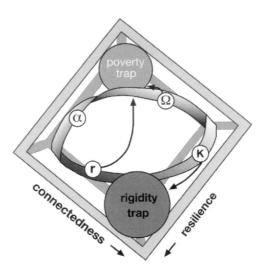

Fig. 6.5. Heuristic model of the adaptive cycle with pathological states of the Poverty Trap and the Rigidity Trap shown. The Poverty Trap has low levels of all three properties and lies below the adaptive cycle in the figure whereas the Rigidity Trap has high levels of all properties and lies above the adaptive cycle in the figure. The Poverty Trap may be most easily entered from the release (Ω) or exploitation (r) phase of the adaptive cycle shown by the arrows in the figure. *Source:* Gunderson and Holling (2002)

and reorganisation) because it would require a change from high levels to low levels in two properties. Conversely, it is easier to enter the Rigidity Trap from either the reorganisation (α) or conservation phase (K). An example of a Rigidity Trap may occur in social systems in which the members of organisations and their institutions become so tightly connected that they are highly resilient to change and become rigid and inflexible, such as some bureaucracies. Holling *et al.* (2002c) contended that one example of a Rigidity Trap may be found in the agriculture industry, where command and control have squeezed out diversity, and power, politics and profit have reinforced one another. The two other possible alternative pathological states were not described. It is proposed here that one of the undescribed pathological states could be labelled the Lock-in Trap, which is characterised by low potential for change, high connectedness and high resilience (Table 6.6). The Lock-in Trap is most likely to occur by changes in the conservation (K) phase shown by the curving arrow in Figure 6.6. This proposition is developed below.

Pathological traps and biophysical resilience thresholds may be avoided through human innovations that effectively redefine the system by extending

Table 6.6. *The level of each of the three variables that characterise the two identified pathological states called the Poverty Trap and the Rigidity Trap and the proposed Lock-in Trap*

Pathological state	Potential	Connectedness	Resilience
Poverty Trap	low	low	low
Rigidity Trap	high	high	high
Lock–in Trap	low	high	high
?	high	low	low

Source: derived from Gunderson and Holling (2002)

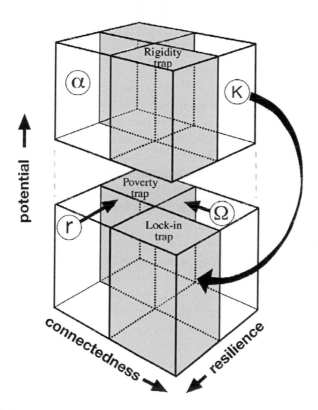

Fig. 6.6. A heuristic model showing eight possible phases of the adaptive cycle. Four phases that make up the adaptive cycle are shown by the white boxes and labelled r, K, Ω, α. The four grey boxes are alternative phases, two of which were identified by Holling *et al.* (2002c) as pathological traps, the Poverty Trap and the Rigidity Trap. A third alternative phase we have identified as the Lock-in Trap.

the boundaries of the thresholds outward (Walker *et al.*, 2002). Human innovation can take a number of forms, for example, technical or institutional change. In the WA agricultural region technical advances in fertilisers and improvement in wheat varieties increased wheat production over time, essentially masking the reductions in land degradation including the reduced productive area caused by increased soil salinity, now approximately 16% of the WA agricultural region.

The ecosystem has been changed from a species rich system to a specialised commodity system with low species richness and loss of system function, for example, flood mitigation and water purification. The costs of loss of system function are the costs to maintain and increase productivity (for example, the costs of fertilisers, herbicides, pesticides, new wheat varieties and mitigation of soil degradation, including acidification and erosion, drainage, and revegetation). It is proposed that the WA agricultural region has lost important system components involved with the hydrological cycle and that the system has been irreversibly modified, which potentially will require a continuous stream of increasing and additional inputs to control the symptoms. For example, pumping to keep freshwater wetlands from becoming saline and the digging of drainage channels to prevent land becoming saline.

The reference modes described the WA agricultural region as a SES with the unintended effects of resource depletion, environmental pollution and social decline. Why has there not been a profound collapse of the system? Holling *et al.* (2002c) proposed that an adaptive cycle will collapse because the potential and diversity have been eradicated by misuse or an external force, illustrated by an example of an irreversible eroding state of a savanna (Holling and Gunderson, 2002). Human activity may 'mine' the resource (for example, depleting the soil through erosion) in a situation in which the land manager is under greater and greater pressure to produce more while the economic return from the land diminishes, either because of lowered productivity or reducing terms of trade or both. Ultimately the ecological system will become severely impoverished, causing the resilience to increase because the system has reached such a depauperate state that it is extremely stable or perhaps irreversibly stable. We suggest that this situation is represented by one of the remaining two unaccounted for pathological states. This state we have labelled the Lock-in Trap in which an industry or enterprise has high amounts of 'sunk-costs' causing it to continue to degrade the resource it relies upon until the natural resource capital is totally removed. The concept of 'sunk-cost' is well defined in the economic literature as that part of any cost that has been incurred in the past (or that part of a cost resulting from a commitment entered into in the past) that cannot be eliminated or recovered by present and future actions (Baumol *et al.*, 1992). This type of relationship is characterised by reinvestment at the macroeconomic scale in agriculture in terms of technology and at the microeconomic scale by investment by the individual in, for example, plant, equipment and intellectual property. The Lock-in Trap has low potential for change, high connectedness and high resilience. High resilience would mean a great ability for the system to resist external disturbances and persist due to the depauperate ecological system. It can be deduced from resilience theory that some subregions or catchments of the WA agricultural region with the most productive soils and not prone to soil salinity will be adaptive and others may well get caught in one or other of the pathological traps through a combination of factors but ultimately through natural resource degradation.

Long-wave economic cycles cause build up and collapse in societies. Records for ancient societies show that in some cases renewal from collapse was possible while in other cases recovery was not possible (Janssen *et al.*, 2002). It is proposed that some societies may become fragile and vulnerable to collapse from a phenomenon known as the 'sunk-cost effect' (Janssen *et al.*, 2002; Tainter, 1988). This phenomenon is attributed to a society that becomes highly interconnected and may not be flexible enough to react to unfavourable climatic events such as drought (Janssen *et al.*, 2002). Such a society has lost its resilience to be able to respond to sudden changes and a threshold may be crossed. This event has also been described as a tipping point (Gladwell, 2002). Tainter (1988) developed an argument of diminishing returns to increasing complexity and ascribed to this cause the collapse of 24 societies. Tainter (1988) proposed that increasing complexity was beneficial up to a certain degree, beyond which the effects were detrimental. Tainter (1988) argued that the development of complexity was an economic process and that society evolved along the marginal return curve in a phenomenon known as 'the law of diminishing returns'. That is to say, at a certain level of complexity the ratio of returns to costs diminishes resulting in negative returns to investment. At this tipping point a society may become extremely vulnerable to collapse.

6.5 Organisation and change

The history of the WA agricultural region and the negative impact of current management practices on natural resources demonstrates the practical difficulties that have arisen from attempting to manage ecological systems. Natural resource management continues to be problematic because it is rarely possible to consider social systems and ecological systems as separate entities, as commonly managed as such in the past. Resilience theory proposes that the concept of the SESs that emphasises the integration of humans-in-ecosystems will help in our attempts to manage these social-ecological linkages towards more sustainable land management practices. There can be no neat separation into individual systems, which are artefacts of the human mind, not character-istics of the real world (Meadows and Robinson, 1985). Cross-scale dynamics, thresholds, stability and resilience are useful concepts to help explain organ-isation and change in SESs.

6.5.1 Cross-scale dynamics

We suggested that in the WA agricultural region human institutions have not responded adequately to the balancing feedback in ecosystems (that is, the natural resource degradation). Social and economic resilience may be created in the short term, but at the expense of loss of ecological resilience. For example, although the effects of clearing land were known in the early 1900s, the political arena ignored the unintended effects or detrimental externalities. We suggest that the economic system, consisting of fast moving variables, over this 100-year period was linked with rural patterns of demography, another fast moving variable, but not linked with the slow moving hydrolog-ical cycle (a slow system variable). However, this position is now changing as the percentage of unproductive land becomes greater making it a political, social and economic issue. It is no longer reasonable to assume that envi-ronmental feedbacks are not a dynamic component of the economic system (O'Neill *et al.*, 1998). Also at the global scale the extent of resource utilisation by society is increasing, impacting on the dynamics of the ecosystem and the ecological cycle is having an increased impact on the lives and activities of humans. This is now a well-documented concept and many papers in the literature identify the linkages between the socio-economic systems and the ecological system (Daly, 1991; Rosser, 2001; Costanza and Farber, 2002).

The scale of the area under investigation may influence the duration of the adaptive cycle, and may explain the differences reported between this regional study in Western Australia and the Goulburn Broken Catchment (Figure 1.2) study in Victoria, eastern Australia by Walker *et al.* (2002). The duration of the two adaptive cycles in the WA agricultural region is inconsistent with those found for the Goulburn Broken Catchment. In a resilience analysis (Table 6.1) of the dynamics of the Goulburn Broken Catchment, Walker *et al.* (2002) identified four periods of major changes over 110 years (1890 to 2000) and suggested that a general pattern where 75% of a period occupies the forward loop was typical for regional systems and is consistent with the adaptive cycle model. As described above, this finding of Walker *et al.* (2002) is inconsistent with the pattern found in the WA agricultural region in which over the 116-year history in the region only 66% and 57% of the period was spent in the forward loop, or the upwave of the Kondratiev Cycle. One possible explanation for the discrepancy in durations is the difference in spatial scales of the two regions; the Goulburn Broken Catchment has an area of 2.4 million hectares (Goulburn Broken Catchment Management Authority, 2002) whereas the WA agricultural region has an area of 18 million hectares, about 7.5 times greater. The smaller size of the Goulburn Broken Catchment may have resulted in a greater influence of more local events on the dynamics of the cycle; for example the influence of the depression of the 1890s, the regional drought and dust storms, and poor success of stone fruit as identified by the stakeholders in the study by Walker *et al.* (2002). Further studies on regions of different sizes would be beneficial in support of this position.

6.5.2 Thresholds, stability and resilience

A key aim of resilience analysis is to identify thresholds, their nature and what determines how they prevent the system from moving into an undesirable configuration (Walker *et al.*, 2002). Ecosystems of renewable resources threatened by the interactions of economic and social systems may lose resilience (that is, the ability to absorb shocks and disturbances) and may suddenly break down and/or settle into a different system with less resilience (Gunderson and Holling, 2002). This implies that there are thresholds at which the levels of stress will lead to the disruption of the system, the first of the six assumptions ascribed to complex systems shown in Table 5.8 (Walker *et al.*, 2002).

We propose that factors involved with ecological buffering help a system's ability to cope with surprise (Folke *et al.*, 2002) and prevent the system moving into an undesirable state. In the WA agricultural system, areas of native vegetation that once provided refugia for stock in times of drought have been lost, and loss of riparian vegetation has increased soil loss and reduced water quality. In other areas raised watertables have reduced the ecological buffering for episodes of greater than average rainfall, which results in flood events, such as was experienced in the Moore River Catchment in the northern area of the WA agricultural region in 1999 (Water Studies Pty Ltd, 2000) and in the Avon River Catchment in 2000 (Hatton and Ruprecht, 2001). In addition, the predicted changes in the annual total rainfall and distribution for the south-west of Western Australia, as a consequence of global climate change

(CSIRO, 2001), may create a crisis through increasingly extreme climatic events that could have an overwhelming impact on the SES. It is proposed that when there is little or no ecological buffering capacity the control mechanisms shift to regional economic, demographic or social factors (Gunderson *et al.*, 2002a). For the WA agricultural region we hypothesise that the potential impact could be a retraction of the area under annual cropping with areas being abandoned and/or a threshold being reached in the carrying capacity of the number of farmers. Barr (2000) proposed that a major restructure in rural demographics is likely to occur, with the agricultural enterprises at the theoretical economic marginal return curve exiting the industry.

Agricultural intensification was a major feature of the second adaptive cycle. We suggest that agricultural intensification involving changes in technology acted as functional reinforcement across scales (see Table 5.7) effectively masking the degradation of natural resources, and helping to produce the perceived stability in the system. The balancing feedback signals were either hidden or ignored. Novelty in technology effectively redefined the system and so prevented the ecosystem from crossing critical thresholds and changing states. By and large the scientific community has helped to perpetuate the illusion of sustainable development through scientific and technological progress (Ludwig *et al.*, 1993). We suggest that this is largely because humans fail to build self-organisation or adaptive capacities into their technologies (Gunderson *et al.*, 2002a); that is, there is no mechanism to automatically provide balancing feedback.

Technological advances make single variable interventions or create interventions without regard for their impacts on other parts of the system. This has been described as humans' propensity to focus on 'single cause and effect solutions', that is, 'means–ends' logic designed to solve a particular problem (Westley *et al.*, 2002), ultimately with serious implications for continuing resource misuse. For instance, as a solution is found for each problem it will create other effects, referred to as side-effects or perverse and unintended effects. In economics, side-effects are often called negative externalities and a major theme of ecological economics is to estimate the value of these externalities. The creation of new institutions (for example, policies and markets) is being promoted as one way to help to account for the full costs (both positive and negative externalities) to society of land management practices to ensure that critical thresholds are not crossed. Even with the ability to redefine the system by creating novel futures through technological advances, this system will rely on a continuous stream of new technologies, institutions or social adaptations to maintain resilience and the adaptive capacity of the whole system.

6.5.3 Policy responses

When faced with shifting stable states and effects that are perceived as crises, policy and management options fall into one of three general classes of response (Hilborn, 1992). The first is to do nothing and wait and see if the system will return to some acceptable state while sacrificing benefits of the desirable state. The second option is to actively manage the system and try to return it to a desirable state. The third option is to admit that the system is irreversibly changed, and hence the only strategy is to constantly adapt, in a world characterised by crises and changing states. All three of the responses were seen sequentially in the WA agricultural region. The problem of soil salinity was known early in the history of the WA agricultural region, and for economic, social and political reasons the government chose to ignore the scientific advice and released land for agriculture in areas known to be susceptible to soil salinity and in areas known to be marginal for agriculture because of climatic variability and poor soil characteristics. The second response was to put in place actions directed at fixing the symptoms, each new policy responding to the effects (side-effects or unintended effects) of the past policy (described in Chapters 2 to 4). This is a well-known phenomenon known as the 'bite-back' phenomenon in resilience theory of large-scale systems (Gunderson *et al.*, 2002c), which is also described as 'policy resistance' in system dynamics (Sterman, 2000). For instance, many tree planting programs designed to alter the changing hydrological patterns failed and advice on where and what to plant changed as our scientific understanding of the hydrological system improved. The solutions were mostly directed at the symptoms as opposed to actions to address the systemic causes of the problem.

The third and current policy response contains a number of strategic actions aimed at adapting to the current situation. One approach currently being discussed is that of environmental triage (Hobbs *et al.*, 2003; Hobbs and Kristjanson, 2003), in which it is acknowledged that some areas will not be able to be managed positively and no further public funds will be directed to these areas. The second strategy is the introduction of market-based instruments. This is based on the premise that many of the changes including biodiversity loss are caused by inadequate institutions, in particular ill-defined property rights (Hanna and Munasinghe, 1995) and the impact of this on resource use. The design of institutions such as property rights in conjunction with market-based instruments and regionalisation is a major thrust in Australian natural resource policy. Young and McCay (1995) argued that by adding flexibility and renewable structures to property rights regimes they can be adapted to incorporate social and environmental objectives, and this is one way to increase resilience. Critics of the proposed economic solutions argue that complications will arise from the coupling of equilibrium economic market-based solutions in a non-equilibrium world in which the system will usually rebound to the detriment of the natural environment; 'A major challenge is to protect and conserve the natural environment in spite of the political/economic power *status quo*, not to implement policies within the framework of, and reconfirming, that *status quo*.' (K. de Greene personal communication, May 2001). Therefore, the use of market-based instruments for natural resource management is in its infancy and further research is required to better understand the relationships between various property rights regimes and the dynamics of complex systems where the interactions between variables occur at different temporal and spatial scales.

Nonetheless, an important research question would be, 'Are there phases within the economic cycle that provide times of greater leverage for different types of policy?' In other words, is it possible to create policies that are most appropriate for the dynamics of the system, 'Let the policy fit the time'. In the agricultural industry, times of rapid change and restructuring may be the most appropriate period to implement policies that create the greatest change to meet the desired objectives of society, for example, retiring severely degraded land, allocating land for conservation of biodiversity and the maintenance of ecosystem services. This may be particularly relevant if there is a trend away from the family farm towards increasing corporate farm ownership. It is possible, with the use of new precision farming techniques, combining the new information system techniques of global positioning system, yield monitoring on harvesters and geographic information systems, to identify those areas with the highest productivity and those with low productivity that are not cost effective to crop (Passioura, 2002). The latter could be retired out of production to some other land use for increasing ecosystem services. An alternative 'system-fix' approach would be in the form of social institutions such as supply and production limits, certification for best practices, and tax and payments based on stewardship that expand the goals of the natural resource economy to encompass more than the standard definition of efficiency (Sawin *et al.*, 2003).

6.6 Concluding remarks

The adaptive cycle metaphor is applicable to the WA agricultural region and has shown the sequential progression between the phases that maximise production and accumulation and the phases that maximise invention and reassortment. Periods of global technical innovation that have created the upwaves of the Kondratiev Cycles have contributed to redefining the thresholds of the WA agricultural region, allowing the region to remain productive and preventing the potential collapse of the SES. Because the Kondratiev Cycles are based only on economic and political behaviour, the application of resilience theory moves beyond the behaviour of the socio-economic variables and includes the requirement for causal explanations for the behaviour and resilience of the ecological and social systems.

The reference modes showed an increasing area of unproductive land, declining farmer terms of trade, rapidly declining number of farm establishments and an increasing average age of farmers over time. In the past the negative effects were partially masked by technological improvements. These trends are examples of diminished sources of novelty through reduction of natural and social capital, which increases the vulnerability of the system, described by the fourth provisional proposition about large-scale systems (Table 5.7). Using the metaphor of the adaptive cycle we suggest that the nature of the dynamics of the WA agricultural region represents a pathological trap, the Lock-in Trap, which is characterised by low potential for change, high degree of connectedness among the structural variables and, because of the extremely degraded state, a high resilience to change.

We suggest that the current state of the WA agricultural region is the balance between those processes that erode resilience and those institutional processes that have maintained it through the expansion of the thresholds. The changes in land use and the ensuing natural resource degradation are founded in economic, demographic and social changes that link the variables in the ecological system to those in the social system. Through the application of the metaphor of the adaptive cycle, Holling *et al.* (2002a) proposed that ecological collapses and the subsequent need to innovate, create, reorganise and rebuild are inevitable consequences of human interactions with nature. The system will continue to produce the same pattern of behaviour unless there is a change in the structure of the system. The WA agricultural region will require increasing amounts of capital in the form of a continuous stream of new technologies, institutions or social adaptations to maintain resilience and the adaptive capacity of the whole system. The WA agricultural region exhibits the common pattern of large-scale commodity systems in which the stabilisation of the agro-ecosystem has led to the progressive decline of the whole system. At the same time, the trend is not predetermined in systems composed of people, which have the ability to reflect and take action to avoid potentially detrimental situations consistent with the belief of meliorism, the belief that the world can be made better by human effort (Cocks, 1992). We are not locked in to some deterministic future. However, consistent with systems theory, for change to take place it will require a change in the structure of the system in order to effect a change in behaviour.

Based on the diagnosis undertaken in this chapter, in Chapter 7 we use qualitative system dynamics to examine the structural elements of the system, to identify the major reinforcing and balancing feedback loops and to identify areas within the structure of the system where intervention may produce changes in system behaviour away from a pathological trap, towards an adaptive cycle.

7

Model conceptualisation of the Western Australian agricultural region. Part 2: system dynamics

> ... social systems are inherently insensitive to most policy changes that people choose in an effort to alter the behavior of systems. In fact, social systems draw attention to the very points at which an attempt to intervene fails. Human intuition develops from exposure to simple systems. In simple systems, the cause of a trouble is close in both time and space to symptoms of trouble. However, in complex dynamic systems, causes are often far removed both in time and space from symptoms. True causes may lie far back in time and arise from an entirely different part of the system from when and where the symptoms occur. However, the complex system can mislead in devious ways by presenting an apparent cause that meets the expectations derived from simple systems. However, the apparent causes are usually coincident occurrences that, like the trouble symptom itself, are being produced by the feedback loop dynamics of a larger system.
>
> *Jay W. Forrester, 1995*

7.1 Introduction

Regional pathology is a common phenomenon of resource management in social-ecological systems (SESs) (Holling and Meffe, 1996; Holling *et al.*, 2002c; Jansson and Jansson, 2002). Holling (1995) showed that, in 23 cases examined, the conditions that caused growth in natural resource systems and accounted for their success ultimately were the same conditions that were responsible for their collapse. Two pathologies, the Poverty Trap and the Rigidity Trap, have been described that can occur as a result of the collapse of the adaptive cycle (Holling *et al.*, 2002c). However, regional systems do not operate in isolation, hence in modern large-scale systems interactions that occur across multiple scales from the individual to the regional, national and global levels are the norm. Consequently, resilience theory focusses on the interactions between local history and regional, national and global processes to identify the synergies and constraints among nature, economic activities and people in an inter-related system that has been termed a panarchy (Holling, 2003). The metaphor of panarchy was developed as a heuristic model of cross-scale organisation (Holling *et al.*, 2002c) (Chapter 5) and used figuratively as discussed in Section 4.4.3, that is to say it can be used to change how we think about things.

In Chapter 6, using resilience theory within an overarching systemic approach, we developed a conceptual model of the WA agricultural region at a macro-scale and diagnosed a third regional pathology, the Lock-in Trap, which we proposed describes the dynamics of the WA agricultural region. Even though the regional dynamics of growth and recession in the WA agricultural region were shown to be described by the adaptive cycle, the dynamics were also synchronous with the global long-wave Kondratiev Cycles which influenced regional-scale dynamics. This chapter has two objectives, firstly, to use system dynamics to examine the interactions of the WA agricultural region as a commodity system within the cross-scale dynamics; that is, a panarchy, where local history and system state interacts with global processes. The second objective is to identify, if possible, high leverage policy points in the system that might be used to effect lasting change.

The WA agricultural region is highly modified for the production of agricul-tural commodities, which has had positive effects on the regional and national economies and negative impacts on in general natural resources. The attributes of commodity markets and the positive and negative impacts of land clearing on natural resources are sufficiently well known (and the data are plentiful) to support a qualitative description of system behaviour and heuristic modelling. A qualitative model was also chosen because in the natural resource and social systems there are many soft variables (for example, natural capital, social capital, wellbeing) that are not readily quantifiable and present difficulties for quantitative models (Coyle, 2000). Thus a simple model at the macro-level of highly aggregated variables is presented, which has two purposes. Firstly, it complements the resilience analysis made in Chapter 6 as a support for a novel way of understanding the dynamic behaviour of the WA agricultural region. The use of causal loop diagrams in system dynamics is also used as metaphors in a figurative way, to change people's mental models in the style of double-loop learning to establish new goals and new decision rules, not just new decisions (Section 4.7). The second purpose is as a support for policy making in the management of natural resources, and is intimately related to the first purpose. The model will be built up section by section to show firstly, the structure of the commodity system, secondly, the structures of the ecological and social systems and thirdly, their integration into a linked social-ecological system (SES).

Caveat Qualitative system dynamics models are used for general understanding and it is recognised that the reality of the system is considerably more complex. The narrative of the WA agricultural region combined with the principles of resilience theory and system dynamics have been used to identify the important causal relationships or structure of the system and the model presented in the previous sections is the present state of an iterative evolutionary process. The important point to understand is that, by standing back far enough from 'the problem', the problem situation comes into focus. It becomes clear that the structure of the system (within the broader context as the boundaries of the system of interest are expanded) is responsible for the patterns of behaviour, one of the fundamental principles of system dynamics.

7.2 Behaviour of commodity systems

Because commodity systems are so important to agriculture and the socio-economic system, they have been the subject of many investigations and the building of commodity market models (Hathaway, 1963; Meadows and Robinson, 1985; Guvenen *et al.*, 1991; Wallace and Evans, 1993; Weber and Schwaninger, 2002). Commodity markets are also fertile ground for economic analysis. However, many models treat the social and ecological variables as exogenous or exclude them from the model entirely (Guvenen *et al.*, 1991), although there are exceptions within system dynamics practice (Meadows, 1970; Forrester, 1971; Meadows and Robinson, 1985; O'Regan and Moles, 2001). Hence it is very important to be explicit about the underlying assumptions including the boundary of the model, and which parameters are treated endogenously, exogenously, or are considered as environmental variables and are excluded (discussed in Chapter 5).

System dynamics models of commodity markets were developed in the 1970s (Meadows, 1970; Meadows and Robinson, 1985) and were recently investigated in relation to including the construct of sustainability into mainstream modelling of natural resource economies (Sawin *et al.*, 2003). The characteristics of general commodity systems are to produce standardised raw materials (undifferentiated products) for the lowest possible price. This type of production system currently dominates world agriculture (Sawin *et al.*, 2003). A large body of evidence suggests that, in agricultural commodity systems

Table 7.1. *Five characteristics of agriculture commodity systems*

1. Inelastic demand for food (that is, a small increase in the quantity available will lead to a larger proportionate decline in prices and vice versa)
2. Slow growth in total demand
3. Competitive market structure
4. Significant technological change
5. The tendency of resources to become fixed within the agricultural sector

Source: Hathaway (1963)

in particular, five characteristics are the major drivers in the movement of prices for commodities and have served as a basis for constructing models of agricultural commodity markets (Guvenen *et al.*, 1991; Hathaway, 1963; Meadows and Robinson, 1985; Sawin *et al.*, 2003), as shown in Table 7.1. The economic theory that gives rise to these characteristics is well known and was documented in the economic literature in the 1960s (Hathaway, 1963). The identification of just five characteristics that are important in producing system behaviour is consistent with Holling's 'Rule of Hand' (Holling *et al.*, 2000).

The classical economic theory of commodity cycles is the cobweb model (Meadows, 1970), which is a variation of the supply/demand model, and has been used to show cyclical price fluctuations of primary commodities, particularly agricultural products. The model takes its name from the cobweb-like pattern that results from tracing a line between price and demand through time. The cobweb model arises from three factors:

1. a time lag must exist between the decision to produce and the actual realisation of production;
2. planned production is a function of current prices, because of the time lag in the production period, current supply is a function of lagged prices; and
3. current prices are mainly a function of current supply, which in turn is mainly determined by current production.

The consequence of the specific characteristics of agricultural commodity systems is the persistent instability of prices, production, profitability and investment (Guvenen *et al.*, 1991). In addition when these characteristics are coupled with climatic and weather uncertainties, the potential for instability becomes even more significant. The instability of prices caused by the five characteristics of the agricultural commodity system plus the uncertainties of climate are often given as the justification for active intervention by governments in agriculture and food systems (Guvenen *et al.*, 1991) possibly through subsidies or production limits. The introduction of production limits in Western Australia as a result of instability of prices was discussed in Chapter 2.

7.2.1 Commodity growth drivers

Commodity systems and economic growth are complex processes, which are composed of a long series of small actions that accumulate to apply pressure which favours further economic growth. The systemic structure of agricultural commodity systems is described by three reinforcing feedback loops, at a highly aggregated level, each of which causes growth in commodity production (Figure 7.1) (Sawin *et al.*, 2003). A discussion of feedback and causal loop construction can be found in Chapter 5. The three reinforcing feedback loops involved in total commodity production growth are the Capital Growth Loop of total industrial expansion (R1), the Efficiency Boosting Loop of the individual producer (R2) and the Demand Growth Loop of total global demand (R3).

Reinforcing feedback loops are responsible for exponential growth and exponential decline, before the effects of a balancing loop cause the system to approach a plateau or endogenous system goal; for example, the behaviour described by the s-shaped curve in the exploitation phase (r) to the conservation phase (K) in the frontloop of the adaptive cycle. The three commodity growth loops are expanded in Figure 7.2 to show greater detail of the structure.

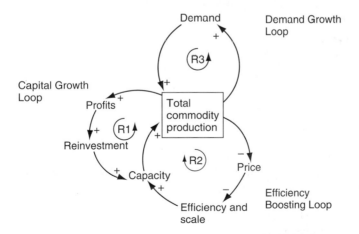

Fig. 7.1. The three positive feedback loops that cause commodity growth: R1, the Reinvestment of Capital Growth Loop; R2, the Efficiency Boosting Loop; and R3, the Demand Growth Loop. *Source:* Sawin *et al.* (2003)

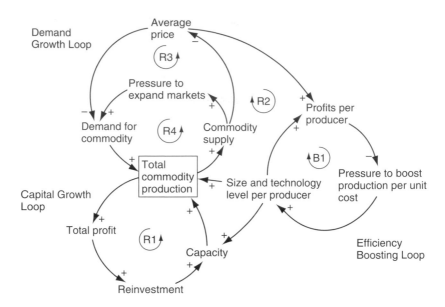

Fig. 7.2. The three positive feedback loops that cause commodity growth shown in Figure 7.1 are expanded to show greater detail of the structure of the feedback loops, the reinvestment of Capital Growth Loop (R1), the Efficiency Boosting Loops (R2 and B1) and the Demand Growth Loops (R3 and R4). *Source:* Sawin *et al.* (2003)

Capital Growth Loop

The Capital Growth Loop (R1) (Figure 7.2) is the process by which global productive capacity leads to the creation of more productive capacity. In these diagrams the capacity is defined only in terms of the capacity of the system to produce the commodity of interest and does not include the ecological capacity and the social capacity. The Capital Growth Loop is considered to be the core driving force of industrial expansion. The description of the loop can be read as: the production creates profit 'Profits', some of which is reinvested 'Reinvestment', which increases global capacity 'Capacity', which is used to increase total production 'Total commodity production'. In this growth process production leads to more capacity for production. Reinvestment may be in the form of capital equipment, for example new harvesting equipment, or collectively in the form of innovation in science and technology. Developments in science and technology, which are components of this loop, were responsible for growth in agriculture in the WA agricultural region just as they were in the growth of long-wave Kondratiev Cycles as described in Chapter 6.

Increasingly the form of reinvestment that is producing growth in agricultural production is biotechnology (Tengerdy and Szakács, 1998; Braun, 2002) in such products as 'Roundup-ready' varieties of wheat. During the seven-year period 1996 to 2002, the global area of genetically modified (GM) crops increased 35-fold, from 1.7 million hectares in 1996 to 58.7 million hectares in 2002. To put this global area of GM crops into context, 58.7 million hectares is equivalent to more than 5% of the total land area of China (956 million hectares) or the USA (981 million hectares), almost 2.5 times the land area of the United Kingdom (24.4 million hectares) (ISAAA), and about 3 times the area of the WA agricultural region. The latest figures show the global area of biotechnology crops is now 81 million hectares, which is a 20% increase over the area in 2003. Australia grew 200 000 hectares of GM crops in 2000, mostly GM cotton in eastern Australia. Field trials in Australia continue to be carried out using cotton, corn, potato and canola (ISAAA). After suffering two years of severe drought, Australia increased its biotechnology cotton hectares 100% to 250 000 hectares in 2004 over the area planted in 2003 (Jones, 2004).

Efficiency Boosting Loop

The Efficiency Boosting Loop comprises two reinforcing loops (R2 and R3) and a balancing loop (B1) (Figure 7.2). This loop can be read as: rising global production means that the 'Commodity supply' available on the market can exceed demand and push the 'Average price' down (R3) through its action on the Demand Growth Loop (R3 + R4). A lower price means lower 'Profits per producer' all else being equal. In times of falling profits the two options available to individual producers trying to maintain profits are to reduce costs and to expand production volume (B1) that is 'Pressure to boost production per unit cost'. Often the route to cutting costs is to expand the 'Size and technology level per producer'. While expanding the operation does reduce costs to the individual operator, thus compensating for falling prices, it also increases the overall production via the reinforcing loop (R2). In agriculture the pressure to keep in business is responded to in three ways:

1. the need to clear more land to put into production;
2. the acquisition of neighbouring farms, for increased economies of scale; and
3. the intensification of production described in Chapter 2.

In combination these processes create a cycle of increasing production and falling prices.

Demand Growth Loop

The Demand Growth Loop can be described in this way: as 'Commodity supply' rises the 'Average price' falls, therefore the demand for the commodity tends to rise as more people can afford the product. Climbing demand gives producers the confidence to invest in increasing production, pushing up supply and pushing down prices, further boosting demand and creating the third reinforcing loop, the Demand Growth Loop (Figure 7.2). The pressure to increase production and decrease costs has been a feature of commodity systems for as long as they have existed and the same pressures exist all over the world wherever commodity systems develop. The consequence of the three reinforcing loops is exponential growth unless one or more balancing loops come into play by applying a strong enough signal (from information flow or material flow) to counteract the reinforcing loops. The case of coffee production has been a recent well-publicised example (Gresser, 2002).

7.2.2 Commodity traps

Balancing feedback loops

In contrast to the behaviour of reinforcing feedback loops that generate growth, balancing feedback loops seek balance, equilibrium and stasis (Sterman, 2000). Balancing feedback loops act to bring the state of the system in line with a goal or a desired state of the system, shown in Figure 7.3. They counteract any disturbances that move the state of that system away from

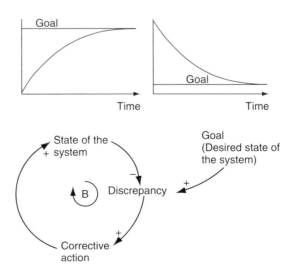

Fig. 7.3. Goal-seeking structure and behaviour of balancing feedback loops. System dynamics causal loop construction conventions are used.

the goal. Every balancing loop includes a process to compare the desired
and actual conditions and take corrective action, shown as the variable
'Discrepancy' in Figure 7.3. The desired state may not be explicit or under
the control of humans; rather it may be endogenous (implicit) within the
structure of the system. The rate at which the state of the system approaches
its goal diminishes as the discrepancy falls. The gradual approach to the goal
arises because large gaps tend to elicit large responses and small gaps tend
to elicit small responses. Balancing feedback also arises from the limitations
caused by erosion of the productive capacity or carrying capacity of a system,
in patterns of behaviour described by the Lotka–Volterra predator–prey
model (Lotka, 1956), modelled in system dynamics by Swart (1990). The
balancing feedback loop may gradually increase in strength, caused by
increasing degradation.

In the absence of limitations of specific desired states applied exogenously
by people to control production (in the form of desired total production goals
of the system) Sawin *et al.* (2003) proposed that three traps exist in commodity
systems, (1) the Resource Depletion Trap, (2) the Environmental Pollution
Trap, and (3) the Social Decline Trap (Figure 7.4). In economic terminology

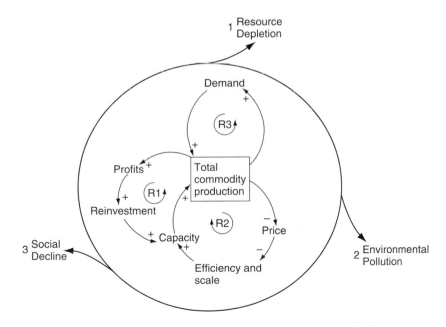

Fig. 7.4. Three commodity system traps: (1) Resource Depletion, (2) Environmental Pollution, and (3) Social Decline. The production growth drivers create
high levels of production and keep costs of commodities low but this comes
at a cost to the other parts of the system, in the form of resource depletion,
environmental pollution and social decline. Source: Sawin *et al.* (2003)

all three traps are negative economic externalities that are not accounted for
in the total cost of producing the commodity.

'Trap' is used in the same metaphorical sense as the maladaptive trap
(Holling *et al.*, 2002c) (Chapter 5). In commodity systems there is the potential over time for one or more of the commodity traps to reduce or prevent
production through resource depletion or environmental pollution as they
place limits on production, in the action of balancing feedback control.
However, rather than allowing the natural resource system to collapse, as
has happened particularly in some open access systems (Buck, 1998; Levin,
1999) and some civilisations (Tainter, 1988; Diamond, 2005), the objective of sustainability policy is to establish social institutions that exert the
balancing feedback effect, which limits the action of the reinforcing feedback
loops.

7.3 The qualitative system dynamics model of the WA agricultural region

The same production growth drivers that are important in world commodities
are responsible for the dynamics of agricultural commodities in the WA agricultural region. Although Australia is predicted to experience a 38% increase
in cereal exports from 1995 to 2020 it remains a relatively small player,
with about 10% of the global market (Dunlop, 2004). For the purpose of this
analysis, wheat is used as the commodity of interest to show the dynamics
of the WA agricultural region, principally because it is Western Australia's
main grain crop making up 37% of the gross value of agricultural commodities produced in WA in 1998–9 year (Australian Bureau of Statistics, 2003).
The global trends for commodities, such as price fluctuation, increasing
productivity and falling prices, are dynamic endogenous responses within
the global wheat commodity market in which the WA agricultural region
operates. Figure 7.5 shows the fluctuations in global wheat prices and the
long-term falling trend in price. The trends for soybeans and corn are shown to
demonstrate that commodity system dynamics apply to these other undifferentiated commodities too. The productivity of wheat in Australia has increased
over time (Figure 6.3 (a)), and the area of wheat production as a land use
increased as a response to price (Figure 7.6) resulting in increasing total
production.

In the global market, Hooper *et al.* (2003) forecast increased grain
production and sluggish growth in demand which are expected to result
in weaker grain prices in 2003–4, one of the common characteristics

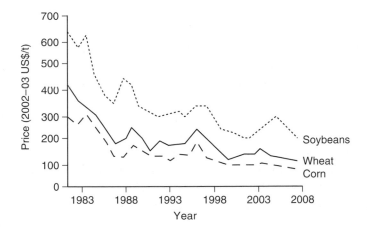

Fig. 7.5. World grain prices with predictions to 2007. *Source:* redrawn from Hooper *et al.* (2003)

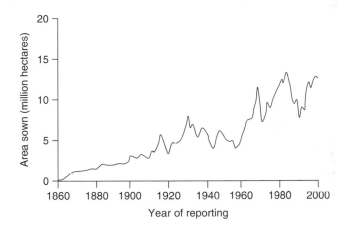

Fig. 7.6. Area of wheat production as a land use in Australia since 1860. *Source:* redrawn from National Land and Water Resources Audit (2001c)

of commodity systems (Table 7.1). Grain production in North America and Australia in 2003–4 year is expected to increase sharply above 2002–3 levels. The Australian wheat crop forecast for 2003–4 is for a near record 24.1 million tonnes compared with just 9.4 million tonnes in the drought affected 2002–3 crop year (Penm *et al.*, 2003), one of the most serious droughts in the past 100 years (Prime Minister of Australia, 2002), which was associated with an El Niño event. Over the next five years world grain prices are projected to decline in real terms as farmers in the major producing countries make further productivity improvements. Increased productivity has enabled grain production to continue to expand, even as prices in real terms have fallen (Hooper *et al.*, 2003). The profitability of Australian agriculture, with its orientation towards export trade, remains closely linked to price fluctuations in global markets (Australian Greenhouse Office, 2000).

The National Land and Water Resources Audit (2001c) reported that in Australia fluctuating prices of commodities may be the primary drivers for changing land use and hence the total production of commodities. Without doubt, market forces in the 1950s to 1960s in the WA agricultural region were among the factors that lead to the increased rates of land clearing as described in Chapter 2. Market forces (that is, the feedback between price, demand and supply) have been effective and efficient in increasing wheat production and in current times are the predominant force in the dynamics of production.

The three reinforcing feedback loops of the commodity system show only one aspect and emphasise only wheat production omitting the structure of other systems involved in the dynamics of the linked social-ecological system (SES). In Section 7.3.1, through a series of causal loop diagrams, we discuss the complex interactions among the commodity system, the social and ecological systems in the WA agricultural region. The model is presented in a series of submodels to progressively create the whole model. Gunderson *et al.* (2002b) proposed that the organisation of regional resource systems emerges from the interaction of a few variables and suggested the number may be as low as three and no more than six. In developing this conceptual model we were guided by this proposition. Only those loops deemed to be the most important, based on the foregoing analysis in Chapters 2, 3 and 6, have been included in the model. There are, of course, others that could be added depending on the objective of the modelling exercise and degree of complexity required.

7.3.1 System dynamics model

Chapters 2 and 3 and the reference modes in Chapter 6 provide the narrative and analysis for the identification of the driving variables and influences used as a basis for developing the qualitative system dynamics model of the WA agricultural region. Based on the trends for the major commodities of wheat and other grains in Australia this model assumes that the characteristics of the general commodity system and the three reinforcing feedback

loops described in Section 7.2 exert the same cause and effect relationships on the WA agricultural region as described in the commodity model
(Figure 7.2).

However, the important difference in the following model is that the
commodity system is set within the boundary of the SES and connected to the
social and the ecological systems through balancing feedback loops (essentially these are the commodity traps). The different model assumptions are
shown by a comparison between the boundary diagrams (Section 5.6.6) for the
commodity system (Figure 7.7) and for the WA agricultural region (Figure 7.8).
The boundary diagrams show in a readily accessible form the assumptions that
underlie the causal loop diagrams. The key point to note in these two diagrams
is the increased number and type of variables now assumed to be endogenous
to the WA agricultural region (including the variables in the commodity traps)
and those that are exogenous. In particular, in the commodity system boundary
diagram the commodity traps are assumed to be exogenous, that is, they are

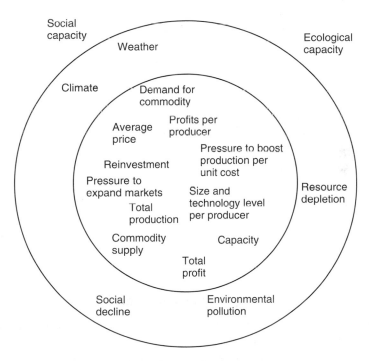

Fig. 7.7. Boundary diagram for the commodity system. The variables in the inner
circle are treated endogenously in this model. Variables in the outer circle are
treated exogenously and those outside the outer circle are omitted from the
model.

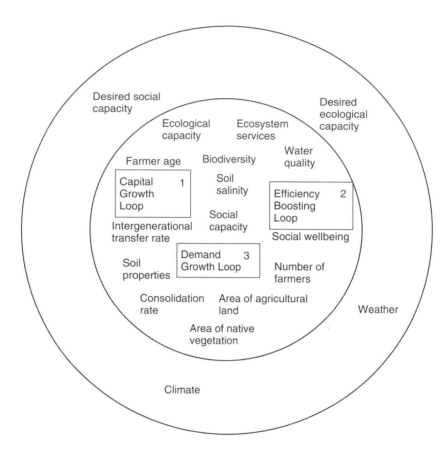

Fig. 7.8. Boundary diagram for the WA agricultural region as a SES, composed of the commodity system, the ecological system and the social system. For simplicity the three commodity growth driver loops are not shown in detail. The variables in the centre circle are considered to be endogenous variables and are within feedback loops. Variables in the outer circle are considered to be exogenous variables and are related to people's values. They are considered to have an effect on the system but are not affected by the system.

a product of the system but do not exert an effect on the system. Also note the addition of the normative variables, namely, the desired ecological and social capacities, the ecological capacity discrepancy and the social capacity discrepancy variables omitted from the boundary diagram for the commodity system. It is assumed that the normative desired system capacities are not affected by the system, although this is questionable, and is beyond the scope of this book. The qualitative model presented here is an attempt to move sustainability into the mainstream of natural resource commodity system economics.

7.3.2 Ecosystem Loop

The Ecosystem Loop (B1) (Figure 7.9) is made up of three loops, the Resource Depletion Loop (made up of B2 and B3) and the Environmental Pollution Loop (B4).

The Resource Depletion Loop (made up of B2 and B3) of the model tracks the effects of the commodity system, through the effects of the variable 'Efficiency and scale', on six state variables in the Ecosystem Loop:

1. Area of agricultural land;
2. Area of native vegetation;
3. Area of salinity;
4. Biodiversity;
5. Ecosystem services; and
6. Ecological capacity.

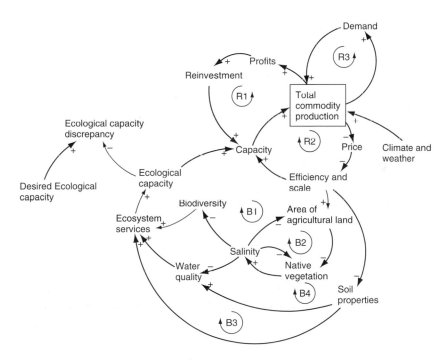

Fig. 7.9. The Ecosystem Loop. Causal loop diagram of the WA agricultural region showing the commodity system and the ecosystem. The Ecosystem Loop (B1) is composed of the Resource Depletion Loops (B2 + B3) and the Environmental Pollution Loop (B4).

These together will affect the capacity of the commodity system. A state variable represents a stock or level in a system and is a point of accumulation. It is often the rate of change in a stock that is responsible for producing oscillations in system behaviour and the development of persistent, undesirable and unintended effects (Sterman, 2000). This may appear as overshoot and collapse in state variables.

In order to read this model we will start with the Efficiency Boosting Loop and the individual producer's need to increase efficiency and scale. The production growth drivers push down prices and the farmer terms of trade, reducing farmers' financial capacity and increasing the need for increasing efficiency and scale. The response is to increase the size of the land holding through land purchase or clearing of land, as shown in the model by the variable 'Efficiency and scale'. The production benefits that can be gained from clearing native vegetation are rarely uniform. The best quality agricultural land, with high production benefits per hectare, was cleared first. As this high quality land becomes scarcer, attention turns to lower quality land where some commercial benefits are still available from clearing (Aitken and Rolfe, 2000). Recent precision farming techniques are now showing that farming these marginal soils has little commercial benefit (Passioura, 2002) and in the process of increasing efficiency it is expected that some of these marginal soils will be retired out of production. However, in some areas increased application of micronutrients will maintain production.

The consequences of the wheat commodity system in the WA agricultural region are the cumulative negative impacts on natural resources, discussed in Chapter 3. Although soil salinity is considered to be one of the most serious off-site consequences of agricultural production (Chapter 3), other depleting mechanisms, such as soil erosion, also occur. The Resource Depletion Loop (B1) identifies some of the important causes and effects of these processes. The Resource Depletion Loop can be described as follows: the need for expansion drives the clearing of native vegetation, which will increase the area affected by soil salinity caused by changes in the hydrological cycle. This is a slowly changing biophysical process, the effects of which may be distant in both time and space. Increased soil salinity has four causal pathways. Firstly, it reduces the area of native vegetation; secondly, it reduces the area of productive agricultural land; thirdly, it reduces biodiversity; and fourthly, it impacts on water quality. Loss of biodiversity and poor water quality will reduce ecosystem services and thus the ecological capacity. Resource depletion includes the impact on soil properties, for instance increasing soil erosion, soil acidity and sodicity, which are the effects of agricultural production and which reduce ecosystem services. The protection of native vegetation is important, not only because of its biological diversity and uniqueness, but also because of the part it plays in maintenance of ecosystem processes.

The Environmental Pollution Loop (Figure 7.9, B4) tracks the effects of the commodity system (through the variable 'Efficiency and scale') on soil and water properties and ecosystem services, which together reduce the ecological capacity. The Environmental Pollution Loop can be described thus: increases in the variable 'Efficiency and scale' may cause impacts through greater intensification of farming. Land management practices may be intensified and cause changes in soil properties, for example, through increased fertiliser, pesticide and herbicide application which have both on- and off-site effects. Runoff can affect water quality through the process of eutrophication of waterways, an externality in economic terms reducing ecosystem services. The multiple feedback loops will combine to impact on ecosystem services and ecological capacity. Depending on the strength of the reinvestment reinforcing loop in the commodity system, the reduction in ecological capacity may cause an impact on the productive capacity of the commodity system.

The Resource Depletion and Environmental Pollution Loops are balancing loops which may act to limit total commodity production and bring about equilibrium and stasis, and may in time become a strong signal within the system through either information flow or material flow. However, at the present time the feedback signal is weak in material flow and largely ignored as information flow or both. There are potentially two reasons for the weakness in strength of the signal. Firstly, its weakness is related in part to the long time delay in the development of symptoms in the ecosystem, and in symptoms becoming visible and at a great enough level to be considered a significant problem. The delay is in the order of a few years to 300 years for significant areas of soil salinity to develop following the clearing of native vegetation (Hodgson *et al.*, 2004). Secondly, often the cause and effect are not only distant in time but also distant in space, the symptoms appearing in different parts of the ecosystem.

Desired states (goals) of the systems are an integral part of all balancing feedback loops and in terms of resilience theory. For example, in Figure 7.9 as resources are depleted and environmental pollution occurs, ecosystem services and ecological capacity are reduced and may cause the system to eventually reach a new state or endogenous goal of the system. The discrepancy in the ecological capacity is the difference between the socially desired state of ecological capacity and its actual state. The desired ecological capacity is culturally and temporally defined. For example, the increasing shortfall in the ecological capacity in Australia was responsible for the Landcare movement described in Chapter 2.

7.3.3 Social Capacity Loop

There is a growing interest in the constructs of social capacity and the related concepts of social capital, human capital and social wellbeing. The interest arises from the interface of the constructs with policy in general (Jacobsen *et al.*, 2002; Petrie, 2002; Productivity Commission, 2003), and rural policy in particular (Land and Water Resources Research and Development Corporation, 1999; Pretty and Frank, 2000; Cary *et al.*, 2002) and the way in which they influence and shape human and social capacity to effect change. A major provider of funds for natural resources management research in Australia prefaced its social and institutional research program information with the statement: 'More than ten years experience in funding natural resource research and development has demonstrated to the Corporation that the most crucial barriers to improved use or management of natural resources are social and institutional factors and not lack of scientific knowledge' (Land and Water Resources Research and Development Corporation, 1999). When managing ecosystems, managers and policy makers must deal with a social system as complex and dynamic as the ecological system, which adopts transformations resembling the adaptive cycle (Section 5.6.4), with four phases identified as polarised, institutionalised, scattered and mobilised (Scheffer *et al.*, 2002). See also the discussion on organisation in Chapter 4. The Productivity Commission (2003) reviewed the literature on the conceptual basis and the empirical evidence for social capital and found that differences in definitions made analysis difficult. Only those constructs that are central to understanding the causal explanations in the system dynamics diagrams are introduced here.

Social capital includes the institutions, relationships, attitudes and values that govern interactions among people and contribute to economic and social development. Social capital, however, is not simply the sum of institutions that underpin society, but also the glue that holds them together. It includes the shared values and rules for social conduct expressed in personal relationships, trust, reciprocity, common rules, norms and sanctions, connectedness in institutions and a common sense of 'civic' responsibility, which make society more than just a collection of individuals (World Bank, 1998; Pretty and Howard, 2001; Productivity Commission, 2003).

For as long as people have managed natural resources, they have engaged in collective action and the rural industry is no exception. The term social capacity is used here as a society's capability for collective action in a variety of spheres, including non-market and market, and involving voluntary interactions, as well as the use of the policy of the country or state (Petrie, 2002; Scheffer *et al.*, 2002). In this broad sense social capacity subsumes the notion of social cohesion; a more cohesive society will, in general, have a higher level of social capacity. For example, it will be able to support a wider range of market exchanges and non-market interactions and institutions. However, natural resource management has paid too little attention to how social capacity affects environmental outcomes.

Although it is assumed that increasing social capacity will produce more desirable outcomes (for example, sustainable natural resource management) there is evidence to suggest that this may not always be the case (Barr and Cary, 2000). On the one hand, it is proposed that social capital serves as a resource to provide robustness to an existing system or to make possible the composition of a new system when the potential within the system is great enough (Resilience Alliance, 2002). On the other hand, increased social capacity may create tension between social norms, institutions and wellbeing (Petrie, 2002). The notion of wellbeing is a complex construct related to social capacity and productive capacity (Petrie, 2002). For example, strong group bonds can make organisations exclusive, prioritising the group's goals to the detriment of the broader society, as has been suggested to occur in the agriculture industry (Holling and Gunderson, 2002). In some instances group norms over time may be detrimental and reduce the potential for innovation. Thus there may be many complex feedback effects between social capital, its sources and its effects (Productivity Commission, 2003). These two dichotomies, between the benefits and detrimental effects, corroborate ideas inherent in the adaptive cycle that (1) increasing connectivity produces the structures for success, and (2) beyond a certain degree of connectivity, organisations may become overly rigid and lack flexibility, and increasing connectivity precipitates a collapse or crisis within an organisation (discussed in Section 5.6.4). These aspects of social capacity are now incorporated into the model of the WA agricultural region.

One of the seven themes of Australia's National Land and Water Resources Audit was an investigation of the capacity of, and opportunity for, farmers and other natural resource managers to implement change (Table 3.1) (Cary *et al.*, 2001, 2002). These studies focussed on human capacity, that is, the characteristics that influence an individual landholder's capacity to change and adopt more sustainable land management practices. It is introduced here because it is one of the components involved in the overarching construct, social capacity. However, a comprehensive discussion on the psychology and sociology of an individual's decision making is beyond the subject of this book. Cary *et al.* (2002) concluded that human capacity to adopt sustainable land management practices was context dependent and hence it was difficult to make any generalisations in this regard. These findings are consistent with the argument of Gallopin (2002) in which capacity is only one of three interacting factors that are involved in change; the other two are willingness and understanding. Cary *et al.* (2002) contended that there was potential for significant structural change within parts of rural Australia, caused by a cohort of older farmers potentially exiting the industry, and proposed that this may have significant consequences, not only for natural resource management but also for community wellbeing in these regions. They recommended the need for improved monitoring of ongoing structural change in rural Australia. Cary *et al.* (2002) inferred a relationship between rural reconstruction and community wellbeing, but the nature of the relationship was not made explicit. In an extensive review of Australian rural producers, it was found that human capacity to change to more sustainable practices varied across the regions and localities of agricultural landscapes. Therefore, to effect change it is critical that future natural resource management policy needs to take account of these differing social capacities (Table 7.2) which reflect differing socio-economic characteristics and locality advantages (Cary *et al.*, 2002).

Table 7.2. *Factors influencing rural producers' capacity to change to sustainable practices*

1. The use of sustainable practices will depend on how landholders assess the value of recommended practices.
2. Landholders seek to reduce the risk of adopting a new practice.
3. Socio-economic factors which can influence adoption of sustainable practices include farm income, age, training, having a farm plan, perception of financial security and community Landcare membership.
4. Pro-environmental stewardship values and attitudes have a relatively minor influence on the adoption of sustainable practices.
5. Future structural and social changes in agriculture will influence the capacity of landholders to adopt more sustainable land use practices.
6. There is a need to adopt, identify and develop locally applicable sustainable practices.

Source: Cary *et al.* (2002)

It is contended (and sometimes assumed) that the use of what are considered to be sustainable practices (Cary *et al.*, 2002) will lead to more sustainable resource management. However, this association is often constrained and is likely to vary for different localities. There may be long time lags before the use of a sustainable practice results in a more sustainable state being achieved. Human behaviour related to implementing sustainable practices is adaptive, rather than simply reactive, in its nature. Appraisal and implementation of these practices will depend on assessment of, and experience with, the use of such practices. Therefore, the difficulty for landholders in observing linkages between many recommended sustainable practices and desired sustainable outcomes lies in the fact that the benefits may be intergenerational and will not accrue to the individual in the short term. Cary *et al.* (2002) proposed that broader conceptions of sustainable management embrace the need for strategies for sustaining both food security and the need to conserve natural resources. This last conception requires the adoption of different model boundaries and assumptions about endogenous model variables. The qualitative model presented here is an attempt to broaden the conception by moving sustainability into the mainstream of natural resource commodity system economics.

Figure 7.10 shows the causal loop diagram of the WA agricultural region including the commodity system and the Social Capacity Loop which is made up of loops B1 and B2, and the additional variable 'Desired Social Capacity'. The commodity system is linked to the social system through the variable

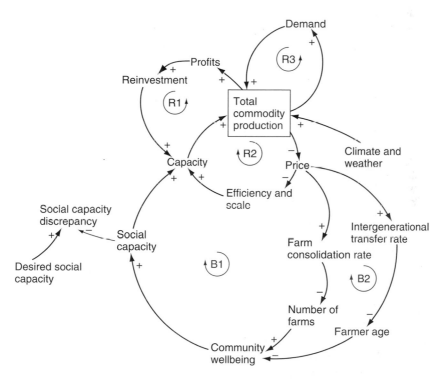

Fig. 7.10. Causal loop diagram of the WA agricultural region showing the commodity system and the social system. The Social Capacity Loop is composed of loops B1 and B2. System dynamics causal loop construction conventions are used.

'Price' in the commodity system. The model is read as follows: Loop B1 – high commodity prices increase land sales (through the expectation of future gain) and increase the rate of farm consolidation, reducing the number of farmers, and potentially the total rural population in the broadacre areas of the WA agricultural region. One way this can be interpreted is that a reduced number of farmers reduces the social capacity through the reduction in the number of relationships between farmers, which in turn reduces the overall community wellbeing and potentially the social capacity. Further research is required to fully understand the complex social relationships and their outcomes (Tonts and Black, 2002).

In the WA agricultural region the number of farm establishments dropped from approximately 23 000 in the late 1960s to less than 10 000 in 2000. Higher land values in general shadowed commodity prices and tended to provide a greater incentive to sell small farms and thus farm consolidation rates increased during buoyant seasons (Cary *et al.*, 2002). During low commodity price periods the incentives for farm consolidation were greatly reduced (Barr, 2000). The growing body of literature in rural sociology suggests that agriculture in North America and Australasia is experiencing a gradual shift away from traditional family farms towards farm business structures that are more corporately orientated (Tonts and Black, 2002; Cary *et al.*, 2002). Corporate farming takes two common forms: either the corporate farm is owned by a diverse group of shareholders or contract farming is used (Tonts and Black, 2002). However, in some areas the consolidation rate has not been as rapid as anticipated as a result of a reduction in the rate of inter-generational transfer (Loop B2). Low profit levels of family farm enterprises reduce the rate of transfer of the farm from father to son, resulting in older farmers continuing to remain in the industry (Barr, 2000), most commonly in the medium sized farms in the broadacre regions. In recent years, however, inter-generational transfer appeared to be unrelated to commodity price fluctuations and reflected a deeper social trend in the lifestyle preferences of younger generations and the attraction of alternative career paths through improved educational levels (Cary *et al.*, 2002).

In this model, the price is linked through the number of farmers to community wellbeing and through to social capacity, although the difficulties with this cause and effect are recognised as community wellbeing is a complex index. In macroeconomics one measure of community wellbeing is reported, in terms of Gross Domestic Product (GDP). This translates to higher growth in per capita income, and better living and environmental standards (Department of Foreign Affairs and Trade, 2003). However, this is not the only index. The United Nations Development Programme's Human Development Index (HDI) has been proposed since the early 1990s as an alternative international index of standards of living, incorporating social indicators and economic output, while other indices that incorporate both consumption and life expectancy have been also been suggested (Dowrick *et al.*, 2003).

The consolidation rate reduces the number of farm establishments and the number of farmers in the region. As the number of farmers declines there may also be a decline in the associated social services provided to a lower population size as, for example, is occurring in the hospital and banking sectors in Western Australia. This will potentially reduce the interactions, the social capital and cohesion of the rural communities based on the assumptions made above and from resilience theory, discussed in Chapter 6. Consequently social capacity may be reduced under these conditions. Tonts and Black (2002) reviewed the literature on the effect of changing farm business structures on rural communities and found that little research had been undertaken in Australia to examine the impacts of changing farm structure on community wellbeing and regional capacity. In comparison much of the research in this area undertaken in North America links the expansion of corporate and contract farming with radical changes in community structure and social interaction (Tonts and Black, 2002). Although anecdotally it was thought that community wellbeing might be undermined through the introduction of a large-scale seasonal and mobile labour force, an alternative view was that more vibrant communities may be created through new opportunities for downstream processing and support services (Tonts and Black, 2002). However, no research in Australia exists to substantiate either position (Tonts and Black, 2002).

7.4 Integration of resilience analysis and system dynamics analysis

Recognising the different variables that control each of the four phases of the adaptive cycle deepens our understanding of the dynamics of the WA agricultural region. The conceptual model of the WA agricultural region can now be completed through the integration of resilience analysis and system dynamics analysis. Figure 7.11 shows the complete model of the WA agricultural region as a large-scale SES at a high level of aggregation. The Resource Depletion Loop and the Environmental Pollution Loop have been combined into the Ecological Capacity Loop (B1), and additions include the desired state of the SES, and the SES discrepancy.

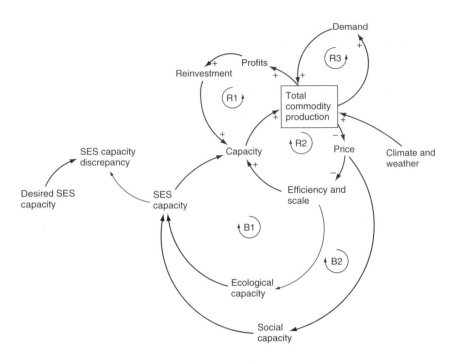

Fig. 7.11. Causal loop diagram of the WA agricultural region showing a summary of the three production growth (reinforcing feedback loop) drivers of the commodity system and the combined Ecological capacity (B1) and Social capacity (B2) balancing feedback loops.

7.4.1 Panarchy and delays

Material and information delays are often responsible for oscillations in the system. It is also possible that subsystems that have delays, that is to say, different time lags between cause and effect, may cause nonlinear dynamics through the action of multiple feedback loops. In this system there are a number of important delays at different timescales in the economic, social and ecological systems. An example in each system is described here. For example there is an economic lag between price and the change in land use. This delay is expected to be approximately two years to change from one grain commodity to another or from sheep to grain. The lag may be dependent on information delay as well as material or production delay. The second example from the social system involves the farmer age. The WA agricultural region is experiencing an increasing average age of farmers, which may be underestimated because, although a son may be the formal owner of the property, the father may still be the decision maker. This generational (social) lag may be in the order of 30 or more years. The third delay in the system is the ecological lag, or the response of the ecological system to land management practices. Current modelling estimates the lag in cause and effect (the lag to a new hydrological equilibrium) to be up to 300 years depending on the geography and position in the landscape (Hodgson *et al.*, 2004). As described in Chapter 3 the cause and effect of native vegetation removal and soil salinity have been known since the early 1900s and scientists have tried to influence policy since that time.

7.5 Policy implications

7.5.1 Structural and high leverage interventions

The effect of the three reinforcing loops of the commodity system is continuous growth and increasing total production. In order to place the commodity system within the matrix of SES, two additional loops are included in the model. These are the Ecological Capacity Loop and the Social Capacity Loop. This whole SES has goals other than that of commodity production. These competing goals are expressed by the desired states of the ecological and social systems in Figures 7.9 and 7.10 and the desired state of the SES in Figure 7.11. These goals are exogenous goals expressed by society. The social and ecological loops are balancing feedback loops that may apply constraints on the commodity system. The system objective is to bring about transformation by balancing the productivity of the commodity system with the desired goals of the other systems, through structural change in the relationship between the variables of the system.

Past and current natural resource policy targeted actions to effect change only in the ecological system at the individual events level. Attempting to effect change at the events level provides low leverage for solutions, while policy prescriptions that effect change at the structural level are systemic, and will provide long-term change. Structural change involves changing rules, incentives or penalties (that is, institutions) linked to social and ecological desired states. Achieving sustainable development will require significant changes in the way economic institutions and activities are organised (ESRC Global Environmental Change Programme, 2000).

Proximal indicators and distal events

Issues of policy are complicated by the differences in spatial and temporal scales. Policy decisions must be made on proximal indicators, which through policy implementation will have an effect, usually on distal events, particularly in ecological and social systems. This is, of course, one of the most enduring problems that society faces. That is, we must take action now that requires knowledge of the future, and the future is more complex and uncertain that ever it was. Further difficulty in application of policy is caused by the common dynamics of systems, in which the consequences of sustainable policy may cause the state of the system to get worse before it gets better.

7.5.2 Examples of natural resource economies that incorporate social and environmental goals

For many commodities, including wheat, that are classified as undifferentiated products that serve as raw materials for other products and do not go directly to the consumer, it is very difficult to employ any of the possible policy measures, such as collective agreements, certification or government taxes and payments, prescribed to incorporate social and environmental goals. This is because the wheat market is global and producers from nations with differing environmental and social standards compete to sell to the same buyers. Thus competition tends to reward those places with the least cost standards. These possible policy prescriptions are effective only when the boundary of the solution includes all the producer communities that compete within the same market. The solution must be within the boundary of the system and thus must be enacted through policies at an international level.

In contrast some commodity systems with particular characteristics have successfully incorporated social and ecological goals. These policy prescriptions have changed the rules through collective agreements, certification and government taxes and payments (Sawin *et al.*, 2003). One such successful example is found in Western Australia. Although natural resource commodity systems commonly deplete the resource, especially in open systems such as fisheries, the Western Australian rock lobster industry is a notable exception. This industry has achieved sustainable harvesting limits in a cooperative approach between industry and government. The rock lobster industry in Western Australia is a limited entry fishery implemented through a collective agreement. In March 2000, the fishery became the first in the world to gain Marine Stewardship Council certification as a sustainable well-managed fishery (Western Australian Fishing Industry Council, 2003). Collective agreements have also operated in tobacco markets in the USA to maintain the price of tobacco and control the numbers of producers in the industry (Burley Tobacco Growers Cooperative Association, 2003).

7.6 Concluding remarks

The greatest advantage of adopting a qualitative system dynamic method as an analytical tool is that it exposes the many interrelationships (the structure of the system) which influence the behaviour of a complex system. In a complex system such as the WA agricultural region, causal loop diagrams are a useful addition to policy evaluation techniques through their effectiveness in capturing and exposing the structure of the system that produces system behaviour.

Another major benefit of this model is that it makes explicit the user's fundamental assumptions, which are then open to examination. It incorporates theories that relate visible dynamic patterns in systems to invisible feedback loop structures, explicitly through the model. If these assumptions are disagreed with, they can be modified by changing the model structure and the consequences can be examined through the logic of the model. This is in contrast to 'black box' models in which the model assumptions are implicit and may be obscured. System dynamic models greatly simplify reality for the sake of clarity in order to identify general relationships, not those that are particular to one system, and highlight system structure as a catalyst for debate, change and adaptive management. By itself the model does not provide definitive answers; instead it is a learning device, an aid to understanding. It does not replace other disciplinary-based analyses but rather it is complementary to them and provides a different context in which to place natural resource management and policy, a context that expands and integrates the boundaries between disciplines, time and space. This technique is particularly useful for policy makers as it provides an analytical tool for designing the best mix of policies to achieve the government's aims in line with commitments to develop sustainability strategies that integrate social, ecological and economic outcomes (Government of Western Australia, 2002a).

Using resilience theory and system dynamics, we hypothesise that the WA agricultural region shows characteristics of what is termed a Lock-in Trap. The characteristics of the Lock-in Trap are low potential for change as a result of the commodity system traps, high connectedness between farmers and the wider agriculture industry and high resilience caused by a reduction in species diversity (Table 6.6). All else being equal, the three commodity system drivers will continue to dominate the WA agricultural region, producing fluctuations in commodity prices, falling prices, resource depletion, environmental pollution and decline in rural populations. The current interest and progress in biotechnology, which is part of the reinvestment loop (one of the three commodity drivers), will cause an increase in the total production of the commodity system, and therefore will have the effect of expanding the threshold of the SES. The SES will increase the capacity of the commodity system to increase total production causing further resource depletion and environmental pollution. We suggest that the expansion of thresholds through changes in technology is a principle explanation for Holling's paradox of the pathology of regional resource and ecosystem management. What Holling observed was that new policies and development usually succeed initially, but they lead to agencies that gradually become rigid and myopic, economic sectors that become slavishly dependent, ecosystems that are more fragile and a public that loses trust in governance.

The application of policy instruments aimed at the mitigation of any or all of the three symptoms of the commodity system may produce short-term changes. However, as described above, policy resistance will most likely occur. In contrast, for systemic change to occur, Gallopin (2002) suggests that three pillars of decision making – willingness, capacity and understanding – must be applied. Any change in these three areas will require the application of ultimate drivers that shape the fundamental structure of values, knowledge and empowerment.

8

Synthesis

Paradigms are the sources of systems.
Donella Meadows, 1999

This chapter summarises the findings of the previous chapters and we discuss their implications for natural resources management in the WA agricultural region and in general. We outline the key areas in which changes are taking place in our understanding of science in response to the complex issues of the impacts of human activity on the natural environment. Many of the most serious global impacts, including natural resource degradation, have emerged from the interaction of human activities in the scientific–technical–industrial system. The need for change to more sustainable practices is now well recognised in order to manage the negative impacts caused by the linkages across large temporal and spatial scales (Lubchenco, 1998; Jasanoff *et al.*, 1997), and new directions in science have emerged to meet this challenge (Forrester, 1971; Holling *et al.*, 2002a; Ravetz, 2002). Post-normal science, with a new epistemology, has been developed to help us understand complexity within the social context. This paradigmatic shift currently taking place in science is contributing to the development of theory and practice: in particular the challenge for scientists in conceptualising and understanding the dynamics of large-scale social-ecological systems (SESs), and the challenge for land managers attempting to practise sustainable natural resource management embedded within the SES. We show how the integration of the theories of resilience and system dynamics can help to understand the dynamics of the WA agricultural region as a SES to investigate places in the whole system that might be sensitive to policy intervention and management. Also, we make some recommendations that emerge from this research in relation to implications for natural resource management in general and for the training of scientists in post-normal science.

8.1 Contributions to natural resource management

There are potentially eight major contributions that this book makes to natural resource management in general and to the WA agricultural region specifically, to help to move towards establishing sustainable natural resource management.

1. We articulate the integration of social science and natural resource management within post-normal science.
2. We identify the basic principles and concepts of the systemic approach that apply to social and ecological sciences.
3. We place the management of natural resources in the WA agricultural region in its social context and the wider global perspective.
4. We identify the variables that are responsible for the organisation of the WA agricultural region as a SES including the commodity system drivers, the key indicators and the system traps.
5. The conceptual models of the WA agricultural region present the economic, social and ecological information in an easily understood and integrated format.
6. We identify that the WA agricultural region is in a Lock-in Trap which has low potential, high connectivity and high resilience.
7. The conceptual model of the WA agricultural region can provide a focus for discussion that can challenge people's assumptions and mental constructs of 'reality' and plausible futures for the region.
8. We clearly identify the need for changes to human-created institutions responsible for natural resource management.

These contributions are synthesised in the following sections.

8.2 Post-normal science paradigm

This synthesis includes the first study of the combined application of resilience theory and system dynamics to an agricultural region. Chapters 2, 3 and 4 identify the historical, policy-making and scientific contexts for natural resource management, and we use them to understand the problem situation; that is, how 'the problem' fits within the wider context or panarchy. The overarching question was 'Is the WA agricultural region a resilient social-ecological system (SES)?' From this initial question it was clear that the selection of the appropriate epistemology for the type of problem required investigation before we could successfully address the research question.

The methodology of normal science has increased the need for specialisation and the need to test the significance of results in order to reduce the
chance of reporting an effect when there is not an effect (a Type II error),
on the basis of probability. Consequently, it only takes one good piece of
evidence to reject a hypothesis but requires a data-rich environment, over
long time periods, to prove that an effect is 'real'. This process may lead
to the possibility that the answers are found too late to make an effective
decision, particularly in ecological systems. The cost of the Type II errors in
scientific method is counted in damage to the environment (Burgman, 2002).
The need for the Precautionary Principle is one result of this deficiency in
normal science. We now know that applying a precautionary approach in
natural resources management is essential (Cooney, 2003) for at least two
reasons: (1) the time-dependent nature of problems in economic-ecological
systems; and (2) mismatches of scale in human responsibility and natural
interactions. Natural resource management problems are complex with uncertainty a predominant characteristic; they defy reduction and empirical testing
by normal scientific method (Chapter 5).

Normal science situations are ascribed with low uncertainty, values are
not in dispute and decision stakes are low. Alternatively, situations where
uncertainty is high, values are in dispute and the decision stakes are high
(Funtowicz and Ravetz, 1990) require a different epistemology and post-
normal science has been proposed as a more appropriate paradigm. Although
the research approach adopted is different from the fundamental normal
applied science paradigm, it is also reliant upon the information that is
acquired from normal science and the two paradigms are considered to be
complementary. As detailed in Chapter 5 through the use of the Normative Information Model-based Analysis and Design Framework (Jayaratna,
1994), we showed that the potential tension that exists between normal and
post-normal science (Soulé, 1995) is resolved by an evaluation of three
factors: the problem situation, the selection of the appropriate method used to
address it, and the mental construct of the person who is attempting to solve
'the problem'. Problems of complexity require an inter- or transdisciplinary
approach and researchers whose mental constructs have been changed and
evolved by a breadth of expertise (Jasanoff *et al.*, 1997).

A framework made up of levels of organisation or a hierarchy is a central
theme in both ecology and social science. In ecology this framework links
the smallest level, the individual, to the greatest level, the global level, and
in sociological theory it is the systematic analysis of the structural components of large-scale and complex societies. Both are based on the premise
that systems are organised. The theory of organisation and the definition of

constructs of effectiveness, resilience and sustainability are areas that produce tension for policy and practice, as detailed in Chapter 4. The focus for organisation at times swings towards the process or the means, at other times towards the ends or the goals (Quinn and Rohrbaugh, 1983) and oft times the means have been confused with the ends in natural resource management (Wallace, 2003). For example, Landcare in the 1990s in the WA agricultural region was process-orientated and it was not until 1997 that the first national comprehensive assessment of the quality of natural resources (the ends) and how farmers relate to management was initiated (National Land and Water Resources Audit, 1997). The early conceptualisation of social organisation was structural differentiation about two dichotomous axes, which defined four functional paradigms considered in some cases to be incommensurable (Burrell and Morgan, 1979). Later theoreticians, however, accepted that alternative paradigms could be commensurable and able to be practised together.

Applying extant theory of the normal science paradigm to large-scale systems made up of people and nature clearly demonstrated our lagging ability to solve the recurring problems that society was responsible for creating. Multiple difficulties existed in concepts and theories, and in the rhetoric between theory and practice (Patterson and Williams, 1998; Bellamy and Johnson, 2000). The frustration caused by the inappropriateness and inadequacy of extant theory provided the impetus for the nascent theory of resilience (Gunderson and Holling, 2002). The blending of the tension between the static frameworks of organisation and the dynamic and flowing metaphor of the adaptive cycle (Holling and Gunderson, 2002) resolved many of the early difficulties surrounding the constructs of effectiveness, resilience and sustainability (Parsons, 1959; Quinn and Rohrbaugh, 1983) discussed in Chapter 4. The differentiated phases became connected and related in a dynamic systemic framework. The heuristic metaphor of the adaptive cycle describes the dynamics of organisation through four phases – exploitation, conservation, release and reorganisation – that account for periods of growth and stability interspersed with periods of release and reorganisation. Not one phase by itself is perpetual. All four phases are required for an effective, resilient and sustainable system made up of people and nature, which in system dynamics language is called self-organisation. It is the ability of a living or social system to change itself utterly by creating whole new structures and behaviour (Sterman, 2000).

8.3 The WA agricultural region

Natural resource policy and management in the WA agricultural region has failed to resolve natural resource management problems at the regional level

(Chapters 2 to 4). Analysis from separate social, ecological and economic perspectives provides a suite of reasons why the problems have persisted: a pro-development ethos, little coordination between institutions responsible in part for natural resource management, lack of an integrated strategy and lack of financial means to adopt sustainable land management practices. All are good reasons and all are part of the problem situation.

Until quite recently it was assumed that science informed policy and was translated into best management practice and adopted – but was this the case? An analysis of the history and policy of natural resource management in the WA agricultural region over the past 116 years showed that farmers and the extensive agri-industry have been successful in achieving increasing productivity through agronomy and genetic improvements, countering many adverse conditions, such as vermin, weeds and soil infertility. The latest improvements in agronomy are technically highly sophisticated and expensive, particularly precision farming techniques that can identify the most productive soils. Farmers are quick to adopt techniques that confer an economic advantage, when they are for direct productivity (Barr and Cary, 2000). In contrast to this is the overwhelming scientific advice for the maintenance of biodiversity and ecosystem services through the retention of native vegetation and its protection, by fencing, from being grazed by stock. Although some fencing has occurred, in many instances the protection of native vegetation is not perceived to confer an economic advantage, and many remnants of native vegetation remain unfenced. These remnants are under threat, in the short term from grazing, and in the long term, whether fenced or not in high risk areas, through rising watertables and soil salinity and other degrading processes, such as weeds.

Natural resource degradation was a concern for many scientists throughout the region's history and warnings were reported to government, as detailed in Chapter 2. Although legislation was proclaimed to mitigate the negative impacts, and economic estimates were made of losses to production and costs of repair to solve the problems, degrading processes such as soil salinity, loss of biodiversity and ecosystem services in the WA agricultural region have continued and are now considered to be intractable. Problems that persist in the face of remedial actions or policies can indicate areas in which our models and our assumptions about reality consistently fail. Although policies have changed over the years there has been a failure to critically examine the epistemological assumptions of science and policy and to make the necessary changes to the methods. The first policies to address the problems of natural resource degradation were command and control policies (CCP) laid down in statute and administered by institutions at the local, state and national levels (summarised in Figure 2.1). The conservation attitudes and ethos that began to emerge in the 1970s resulted in a national strategy to change farmers' attitudes in order to adopt more sustainable land management practices. As part of this movement significant change occurred in Western Australia from the late 1980s when a collection of approaches was introduced and practised under the rubric of integrated natural resource management. An examination of the issues and problems that are identified as natural resource management has revealed a number of weaknesses. There is no evidence to date to justify the rhetoric that adaptive management and integrated or participatory management of natural resources have improved natural resource management in the WA agricultural region.

Adaptive management, however, may have been less than successful in the WA agricultural region for a number of reasons. Firstly, the adaptive management process is now over 20 years old and in Western Australia has been adopted as a method for natural resources management since the late 1980s. There are three domains in which a method exists – creation, selection and action – and in each domain there is the method, the problem situation and the method user as discussed in Chapter 5. The mental construct of the creator of the method may be quite different from that of the person who selects the method for use and then puts it into the hands of the natural resource manager who has to deal with 'the problem' in the context of the WA agricultural region. In addition resilience theory has evolved to include a series of complex concepts perhaps still restricted to academic circles and not yet widely known or adopted by people in policy and management. We suggest that it is questionable that policy and management are adopting the latest science for sustainable natural resource management and in Section 8.4 propose theoretically why this occurs.

While throughout most of the twentieth century the focus was primarily on the symptoms of natural resource management problems, as we described in Chapters 2 and 3, we suggested in Chapters 5 to 7 that the symptoms must be viewed within the whole context. This poses problems for the choice of boundary for enquiry and requires changing our mental construct from thinking about 'the problem' to 'the problem situation'. In order to understand 'the problem situation' from a conceptual basis (Chapter 5), we constructed a framework founded on a post-normal epistemology that is proposed to help understand complex problems. The framework is based on a post-normal science paradigm using systemic assumptions and notions applied to a perspective of complex systems. These complex systems are composed of multiple feedback loops between the behaviour of humans and the environment. Instead of analysing and gathering data on as many separate components of a system as possible and how they interact, the qualitative system dynamics and resilience analysis approaches identify the dynamics of the system from a small number of key variables (Holling's Rule of Hand) at a highly aggregate level. This synthesis involves the suppression of detail to search for general, broadly explanatory patterns. Resilience theory posits that vulnerability increases as sources of novelty are eliminated and as functional diversity and cross-scale functional replication are reduced. In the WA agricultural region, loss of ecosystem services, loss of biodiversity and loss of rural population may contribute to increasing vulnerability of the linked SES.

Patterns of behaviour in the WA agricultural region were extracted from the historical analysis (Chapter 2). The initial steps of resilience analysis and system dynamics both involve a modelling process that seeks to characterise 'the problem' dynamically, to show from history how 'the problem' may have emerged over long time periods, and to encourage the adoption of a longer-term perspective by the investigator. This is particularly important because cause and effect are likely to be separate both in time and space, and delays in either information or material flows are likely to cause oscillations in the system. In this study the choice of only five variables – land use change, the number of agricultural establishments, farmer age, farmer terms of trade, and the wheat yield – that we used to describe the WA agricultural region is consistent with resilience theory. Resilience theory proposes that understanding a panarchy and its adaptive cycles requires a model of at least three to five key interacting components, at three qualitatively different speeds, and non-linear causation. For example, the creation of reference modes of five key variables that portray system behaviour (Chapter 6) illustrated two key factors. Firstly, there were differences in the dynamic patterns of the ecological factors and socio-economic factors, and secondly, there was a declining trend in ecosystem and social capacity.

The historical patterns were interpreted through a comparison of the adaptive cycle and long-wave economic cycles (Kondratiev Cycles), which were shown to be more or less synchronous. The 116-year history of the WA agricultural region shows recurring patterns of growth and decline. In contrast to rapid cycles of boom and bust in the economic factors, farm numbers showed one cycle reaching a maximum of approximately 23 000 in 1968 and subsequent decline to around 9000 in 2000, demonstrating a rapid response to changing economic conditions. The hydrological cycle showed a slow decline, which it is proposed may reach a new equilibrium between 50 and 300 years from now. This process is non-linear and demonstrates hysteresis. This means that if a system is able to return to its prior state, it will be by means of a different path of recovery and timescale. In this case vegetation replacement at a scale and rate that are feasible will be unable to halt or reverse the hydrological processes. In the WA agricultural region the processes in the economic, social and ecological systems are operating at different temporal scales. These three variables represent three selected levels of a panarchy that follow their own adaptive cycle, the fundamental unit of dynamic change described in resilience theory.

In resilience theory it is posited that vulnerability and resilience of the system change with the slow variables (Table 5.7). Resilience is about characterising and understanding change in complex systems, and in particular how human intervention results in ecosystem change. Human interventions and practices decrease ecological resilience through at least four processes: mining of ecosystem capital (for example, depletion of soil), eutrophication, modifying key ecosystem relationships and homogenising temporal and spatial variability. All four processes are described for the WA agricultural region in Chapters 2, 3, 6 and 7.

The most recent definition of social-ecological resilience has three defining characteristics: the amount of change the system can undergo and still retain the same controls on function and structure, or still be in the same state; the degree to which the system is capable of self-organisation; and the ability to build and increase the capacity for learning and adaptation (Resilience Alliance, 2002). Applying this definition to the WA agricultural region, we can make the following observations. At the regional scale the WA agricultural region is in a Lock-in Trap driven by the three commodity system drivers that continue to deplete natural resources, increase environmental pollution and cause social decline.

In response to system changes there are three management options: do nothing and wait and see; actively manage to return the system to a desired state; and manage or adapt to the new and altered system. The most common response has been the second option founded on the command and control philosophy, with the assumptions that we understand the causes, can predict with certainty and can control the processes. New theories on complexity and resilience replace these with contrasting notions that the future is uncertain and surprises are inevitable in self-organising systems which have emergent properties. The concepts of uncertainty and surprise as the characteristics of SESs contest the previously held assumptions that SESs are ordered, knowable and controllable and that scientists, politicians and land managers must be able to order, know and control the factors.

8.3.1 The WA agricultural region: management implications

Natural resource management policy has been generated with the assumption that if applied correctly the intervention will improve the identified problem situation. Policy interventions are directed at attempting to change individual behaviour; however, this on its own has proven to be ineffective. The rural sociology literature has shown that, although education has changed people's understanding and attitudes towards natural resource degradation problems, changed attitudes have not increased the wide-scale adoption of sustainable land practices. In SESs there are four domains that describe the intersection between feasibility space and decision processes involved in overcoming obstacles to change – willingness, understanding, capacity and what is physically possible – (Gallopin, 2002) as shown in Figure 8.1. Taking appropriate action is a complex decision-making process in which a person has to be willing, able and wise.

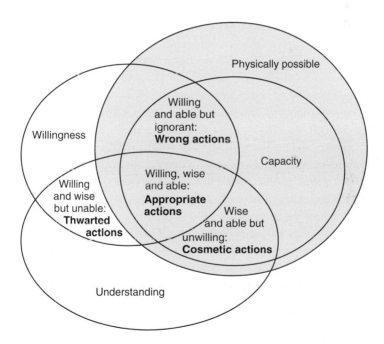

Fig. 8.1. Intersection between physical feasibility and decision processes. The capacity to do what is physically impossible cannot exist (by definition). Understanding generally allows for a realisation of what is and is not possible, although in some cases, people are willing to implement actions that will not result in change, because they violate physical laws or constraints. *Source:* derived from Gallopin (2002)

In Chapter 7, we described the general characteristics of aggregate commodity markets, including the three production growth drivers that account for the dynamics of the markets, and the three commodity traps. Three positive reinforcing feedback loops are responsible for the relationships between increasing productivity, prices and demand for wheat. If the structure of the system remains the same, it is proposed that the three commodity system drivers will continue to dominate the dynamics of the WA agricultural region, producing resource depletion, environmental pollution and decline in rural populations. To avoid policy resistance and find high leverage policies, we need to expand the boundaries of our models, exposing our assumptions for examination, so that we become aware of and understand the implications of the feedback loops operating at various scales in the spatial and temporal panarchies. We must learn about the structure and the dynamics of the increasingly complex system in which we are embedded. This requires altering the boundary of the system to include factors considered to be key structural variables of the whole system and not just of the subsystem in which 'the problem' is located. What this means is that the individual farmer in the WA agricultural region is one 'actor' or a 'pawn' in a large-scale, complex, self-organising SES that is tightly connected to global markets. Australian national policies are often seen as applied exogenously and are not often appreciated as being part of and driven by the larger system (that is, they are endogenous within the larger global system). Here then is one of the most difficult steps for science and management, that is, the choice of system boundary and the determination of policy makers with the appropriate understanding of system behaviour who can design effective policy that will change the structure and hence the behaviour of the system.

One of the assumptions of feedback control theory is that balancing feed-back loops control the exponential growth produced by reinforcing feedback loops. Nature evolves balancing feedback loops and humans invent them as controls to keep important system states within safe bounds. Whole system goals are not what we think of as goals in the individual motivational sense. They are not static, well structured or clearly defined (for example, the new hydrological equilibrium of the WA agricultural region). In the WA agri-cultural region the signals from the balancing feedback loops of resource depletion, environmental pollution and social decline have been ignored. Human innovation in the interaction of the science–technology–industry system has effectively redefined the threshold of the SES by extending its boundary outward, maintaining short-term productivity in a system that is self-organising. These balancing loops are weak and therefore do not indi-cate points of high leverage, where intervention will change the dynamics of the system, at least not at the present time. In feedback theory all balancing loops have a goal (Figure 7.3) either explicitly defined and based on human values, or implicit within the system structure (endogenous). Alternatively the endogenous system goal may be replaced with one based on the values of society, shown in Figures 7.9, 7.10 and 7.11 as the desired system states. These are exogenous to the system and are normative factors based on human values, for example, the level of biodiversity that is socially desirable. However, an appropriate response to the dynamics of the powerful reinforcing feedback loops of the commodity system will require more than the identification of explicit goals (Ravetz, 1997; Meadows, 1999).

8.3.2 Four scenarios

Extending the dynamic hypothesis described in Chapter 6, it is possible to suggest the following four scenarios for the future of land use change in the WA agricultural region which are an extension of the dynamic hypothesis based on Figure 6.2. A simple integrated model of resilience theory and system dynamics is used to explore different plausible futures. Four hypothetical scenarios – Dystopia, Conventional, Policy Reform and Transformational – are shown in Figure 8.2. System dynamics theory states that there has to be a structural change in the system variables, that is, a change in the relationship between the variables for a change to occur in the behaviour.

Dystopia scenario

Dystopia (Figure 8.2) may be considered as a reference mode in which the system structure remains unchanged, with a caveat that the timing of changes would be uncertain. If we do not act on available information, the commodity system will continue to be driven endogenously and consequently in the WA agricultural region many farmers do not know if they will be farming five and ten years from now, as they deal with a reduction in real terms of the prices of their commodities.

Rising watertables will reach their new equilibrium, with an impact on the land itself and on rural infrastructure such as town buildings and roads. By 2050, rising watertables will not only affect productive agricultural land but also lead to increased flood risk in many areas. In addition, sealed road life expectancy will be reduced by up to 75%, resulting in high public expenditure for repair to salt-affected infrastructure (Parliamentary Liberal Party, 2002). From hydrological modelling it is predicted that a new equilibrium of 33% salt affected land may be reached in 50 to 300 years, and so we have taken 33% as the minimum likely level of unproductive land. In this scenario the pattern of the first 100

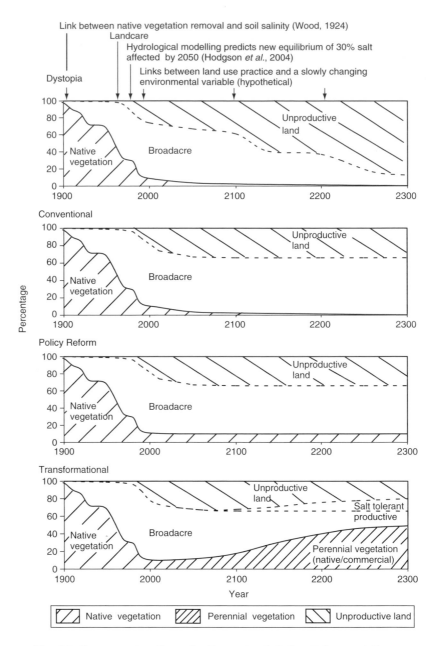

Fig. 8.2. Four scenarios, Dystopia, Conventional, Policy Reform and Transformational, illustrating the potential dynamics of land use change in the WA agricultural region with different combinations of native vegetation, broadacre, unproductive land, perennial vegetation (made up of additional native vegetation and commercial species). Further explanation is given in the text.

years (approximately) from 1900 to 2000 has been repeated twice. That is, land use has caused a change in a further two slowly emerging ecosystem variables sequentially, described by the series of s-shaped curves, which will increase the area of unproductive land through resource depletion and environmental pollution. Such behaviour may be produced by one or more reinforcing loops that drive the system into decline. Although the symptoms may be recognised early in their development, in similar circumstances to soil salinity, without sufficient evidence and without the symptoms being perceived as a significant problem, the endogenous system goal will eventually be reached, as shown in the causal loop diagram in Figure 5.8. The system is driven endogenously with the dominant goal being maximum total production of wheat and efficiency of the system, as shown by the production growth drivers in Chapter 7.

The endogenous goals of the ecological system and the social system are resource depletion, environmental pollution and social decline, unless they are replaced with explicit externally created human goals that are not subordinated to the endogenous goal of the production system. In this scenario much of the remnant native vegetation will be lost without remedial programmes to reduce the degrading processes in the agricultural catchments in which they are located (George et al., 1996; Saunders et al., 2003). The broadacre areas will continue to increase production through changes in technology. In the past ten years Australia has achieved its highest rate of average yield for wheat production through agronomy and improvement in wheat cultivars (Figure 6.3 (a)) and it is predicted that the sustained rate of increase in productivity may continue at roughly 1% a year (Passioura, 2002). Productivity gains will be essential to sustain total production if there is a concomitant decrease in the area available for productive purposes.

Conventional and Policy Reform scenarios

The Conventional and Policy Reform scenarios (Figure 8.2) do not deviate markedly from the present and represent a continuation of generally extant processes and forces with some cosmetic action (Figure 8.1). It is assumed that we have the information and are able to act but are unwilling to do so. The major assumption in these two scenarios is that the commodity system structure is changed to reduce the impacts of the three commodity traps. In the Conventional scenario the current predictions suggest that a new equilibrium of 33% of the WA agricultural region will become saline over the next 300 years and is shown as remaining stable at this level. Additional assumptions in this scenario are: no additional degrading processes will further degrade the soils to reduce the area of unproductive land further; and native vegetation will continue to decline. The Policy Reform scenario is similar with the addition of management to retain the area of native vegetation or to revegetate to maintain the current area.

Transformational scenario

We presented a conceptual model of land use change in Figure 6.1 in which commercial land use change could be accommodated through changes between cropland, pasture land and commercial forestry, including agro-forestry. Based on this conceptual model and the current agro-forestry strategies, the Transformational scenario may occur if there is a significant revegetation program with species that have a commercial benefit. Part of the revegetation will occur under the auspices of one current project, the Oil Mallee Project, which aims to develop an industry that produces eucalyptus oil, charcoal, activated carbon and 'green electricity' as bulk industrial products from selected eucalyptus species across a range of WA agricultural region conditions (Oil Mallee Association of Western Australia, 2001). The Oil Mallee Project has target plantings of 500 million mallees, to be planted over one million hectares, by the year 2025. This is approximately one-third of the three million hectare revegetation preliminary target set by the State Salinity Council in the Salinity Strategy for the south-west of Western Australia, an area of approximately 24 million hectares (Government of Western Australia, 2000). Other planting may take place under share-farming schemes with the Department of Conservation and Land Management using such species as the Tasmanian bluegum (*Eucalyptus globulus*) in the greater than 600 mm annual rainfall zone and the Maritime pine (*Pinus pinaster*) particularly in the light sandy soils in the 400 to 600 mm annual rainfall zone (Shea *et al.*, 1998). It is predicted that some land of marginal agricultural potential (based on precision farming techniques) may be taken out of production and potentially could be replanted with native vegetation to help meet the State Salinity Strategy target of 1.25 million hectares of land conservation and biodiversity plantings. Even if these strategies meet their targets for plantings, the cumulative revegetation total will only be approximately 12% of the area. It is assumed that even with a level of 50% of the area revegetated, the area of salinity affected land will not be substantially reduced, although there may be changes in hydrological processes that reduce watertables at the local scale (Pannell *et al.*, 2001).

8.3.3 The Sustainability Paradox of the behaviour of complex social-ecological systems

In Chapter 7, we showed how the structure of the generic commodity cycle will produce a pattern of response and will continue to achieve the single goal of commodity systems – the provision of a plentiful and inexpensive raw material. This uni-polar orientation of commodity markets causes trouble because the two basic rules of commodity markets are (1) commodity systems standardise the characteristics of the raw commodity, and (2) the producer with the lowest price makes the sale (Sawin *et al.*, 2003). If the focus of competition is only on the volume and cost of production without information about how the commodity was produced, commodity systems will continue to produce the three commodity traps, resource depletion, environmental pollution and social decline, producing the Sustainability Paradox.

We now have the information on the negative as well as the positive effects of the agricultural commodity system on the WA agricultural region, discussed in Chapters 2, 3 and 6. The question is, 'What are we going to do with this information?' We used the scenarios to show four possible long-term future scenarios to emphasise the Sustainability Paradox and the need to balance the short-term efficiency with the long-term survival. Are we willing to change the rules of human institutions, markets and commodity systems to take account of the information feedback on the external costs of production, soil erosion, soil salinity, loss of biodiversity, loss of ecosystem function, salinisation of waterways and rural decline? In other words can we effect a change to the short-term efficiency and need for greater production to achieve long-term sustainability.

8.3.4 Surprisingly unsurprising or is the surprise still to come?

In this synthesis we applied resilience theory, the adaptive cycle and the concept of panarchy to the WA agricultural region and found a general conformity with the paradoxes, provisional propositions and conclusions of these approaches, except for one conclusion – that management has to deal with surprise (Holling *et al.*, 2002a). In the WA agricultural region there has been no major surprise. Given that the causation between native vegetation removal and the appearance of soil salinity was known in 1924 (Wood, 1924), the dynamics of commodity systems has been known and modelled since the 1960s (Hathaway, 1963; Meadows, 1970), and system dynamics and feedback theory have been considered since the 1960s, the dynamics of the WA agricultural region may be more predictable than surprising. In the WA agricultural region the crossing of thresholds has been avoided by human innovation, metaphorically extending the thresholds outwards, preventing rapid system change and yielding no surprises in the dynamics of the WA agricultural region.

8.4 Governance, institutions and resilience: policy change, real world constraints and possibilities

We ground our politics, economic theory, education and societal values in the science of our times. Systems thinking provides a very different way of seeing the world – of setting boundaries, governing, organising and decision making for the future. In normal circumstances a policy problem or issue will be dealt with by reference to an existing practice or the existing knowledge base, in what has been described as incremental change and a continuation of past policies and practices. In general the substance of 'normal' policy making describes policy evolution in relation to natural resource management between 1889 and 1990 in Western Australia. The normal pattern of incremental change can be explained by the fact that the same set of policy makers are involved in the policy process over a long period of time, founded on the same shared values, culture, beliefs and paradigms. The policy makers' understanding of the nature of the 'problem' and the acceptable or feasible solutions to it are constrained by past solutions and their mental models of how the world works.

A second pattern of policy change, paradigmatic change, represents a major re-conceptualisation and restructuring of policy and may occur either over short or longer time periods. Paradigmatic change is seen as involving periods of stability and incremental adaptations interspersed by periods of revolutionary upheaval or what often has been referred to as a punctuated equilibrium pattern (Howlett and Ramesh, 1998). Fast paradigmatic policy change is infrequent because two conditions have to be met: a change in ideas and understanding and a change in the key actors/interests. Slow paradigmatic change may occur more often when only one of the conditions is present, for example, a change in knowledge without a change in the key actors and their interests that impede any change (Howlett and Ramesh, 1998).

Applying paradigmatic change theory to the WA agricultural region, we suggest that slow paradigmatic change is the model for natural resource management in Western Australia. As we suggested in Chapters 2 and 4, integrated natural resource management was adopted as the overarching policy model in 1987, including the adaptive management approach. This constituted a change in the knowledge base and for a short period of four years between 1990 and 1994 was facilitated by the Office of Catchment Management (OCM) as described in Section 2.2.6. In 1994 the integrating function of the OCM was essentially lost when the function was assigned to joint implementation by the four natural resource agencies, the Department of Agriculture, the Department of Conservation and Land Management, the Environmental Protection Authority and the Waterways Commission (the latter now merged into the Department of Environment). We suggest that the second condition required for paradigmatic change is missing in Western Australia; that is, there has been no change in the key actors/interests. Consequently only a slow paradigmatic change may currently be possible.

Slow paradigmatic change may occur for two reasons. Firstly, the key actors may retain the mental constructs of an older paradigm. A good analogy is drawn from music. The mental models of the users may be compelling them, metaphorically, to perform the steps to the waltz when dancing to the beat of a rock and roll song (Alfred and Allen, 1955). Although the tune has changed, those trained in an older version of a method may still go through the steps however awkward it may seem to observers, because the dancers cannot pick up the beat. This is particularly relevant to the adoption and practice of adaptive management in the WA agricultural region. Secondly, the new paradigm may challenge the interests of the key players, their positions, authority and power. For example, it was proposed by Capp (1997a) that a draft report, which was never finalised, that made recommendations on natural resource management and viability of agriculture in Western Australia threatened the primacy of the Department of Agriculture as the lead agency in agricultural land management and that it drew criticism from agricultural lobby groups and producer organisations (Parker, 2002). Similarly, the function of the OCM threatened the primacy of four government departments and its function was absorbed into the relevant departments.

8.4.1 The enigma of cross-scale interactions, self-organisation and the capacity for change

In modern agriculture the cross-scale interactions vary from the very small and fast to the very big and slow, and from the individual, local, regional and to the global scale. There can scarcely be any single appropriate scale at which to manage. This is analogous to system boundary identification, a fundamental issue in systems analysis. Systems in which interactions occur across broad scales have been defined as large-scale systems. Hence the WA agricultural region is considered to be a large-scale system which has interactions from the individual farmer level to the global level in commodity markets. Systems theory explains behaviour though the concept of feedback loops in which strong balancing feedback balances the effects of reinforcing feedback. If cause and effect are closely linked in time and space the feedback mechanisms are intuitive and the limiting factors can be reorganised. In comparison, when cause and effect are separated in time and space across large scales and are composed of multiple feedback loops, the cause and effect may become counterintuitive, the limiting factor(s) are more difficult to recognise and feedback signals can become weak.

Resilience is the capacity to lead to continued existence and to self-organise by incorporating change. It stresses the importance of assuming change and explaining stability instead of assuming stability and explaining change. When faced with the notions of self-organising systems, the power of the positive feedback loops in the commodity system, the lack of uptake of sustainable land management practices, farmers' declining profitability, technology and substitution altering thresholds, and the weak signals in the balancing feedback loops, we must question the ability of the social and ecological systems to place constraints on the behaviour of the commodity system, and query what cross-scale level intervention is required for transformational learning and change. Transformational learning involves awareness and understanding of the dynamics within and between several levels in a panarchy, not simply one level. In these cases, learning involves acquiring an ability to identify the tractable problems from among sets of complex variables. The most dramatic type of change is transformational, that is, a change in the structure and dynamics of the system. Management in these circumstances requires a fundamental understanding of cross-scale interactions.

8.4.2 Do we understand the dynamic behaviour of the system?

The challenge of developing sustainable natural resource management in agricultural systems is not primarily technical or scientific, for example, developing new technologies or disease resistant or ecologically friendly crop varieties (Röling and Wagemakers, 1998), nor is it an analytical challenge of developing appropriate policy and economic instruments. Röling and Wagemakers (1998) place agriculture within complex adaptive SESs, where multiple perspectives, values and ecological complexity defy reductionism. We suggest that post-normal science, resilience theory and qualitative system dynamics may be used in combination as a decision-support tool. It may be used to change people's mental models in the mode of double-loop learning on the issues of natural resource management, thus achieving a deeper understanding of the situation, the options available and their implications.

8.4.3 Is it physically possible to change the ecological systems?

The gradual change in the slow hydrological system is currently beyond human capacity to reverse, and a new hydrological equilibrium may be reached largely unaffected by any feasible intervention. Higher watertables reduce the buffering capacity of the hydrological system against greater than average rainfall events, causing flooding in river systems such as has occurred in the Moore River Catchment and the Avon River Catchment. The system is losing its buffering capacity and becoming susceptible to external disturbances such as climatic extremes. Increasing the size of a buffer is one way to stabilise a system; however, when it is a physical entity such as the subsurface aquifers it is not easily or quickly changed.

At the broadscale context in the WA agricultural region, hydrological modelling predicts that a new hydrological equilibrium will be reached over the next 50 to 300 years depending on position in the landscape and location in the region (Hodgson *et al.*, 2004). Areas with a low probability of long-term persistence or system recovery and a high level of threat will change to a different stable state (Cramer and Hobbs, 2002). It is anticipated that at the large-scale context, 33% of the WA agricultural region will change to a different stable state, affected by salinity and waterlogging. Under these conditions the land will have no or little commercial productivity. The once close linkages between vegetation, soil and rainfall that maintained a delicate hydrological balance across the region have been irreversibly altered (McFarlane *et al.*, 1993). Under the current conditions there is no immediate or long-term technical solution to fix the problem. The current Australian natural resource policies, which focus on management intervention at the broadscale regional levels, and more specifically on altering hydrological regimes for the protection of native vegetation, are therefore questionable in their effectiveness because it is not physically possible to intervene at a large enough scale or fast enough.

8.4.4 Are we willing to make the necessary changes?

Recent literature in natural resource management and complexity has included a discussion on the role of values, an emphasis on different ways of knowing, and new paradigms (Meadows, 1999; De Greene, 2000; Beresford *et al.*, 2001; Folke *et al.*, 2002; Hamilton, 2003; Monbiot, 2003), central themes in social organisation. As we discussed in Chapter 4, effectiveness of social organisation is a complex interrelationship of three competing value dimensions (Quinn and Rohrbaugh, 1983): organisation focus (internal–external), organisational structure (flexibility–control), and organisation means and ends (processes–outcomes) shown in Figure 4.3. Just like natural systems, social systems must fulfil key functions dictated by competing values. They may at times be orientated towards certain goals or objectives and at other times towards the means or processes. Whether we are willing to make a change depends on sets of rules, based on the values we hold as a society. Society's rules are composed in a hierarchy of values, traditions, policies, law, constitution and culture (Westley *et al.*, 2002) set in a panarchy across temporal and spatial dimensions in a similar way to natural systems.

Another distinguishing feature of social systems compared with natural systems is the capacity to reflect, as introduced in Chapter 6. Social rules and values can be changed as a result of that reflection. For example, a society could change its laws to better account for environmental externalities created by its commodity markets. Such changes have been proposed for the rules that govern global society under international conventions and institutions, such as the World Trade Organisation which deals with the rules that govern trade between nations (Cash and Moser, 2000; Hamilton, 2003; Monbiot, 2003). To those who hold the power in these trading systems, some of the proposed measures may seem revolutionary and would in fact constitute a change in the structure of the system. Changes in the rules that govern the structure of self-organising systems are considered by system dynamicists to be one of the most powerful leverage points in the system, and because of this they are also the most resistant to change (Meadows, 1999).

8.5 Implications for other broadacre agricultural regions

Globally the demand for agricultural products comes from the demand for food to feed a growing global population. It is projected that there will be a 40% global increase in cereal consumption by 2020 relative to 1995 levels (Pinstrup-Andersen *et al.*, 1999). Linked to this trend, increasing total production will continue to be the endogenous goal for the commodity system. The WA agricultural region characterises a system that is part of a global commodity system. It is particularly susceptible to global dynamics because it is primarily export orientated. The dynamics experienced in Western Australia is mirrored by Australian agricultural statistics (Productivity Commission, 2005). For example in the whole of Australia there is a continuing decline in the number of farms, which fell by about a quarter – almost 46 000 farms – over the 20 years to 2002–3. While the number of farms fell, the size of farms increased by an average of 23% (Productivity Commission, 2005). Australia's population is small and growth rates have slowed, consequently Australian agriculture will continue to be export dependent, around two-thirds of agricultural production is now either directly or indirectly exported, and future expansion will come from export markets (Productivity Commission, 2005). Australian agriculture with its export-dependent characteristics will continue on the current trajectory dominated by global market dynamics. Similar globalisation trends are recorded in agriculture worldwide particularly over the past 20 years as trade liberalisation allows the market to set prices and production levels (Hamilton, 2003; Buckland, 2004; Productivity Commission, 2005).

Although the history of the WA agricultural region is unique in terms of its specific influence at the regional level, it is linked to global-scale dynamics through the concept of the panarchy by the dynamics of the commodity cycle. Similarly the Goulburn Broken Catchment has local- and regional-scale influences that produce the regional dynamics, which may modify the impact of the global-scale dynamics of the commodity markets. The desire to understand systems and to design policies persists even though we recognise that the systems that we try to modify are complex within the panarchy. Holling's adaptive cycle provides one of the few well-defined, well-supported interpretations of complex systems (Cumming and Collier, 2005).

8.6 Further research

The ideas in this book are useful for making science relevant within a social and ecological context. The book also includes a powerful set of tools for communicating knowledge in an integrated fashion to inform policy and management decisions. To bring these ideas to a wider audience, a number of further steps will be required:

1. an expansion of the scope of the model from its limited representation of the social, ecological and commodity systems;
2. the incorporation of integrative science thinking into the sustainable regional development cycle for learning and adapting;
3. the development of the model with a user-friendly front-end as an education tool that can address 'What if . . .' questions about the future of the WA agricultural region within the global context and with a long-term perspective; and
4. fine-tuning the model into a robust tool for policy analysis so that it can be a dependable and a well-known resource for policy decision making.

The ideas will be required to be presented to producers, policy makers and other participants in the system as a starting point for debate on how the whole SES functions, not just the ecological resource system or the economic system or the social system. It is clear that the current economic status of agriculture is well known to Western Australian politicians who issued a position statement that included the words, 'Given fluctuations in the terms of trade for wheat, there may be other more profitable uses for the Wheatbelt areas' (Parliamentary Liberal Party, 2002) and to Australian thinktanks (Hickman and Andrews, 2003) who are requesting an open and transparent evaluation with regard to agriculture's economic viability, environmental impacts, social effects and the priority it is given for access to public money, in particular to drought relief (Botterill and Chapman, 2002).

The development of a more sophisticated system dynamics model is an appropriate response to the new challenges that require a precautionary approach, particularly in relation to policy decisions in natural resource management, producing slowly emerging ecological effects. It would allow an open and transparent evaluation of the problem situation that could be used as a 'what-if' type model in the genre of post-normal science which can deal with uncertainty (Ravetz, 1997). There is a growing practice of building system dynamics models directly with stakeholder groups (Zagonel, 2002). Such an approach would be complementary to the development of the regional strategies that are being used as the basis for public funding for natural resources in the WA agricultural region. Together they could be used to apply public funding for strategic long-term goals within a wider context and inclusive of social issues.

The WA agricultural region is linked through multiple complex feedback loops to the global commodity system and the global technical system (the Kondratiev Cycles discussed in Chapter 6). It is unlikely that local and regional strategies will be effective in changing the current regional dynamics by themselves, although management at all scales is required. The theory of resilience is in its infancy and further research would be beneficial on the role of slowly emerging ecological variables and their implications for the crossing of thresholds and surprises in SESs with different characteristics.

Resilience theory identifies that thresholds or tipping points occur when cycles of different speeds interact that are particularly sensitive to the dynamics of the slow ecological variable. Although there is now a significant body of knowledge and modelling of the slow hydrological variables in the WA agricultural region, further research is required to identify other slowly emerging ecological factors that will, through time, have the potential to cause the area of unproductive land to increase consistent with the Dystopic scenario in Figure 8.2.

Research to identify the total area that will become unproductive or abandoned based on poor economic returns will be important, particularly under potential changes in climate. Improved wheat varieties and improved agronomy have resulted in crop yields moving closer to the levels at which water supply is the major limitation (Passioura, 2002). Consequently, precision farming techniques to further improve agricultural efficiency may identify soil types that produce no economic return for the farmer, resulting in some areas becoming abandoned. Alternatively, once the poorer soils are identified, modifications may be made through application of chemicals to these areas to increase production. In Chapter 6 it was identified that rapid changes can occur when external factors are added to systems that are already under stress; for example, the potential for long-term climate variation to change the economic limits for agriculture may result in further areas being abandoned. This would indicate that further research is required to identify marginal agricultural areas that will be affected by any potential climate changes. Additional case studies that compare the dynamics of agricultural regions of different sizes within Australia, that produce undifferentiated commodities would be beneficial and add strength to the argument that such systems are more predictable than surprising.

8.7 Education: integration of the natural and the social sciences

The central theme uniting this book is the need to understand and conceptualise SESs at scales that include the feedback loops that are involved with the dynamics of the system, in order to navigate and build resilience for complexity and change. Necessarily this '…transcends the sciences, because the issues in focus require collaboration over the boundaries of the natural, social sciences and humanities' (Berkes *et al.*, 2003). It is recognised that we must change the way we teach science to address complex problems using an interdisciplinary approach and to produce individual scientists with a breadth of expertise (Jasanoff *et al.*, 1997; Bammer, 2005). If, as was suggested, universities could be influential for crossing disciplinary and institutional lines (Jasanoff *et al.*, 1997) it will require a deeper understanding by individuals about the epistemology of science and causal explanations of complex, physical, biological and social phenomena. These basic shifts in our understanding of causes will need to be taught throughout the education system and are already in place in some institutions in kindergarten through 12th grade education (Forrester, 1992). At the university level, an example of progress in this direction is the changing ideas about the expertise of graduate training in the sciences, as shown by a program of the Lyman Briggs School, which may provide a potential model for future courses in interdisciplinary study.

The Lyman Briggs School, part of the College of Natural Science at Michigan State University, USA, offers its students a basic education in mathematics and science within their social, historical and philosophical contexts (Lyman Briggs School, 2003). The Lyman Briggs School is a residential learning community devoted to studying the natural sciences and their impact on society. This school provides a liberal arts augmented science program taught by staff from academically diverse backgrounds in the natural and social sciences, mathematics and the humanities. The curriculum is designed to inter-connect biology, physics, chemistry, mathematics, history, sociology and philosophy, to prepare students to excel in a complex, rapidly changing society driven by technology and interdisciplinary collaborations.

8.8 Concluding remarks

Clearly the dynamics of commodity systems are well known and understood (Meadows, 1970; Guvenen *et al.*, 1991). Many great minds including those of Nobel Laureates in economics are addressing distributive issues in economics and the social cost and the management of ecosystem resources (Arrow *et al.*, 1999; Heal, 2000; Costanza and Farber, 2002). System dynamicists have modelled natural resource systems and asked some of the big social questions (Meadows, 1970; Forrester, 1971). Resilience theoreticians have presented heuristic models and metaphors that characterise the dynamics of complex and coupled SESs. The proposed measures from these sources suggest that effecting a change can appear either hopelessly unambitious or hopelessly unrealistic. Without a belief in meliorism – the belief that the world can be made better by human effort – it would be too easy to take a dystopic view of the future. However, we think there is cause for some hope that meliorism is not unrealistic.

Post-normal science is addressing the gap in our knowledge of how we define problems, identify solutions and implement actions. Values and quality shape paradigms and paradigms are the source of systems. Paradigms form the shared reality about how we understand the world around us; they are composed of shared social agreements and institutions. It is from these that we get the system goals and information flows in order to take the necessary action to effect change. Paradigms and systems are creations of the human mind, and therefore we must create resilient social-ecological systems that meet the goal of sustainability. The decisions that we have to make about natural resource management are social decisions. Our purpose is not just about new decisions that tinker at the edges, that allow the system to continue to reach the endogenous goals of resource depletion, environmental pollution and social decline. Our purpose has to be about establishing new decision rules within the human-created institutions, such as commodity systems, to change system structure and to do our utmost to meet the explicit socially derived goals for economic, ecological and social systems.

This analysis clearly identifies that the regional strategies that are being developed under the National Action Plan for Salinity and Water Quality (discussed in Chapter 2) must take into account not only the regional-scale issues but also the cross-scale issues, in particular the linkages between the commodity system drivers and the commodity system traps. In addition, this analysis has indicated ways to provide the information to encourage natural resource policy makers to take long-term and whole system perspectives.

Epilogue

The difference between a good mechanic and a bad one, like the difference between a good mathematician and a bad one, is precisely this ability to *select* the good facts from the bad ones on the basis of quality. He has to *care!* This is an ability about which formal traditional scientific method has nothing to say. It's long past time to take a closer look at this qualitative preselection of facts which has seemed so scrupulously ignored by those who make so much of these facts after they are "observed". I think that it will be found that a formal acknowledgement of the role of Quality in the scientific process doesn't destroy the empirical vision at all. It expands it, strengthens it and brings it far closer to actual scientific practice.

I think the basic fault that underlies the problem of stuckness is traditional rationality's insistence upon "objectivity", a doctrine that there is a divided reality of subject and object. For true science to take place these must be rigidly separate from each other. "You are the mechanic. There is the motorcycle. You are forever apart from one another. You do this to it. You do that to it. These will be the results."

This eternally dualistic subject–object way of approaching the motorcycle sounds right to us because we're used to it. But it's not right. It's always been an artificial interpretation *superimposed* on reality. It's never been reality itself. When this duality is completely accepted a certain nondivided relationship between the mechanic and motorcycle, a craftsmanlike feeling for the work, is destroyed. When rational rationality divides the work into subjects and objects it shuts out Quality, and when you're really stuck it's Quality, not any subjects or objects, that tells you where you ought to go.

By returning our attention onto Quality it is hoped that we can get technological work out of the noncaring subject–object dualism and get back into craftsmanlike self-involved reality again, which will reveal to us the facts we need when we are stuck.

Zen and the Art of Motorcycle Maintenance: An Inquiry
into Values. R. M. Pirsig, 1976

Glossary

Action world The situation in which methodologies are used for bringing about transformations (*see also* thinking worlds) (Jayaratna, 1994).

Adaptive cycle A four-phase adaptive cycle is a heuristic model or metaphor for understanding the process of change in complex systems and can be used to identify structure, patterns and causality in the complex adaptive system. The fundamental conceptual model describes in theoretical terms perpetual and ever-changing time periods of the flow of events through four phases in an ecosystem. These four phases are exploitation, conservation, release and reorganisation (represented by r, K, Ω and α respectively). The relative levels of the three properties – potential, connectedness and resilience – that are characteristic of each of the four phases of the cycle are shown in Table 5.10 (Holling, 1978).

Agro-ecological region A region with a characteristic interrelationship between the agronomy farming system and various environmental features, not just climatic. It is regarded as less specific than an agro-ecosystem (Williams *et al.*, 2002).

Agro-ecosystem An ecosystem manipulated by frequent, marked anthropogenic modifications of its biotic and abiotic environments. Four main types of modifications have been recognised, which are inputs in energy, reduction in biotic diversity to maximise yield of economic products, artificial selection and goal-orientated external control (Williams *et al.*, 2002).

Backloop In the adaptive cycle the backloop stage from reorganisation (Ω), to exploitation (α) is the rapid phase of reorganisation leading to renewal (Gunderson and Holling, 2002).

Boundary The real or abstract delineation between a system and its environment (Clayton and Radcliffe, 1996).

Causal loop diagram Diagram representing a closed loop of causal effect linkages (causal links) that is intended to capture how the variables interrelate. A causal loop diagram is a tool to represent the feedback structure of systems (Sterman, 2000).

Concept An abstraction from observed events, the characteristics of which are either directly observable or easily measured (Quinn and Rohrbaugh, 1983).

Construct An inference at a higher level of abstraction from concrete events and their meaning cannot be easily conveyed by pointing to specific occurrences. Such higher level abstractions are sometimes identified as constructs since they are constructed from concepts at a lower level of abstraction. The highly abstract nature of a construct and the lack of agreement as to its structure account for a major portion of the confusion in the effectiveness literature (Quinn and Rohrbaugh, 1983).

Counterintuitive behaviour A surprising result of policies devised to remedy a problem. Often the presumed 'solution' results in counter-productivity. Thus as troubles increase, efforts are intensified which actually worsen the problem (Gunderson and Holling, 2002).

Delay Time lag between cause and effect. Some elements of some systems take longer to react than others. This means that some events are synchronised. They are entrained but out of phase, while others are part of the same process of cause and effect but happen over different timescales. The degree of lag can itself be subject to threshold or interactive effects (Clayton and Radcliffe, 1996).

Diagnosis An expression of our understanding of a 'situation of concern'. This expression should describe both the logical and the physical aspects of the situation and, most importantly, the state of the 'situation of concern' (Jayaratna, 1994).

Dialectical Used loosely to indicate approval that a person or text shows some sensitivity to the contradiction and complexities of reality (Mann, 1983).

Disciplinary Specialisation in isolation (Light, 2000).

Dynamic hypothesis A working theory that describes how a problem arose (Sterman, 2000).

Ecological system Ecological systems (ecosystems) refer to self-regulating communities of organisms interacting with one another and with their environment. *See also* social systems and social-ecological systems (Berkes *et al.*, 2003).

Ecosystem A system resulting from the interaction of all the living and non-living factors of the environment (Tansley, 1935).

Ecosystem services Ecosystems are capital assets; if properly managed they yield a flow of vital services. Ecosystem services include the production of goods – such as seafood, timber and precursors to many industrial and pharmaceutical products – an important and familiar part of the economy. They also include basic life-support processes (such as pollination, water purification and climate regulation), life-fulfilling conditions (such as serenity, beauty and cultural inspiration), and preservation of options (such as conserving genetic and species diversity for future use) (Daily, 1997).

Emergence The phenomenon that systems have properties that the system components by themselves do not have and cannot be explained by the properties of the subcomponents (Clayton and Radcliffe, 1996).

Endogenous explanation An endogenous theory generates the dynamics of the system through interaction of the variables and agents represented in the model within the feedback loops, that is to say, 'arising from within' (Sterman, 2000).

Entrained The process whereby an endogenous, clock-driven rhythm is synchronised to the rhythm of environmental events. Entrainment of individual cycles is common in the natural world (Walker, 1995).

Epistemology Epistemological issues relate to the nature and understanding of knowledge and require answers to the question 'What is the nature of the relationship between the knower (the inquirer) and the known (or knowledge)?' (Burrell and Morgan, 1979).

Exogenous explanation An exogenous theory generates the dynamics of the system through interaction of the variables and agents not contained within the feedback loops (Sterman, 2000).

Externality (beneficial) Result of an activity that causes incidental benefits to others with no corresponding compensation provided to those who generate the externality (Baumol *et al.*, 1992).

Externality (detrimental) Result of an activity that causes damage with no corresponding compensation paid by those who generate the externality (Baumol *et al.*, 1992).

Feedback Feedback is one of the core concepts in system dynamics. All dynamics in a system arise from the interaction of just two types of feedback loops, positive (or self-reinforcing) and negative (or self-correcting). Reinforcing or positive feedback tends to reinforce or amplify whatever is happening in the system. Balancing or negative feedback counteracts and opposes change (Sterman, 2000).

Flow Rates or rates of change of a stock (Fey, 2002).

Framework A meta-level model (a higher level abstraction) through which a range of concepts, models, techniques and methodologies can either be clarified and/or integrated. A framework is a static model (Jayaratna, 1994).

Frontloop In the adaptive cycle the frontloop from exploitation (r) to conservation (K) is the slow, incremental phase of growth and accumulation (Gunderson and Holling, 2002).

Homeostasis The tendency towards maintenance of relatively stable social conditions among groups with respect to various factors (such as food supply and population among animals) and to competing tendencies and powers within the body politic, to society, to culture among men (Allen, 2000). Originally used in physiology the term is now applied to social and industrial systems and ecosystems (Ford, 1999).

Human nature Human nature concerns the implicit or explicit model of humans and their relationship with the environment (Burrell and Morgan, 1979).

Hysteresis If a system returns to its prior state, it does so by means of a different path of recovery (Gunderson *et al.*, 2002c).

Influence diagram *See* causal loop diagrams.

Interdisciplinary The use of an integrating theory or framework to link two or more disciplines such that experts in each field work together to address a problem, or such that a single researcher draws on the different disciplines to address a problem. Coordination by higher level concept (Mobbs and Dovers, 1999).

Kondratiev Cycle Long-wave rhythm in economic development and political behaviour (Berry, 1991).

Large-scale system Regional-scale system of people and nature composed of panarchies (Gunderson and Pritchard, 2002).

Law of diminishing marginal returns The 'law' that asserts that in a production process, when the amount of any one input is increased, while the amounts of all other inputs are held constant, the marginal returns to the increasing input ultimately diminish along a line called the marginal return curve (Baumol *et al.*, 1992).

Legitimacy Credible and accepted by key stakeholders (or other powerful individuals or institutions) involved (Allen, 2000).

Linearity A relationship that is proportional for all values of the cause and effect and for which the effect of changing two or more variables is the sum of the effects of changing them independently. While some non-linear relationships can be approximated by linear models, in many complex systems the non-linearities are both real and significant (Clayton and Radcliffe, 1996).

Marginal return curve *See* law of diminishing marginal returns.

Meliorism The belief that the world can be made better by human effort (Allen, 2000).

Mental construct It consists of nine elements namely perceptual process, values, ethics, motives and prejudices, structuring process (including methodologies), reasoning ability, roles, skills and knowledge sets, and models and frameworks. These interact to help make sense of situations, guide our actions (Jayaratna, 1994).

Metaphor A description or model that expresses in an indirect form our presuppositions about a problem or situation and its possible solution (Ravetz, 2002).

Methodology An explicit way of structuring one's thinking and actions. Methodologies contain model(s) and reflect particular perspectives of 'reality' based on a set of philosophical paradigms (Jayaratna, 1994).

Model A descriptive intellectual construct (Clayton and Radcliffe, 1996). A complete and coherent set of concepts that can underpin our understanding and actions. If we externalise it then it gives us a chance to examine, understand and analyse its relevance and completeness. Models also help us to design abstract or physical things (Jayaratna, 1994).

Multidisciplinary A process in which more than one discipline is involved and without cooperation (Light, 2000).

Natural resource management The use, development or conservation of rocks and soils; inland waters, estuaries and seas; vegetation (native, introduced, wild and controlled); and fauna (native, introduced, wild and domesticated) (Dore *et al.*, 2000).

Nomothetic methodology A methodology usually identified by four steps: (1) observation and description of a phenomenon or problem; (2) formulation of a hypothesis to explain the phenomenon. In physics, the hypothesis often takes the form of a causal mechanism or a mathematical relation; (3) use of the hypothesis to predict the existence of other phenomena, or to predict quantitatively the results of new observations; and (4) performance of experimental tests of the predictions by several independent experimenters and properly performed experiments. Because of this sequence it is often referred to as a hypothetico-deductive approach or normal science (Stokes, 1998).

Non-linearity A relationship that is not strictly proportional for all values of the cause and the effect or in which the combined effect of changing two or more control variables is not additive (Clayton and Radcliffe, 1996).

Notional system Conceptual model of how a system ought to be rather than how it is. Systems or mental constructs that can be formulated from our 'mental constructs' as being relevant and if designed, built and become operational are expected to bring about change from the 'current state' to the 'desired state' (Jayaratna, 1994).

Ontology Ontological issues relate to the nature of existence, and require answers to the question, 'What is the nature of the knowable, or what is the nature of reality?' (Burrell and Morgan, 1979).

Panarchy The adaptive and evolutionary nature of adaptive cycles that are nested one within the other across space and timescales (Holling *et al.*, 2002c).

Paradigm Universally recognised scientific achievements that for a time provide model problems and solutions to a community of practitioners, emphasising the social and cognitive integration of communities of scientists (Kuhn, 1970).

Paradigmatic change Discoveries or theories that violate the extant paradigm are anomalies which are rejected unless they are too obvious or too important, then they become sources of paradigm stress. Theories that solve intractable problems and relieve these stresses through a re-evaluation of the basic paradigm become threshold points for revolutionary science or paradigm change. Because all of the theories in every field that shares the paradigm depend on the assumptions of the paradigm, they must all be adjusted to the new assumptions, this causes dramatic changes in extant theories (Kuhn, 1970).

Policy resistance A phenomenon in which there is the tendency for interventions to be defeated by the response of the system to the intervention itself (Sterman, 2000).

Post-normal science An approach to problem solving that recognises the value-laden context and inherent uncertainty of science. The approach emphasises the need for quality assurance and expansion of the peer community. Although the concept originated with Gregory Bateson, the term originated with Funtowicz and Ravetz as a contrast to and complementary with normal science (Funtowicz and Ravetz, 1992).

Precaution, the precautionary principle or precautionary approach It is a response to uncertainty, in the face of risks to health or the environment. In general, it involves acting to avoid serious or irreversible potential harm, despite lack of scientific certainty as to the likelihood, magnitude or causation of that harm. Applying precaution in natural resource management and biodiversity conservation is clearly essential (Cooney, 2003).

Problem A problem is a mismatch between the perceived 'current state' of a situation and the perceived 'desired state' for that situation (Jayaratna, 1994).

Problem situation A situation in which people perceive 'problems'. Quotation marks are used to remind us that we should not assume that these are 'problems' (*see* problem) (Jayaratna, 1994).

Problem-solving process The problem-solving process can be considered as consisting of three major phases, namely, a problem formulation phase, a solution design phase and the design implementation phase (Jayaratna, 1994).

Prognosis The expression of our understanding of a 'desired state' for a particular 'situation of concern' including the design elements that will help to bring about the 'desired state' (Jayaratna, 1994).

Proximate driver The proximate drivers draw attention to the direct levers of change. Proximate drivers include those factors that have a direct influence on trends, and are subject to short-term policy intervention. Though the distinction is not always sharp, the grouping of drivers into proximate and ultimate categories is useful for discussing policies and priorities (Raskin *et al.*, 1998).

Rationalism In philosophy the term has been applied to an epistemological doctrine which, in opposition to empiricism, stresses the importance of deductive reasoning and a-priori theory in the creation of knowledge. Knowledge itself is seen as ideally forming a single, logically coherent system (Mann, 1983).

Real world The real world is taken to consist of both the 'thinking world' and the 'action world' of the intended problem solver (Jayaratna, 1994).

Resilience (ecological) Resilience is measured by the magnitude of disturbance that can be absorbed before the system changes its structure by changing the variables and processes that control behaviour. Particularly in systems in which conditions are far from an equilibrium steady state (Gunderson and Holling, 2002).

Resilience (engineering) Resilience is measured as the resistance to disturbance and speed of return to the equilibrium (Gunderson and Holling, 2002).

Scenario A story about the future. It indicates what the future may be like, as well as how events might unfold. Unlike projections and forecasts, which tend to be more quantitative and more limited in their assumptions, scenarios are logical narratives dealing with possibly far reaching changes (Gallopin, 2002).

Second-order cybernetics The science of communication and complex control processes through which self-organising biological and social systems regulate themselves and maintain homeostasis or stability within a given environment (Beer, 1959).

Self-organising The dynamics of systems arise spontaneously from their internal structure. Often, small, random perturbations are amplified and moulded by the feedback structure, generating patterns in space and time (Sterman, 2000).

Situation of concern An expression used to show a part of a situation around which we have drawn a boundary. The content inside the boundary then becomes of interest to us (Jayaratna, 1994).

Skills Skills are our ability to apply knowledge in practice. Skills reflect competence in the use of knowledge. These can be gained from continuous training and experience (Jayaratna, 1994).

Social capacity Social capacity is closely related to social capital and includes the notion of capability to be able to effect change (Cary *et al.*, 2001).

Social capital Social capital includes the institutions, the relationships, the attitudes and values that govern interactions among people and contribute to economic and social development. Social capital, however, is not simply the sum of institutions that underpin society, it is also the glue that holds them together. It includes the shared values and rules for social conduct expressed in personal relationships, trust and a common sense of 'civic' responsibility, that make society more than just a collection of individuals (World Bank, 1998).

Social system Social systems include those systems dealing with governance, institutions including financial and economic, and knowledge systems (Berkes *et al.*, 2003). *See also* ecological systems and social-ecological systems.

Social-ecological system (SES) A term that emphasises the integrated concept of humans-in-nature as opposed to ecological systems and social systems viewed separately (Berkes and Folke, 1998). *See also* social systems and ecological systems.

Soft disaster The gap between hard tools and uncertain issues can lead to soft disasters – environmental and political crises that emerge only slowly but at high costs to society, not least the erosion of public confidence and legitimacy. Examples are the BSE crisis and the GM food debate (ESRC Global Environmental Change Programme, 2000).

Stability The ability of a system to resist perturbation (Clayton and Radcliffe, 1996).

State The state of a system is a complete description of every important aspect of the system at some time. In an unchanging system, the system state is unchanging, whereas in a dynamic system the state constantly changes as the system changes. In modelling systems we typically use equations that describe how one system state gives rise to another, and thus how the system changes over time (Clayton and Radcliffe, 1996).

State cycle A system's complete range of possible combinations (Clayton and Radcliffe, 1996).

State variable Also known as a stock (Sterman, 2000).

Stock A store or quantity of material, energy or information. In economics stocks are also known as levels (Clayton and Radcliffe, 1996).

Structure The set of stocks, flows, loops and delays that define the interconnectedness of a system. A systems structure determines the range of behavioural possibilities. Although structures themselves do adapt, the term is normally used to refer to those elements that are permanent or adjust relatively slowly or infrequently (Clayton and Radcliffe, 1996).

Structuring process A way of making sense of or bringing order to our thoughts and actions. We expect methodologies to help us do this (Clayton and Radcliffe, 1996).

Sunk-cost That part of any cost that has been incurred in the past (or that part of a cost resulting from a commitment entered into in the past) that cannot be eliminated by present and future actions (Baumol *et al.*, 1992).

Synchronous Of the same date or moment, simultaneous. Similarly timed (especially of events coinciding in time but not place) (Fowler and Fowler, 1969).

System An interconnected set of elements, with coherent organisation. A system is characterised by hierarchical structure, emergent properties, communication and control. Some systems can exhibit dynamic, adaptive, goal-seeking, self-preserving or evolutionary behaviour. A subsystem is a component of a system (Clayton and Radcliffe, 1996).

System environment That which lies outside the system boundary (Clayton and Radcliffe, 1996).

Systematic Methodical, according to a plan, not casual or sporadic or unintentional (Fowler and Fowler, 1969).

Systemic analysis The process of problem formulation using the epistemological notion of 'systems'. The critical enquiring process using the notions of 'systems' for defining notional system(s) that is (are) considered as relevant to the 'situation of concern'. The problem formulation phase activities involve the critical examination of the rationale for the current and desired states, formulation of problem statements and hence the identification of relevant notional system(s). Systemic analysis is simply the use of 'systems' notions in the problem formulation phase of the problem-solving process (Jayaratna, 1994).

Systemic design The process of generating solutions using epistemological notions of systems (*see also* systemic analysis) (Jayaratna, 1994).

Systems analysis The study of an existing system in which the boundaries are taken as given (Jayaratna, 1994).

Systems thinking The understanding of a phenomenon within the context of a larger whole. To understand things systemically literally means to put them into a context, to establish the nature of their relationships (Clayton and Radcliffe, 1996).

Teleology The doctrine of final causes, the view that developments are due to the purpose or design that will be fulfilled by them (Fowler and Fowler, 1969).

Terms of trade Falling prices of agricultural commodities in comparison to the price of farm inputs (National Land and Water Resources Audit, 2002).

Thinking world The methodology user's conceptualisation about the intended actions (Jayaratna, 1994).

Threshold A threshold (or tipping point) is a point at which there is a qualitative change in behaviour of an element of a system or the system itself. Threshold effects can appear for a number of reasons, for example, they can appear as a function of several independent constraints, where one constraint is inoperative within the bounds of the other constraint but operative outside of those bounds (Clayton and Radcliffe, 1996).

Transdisciplinary The application of basic laws, principles, concepts and findings across a range of sciences (De Greene, 2000).

Transformational change A fundamental change in the nature and dynamics of the system caused by a change in the structure and relationship of variables in the system (Jayaratna, 1994).

Ultimate driver The ultimate drivers refer to the shape of the fundamental structure of values, knowledge and empowerment. Ultimate drivers are more stable and are a subject for the long-term policy-making agenda. They tend to influence trends indirectly by acting upon proximate drivers. Though the distinction is not always sharp, the grouping of drivers into proximate and ultimate categories is useful for discussing policies and priorities (Raskin *et al.*, 1998).

Values Beliefs that we consider to be 'good'. They are used as criteria for passing judgements about situations, the behaviour of others, and their actions (Jayaratna, 1994).

Yield gap The difference between the value of the yield on land assuming no soil health problems and the value of the yield on land with soil health problems (National Land and Water Resources Audit, 2002).

References

ABARE (2001). *Alternative Policy Approaches to Natural Resource Management. Background Report to the Natural Resource Management Taskforce*. Canberra, Australia: Agriculture, Fisheries and Forestry–Australia.

ABARE (2002). *ABARE-Agsurf*. Australian Bureau of Agricultural and Resource Economics. www.abareconomics.com/interactive/agsurf/aboutagsurf.htm. (Accessed 23 June 2002).

Ackoff, R. L. (1999). *Ackoff's Best: His Classic Writings on Management*. New York, USA: Wiley.

Aitken, L. and Rolfe, J. (2000). Social and economic issues. In Boulter, S. L., Wilson, B. A., Westrup, J., *et al.*, editors, *Native Vegetation Management in Queensland*, pages 97–112. Coorparoo, Australia: Department of Natural Resources, Queensland.

Alfred, R. and Allen, S. (1955). *Rock And Roll Waltz*. New York, USA: The RCA Records Label.

Allen, G. M. and Gould, E. M. (1986). Complexity, wickedness, and public forests. *Journal of Forestry*, **84**(4):20–23.

Allen, R., editor (2000). *The New Penguin English Dictionary*. London, UK: Penguin Books Ltd.

Allison, H. E., Brandenburg, S. A., and Beeston, G. R. (1993). *Natural Resource Zones of the South West Land Division, Western Australia. Technical Series 55*. Perth, Australia: Environmental Protection Authority.

Arrow, K., Daily, G., Dasgupta, P., *et al.* (1999). *Managing Ecosystem Resources*. Stockholm, Sweden: The Beijer International Institute of Ecological Economics.

Attwater, R. (2000). Pluralism, economic rhetoric, and common property. *Systemic Practice and Action Research*, **13**(4):543–557.

Australian Academy of Science (1999). *Sodicity – a dirty word in Australia*. Nova: Science in the news. www.science.org.au/nova/035/035key.htm (Accessed 23 October 2002).

Australian Bureau of Statistics (2003). *Year Book Australia 2003*. Australian Bureau of Statistics. www.abs.gov.au/Ausstats/ (Accessed 23 June 2003).

Australian Greenhouse Office (2000). *Land Clearing: A Social History*. Technical Report No. 4. Canberra, Australia: Australian Greenhouse Office, National Carbon Accounting System.

Australian Institute of Agricultural Science and Technology (1997). Agriculturalists take Monty House to task. *Australian Institute of Agriculture Science and Technology News.*

Ausubel, J. H. (1993). The organizational ecology of science advice in America. *European Review,* **1**(3):249–261.

Bammer, G. (2005). Integration and Implementation Sciences: building a new specialization. *Ecology and Society* **10**(2), 6. www.ecologyandsociety.org/vol10/iss2/art6.

Barath, T. (1998). Models and concepts of effectiveness in public education. In *23rd ATEE Conference,* Limerick, Ireland.

Bardsley, P., Chaudhri, V., and Stoneham, G. (2001). New directions in environmental policy. In *4th Australian Agriculture and Resource Economics Society Annual Symposium,* pages 34–38, Melbourne, Australia: AARES.

Barnabé, F. and Fischer, M. (2002). Group model building at a chemical company: System dynamics for knowledge elicitation and scenario training. In *20th International Conference of the System Dynamics Society, System Dynamics Society,* page 65, Palermo, Italy. 28 July–1 Aug 2002.

Barr, N. (2000). *Structural Change in Australian Agriculture; Implications For Natural Resource Management. Theme 6 Project 3.4.* National Land and Water Resources Audit, Canberra, Australia.

Barr, N. and Cary, J. (2000). *Influencing Improved Natural Resource Management on Farms. A Guide to Understanding Factors Influencing the Adoption of Sustainable Resource Practices.* Canberra, Australia: Department of Agriculture, Fisheries and Forestry–Australia.

Bartlett, R. H., Gardner, A., and Humphries, B., editors (1996). *Water Resources Law and Management in Western Australia.* Perth, Australia: The Centre for Commercial and Resources Law, The University of Western Australia.

Bateson, G. (1979). *Mind and Nature: A Necessary Unity.* London, UK: Dutton.

Baumol, W. J., Blinder, A. S., Gunther, A. W., and Hicks, J. R. L. (1992). *Economics: Principles and Policy.* Sydney, Australia: Harcourt Brace Jovanovich, 2nd Australian edition.

Bawden, R. J., Ison, R. L., Macadam, R. D., Packham, R.G., and Valentine, I. (1985). A research paradigm for systems agriculture. In Remenyi, J. V., editor, *Agricultural Systems Research for Developing Countries,* pages 31–42. Canberra, Australia: ACIAR.

Beer, S. (1959). *Cybernetics and Management.* London, UK: English Universities Press.

Beer, S. (1979). *Heart of the Enterprise.* Chichester, UK: John Wiley & Sons.

Beer, S. (1981). *Brain of the Firm.* Chichester, UK: John Wiley & Sons.

Beeston, B. G. R., Mlodawski, R. G., Sanders, A., and True, D. (1994). *Resource Management Report No. 149.* Perth, Australia: Department of Agriculture.

Bekle, H. (2002). The salinity crisis: Looking back and looking forward. In Bennet, S. J. and Blacklow, M., editors, *International Conference on Prospects for Biodiversity and Rivers in Salinising Landscapes.* Albany, Australia: Centre of Excellence for Natural Resource Management.

Bellamy, J. A. and Johnson, A. K. L. (2000). Integrated resource management: moving from rhetoric to practice in Australian agriculture. *Environmental Management*, **25**(3):265–280.

Bellamy, J. A., McDonald, G. T., Syme, G. J., and Butterworth, J. E. (1999). Evaluating integrated resource management. *Society & Natural Resources*, **12**:337–353.

Bellamy, J. A., Walker, D. H., McDonald, G. T., and Syme, G. J. (2001). A systems approach to the evaluation of natural resource management initiatives. *Journal of Environmental Management*, **63**:407–423.

Beresford, Q., Bekle, H., Phillips, H., and Mulcock, J. (2001). *The Salinity Crisis. Landscapes, Communities and Politics*. Perth, Australia: University of Western Australia Press.

Bergh, van den J. C. J. M., Ferrer-i-Carbonell, A., and Munda, G. (2000). Alternative models of individual behaviour and implications for environmental policy. *Ecological Economics*, **32**:43–61.

Berkes, F. and Folke, C., editors (1998). *Linking Social and Ecological Systems. Management Practices and Social Mechanisms for Building Resilience*. Cambridge, UK: Cambridge University Press.

Berkes, F., Colding, J., and Folke, C., editors (2003). *Navigating Social-Ecological Systems. Building Resilience for Complexity and Change*. Cambridge, UK: Cambridge University Press.

Berkhout, F., Hertin, J., and Jordan, A. (2001). *Socio-Economic Futures in Climate Change Impact Assessment: Using Scenarios as 'Learning Machines'*. Tyndall Centre Working Paper No. 3. University of Sussex, UK.

Berry, B. J. L. (1991). *Long-Wave Rhythms in Economic Development and Political Behavior*. Baltimore, USA: The Johns Hopkins University Press.

Bertalanffy, von L. (1968). *General System Theory: Foundations, Development, Applications*. New York, USA: G. Braziller.

Blackmore, D. J. (1995). Murray-Darling Basin Commission: A case study in integrated catchment management. *Water Science Technology*, **32**(5-6):15–25.

Blann, K. and Light, S. S. (2000a). Science and the new work of the resource practitioners; implications of complexity for natural resource management. www.iatp.org/AEAM/ScienceandtheNewWork.htm (Accessed 12 July 2003).

Blann, K. and Light, S. S. (2000b). *The Path of Last Resort. Adaptive Environmental Assessment and Management. 'Nine Heuristics of Highly Adaptive Managers'*. www.iatp.org/AEAM/primer.htm (Accessed 12 July 2003). Institute for Agriculture and Trade Policy, Adaptive Management Practitioners Workshop.

Bolton, G. (1972). *A Fine Country to Starve in*. Perth, Australia: University of Western Australia Press in association with Edith Cowan University.

Bonanno, G. A., Papa, A., and O'Neill, K. (2001). Loss and human resilience. *Applied & Preventative Psychology*, **10**(3):193–206.

Botterill, L. and Chapman, B. (2002). *Developing Equitable and Affordable Government Responses to Drought in Australia*. Centre for Economic Policy Research, Discussion Paper No. 455, Canberra, Australia.

Bradsen, J. R. (1988). *Soil Conservation Legislation in Australia. Report for the National Soil Conservation Program*. Adelaide, Australia: Faculty of Law, University of Adelaide.

Braun, R. (2002). People's concerns about biotechnology: some problems and some solutions. *Journal of Biotechnology*, **98**(1):3–8.

Brewer, G. B. (1986). Methods for synthesis: policy exercises. In Clark, W. C. and Munn, R. E., editors, *Sustainable Development of the Biosphere*, pages vi, 491. Cambridge, UK: Cambridge University Press for the International Institute for Applied Systems Analysis.

Brussard, P. F., Reed, J. M., and Tracy, C. R. (1998). Ecosystem management: what is it really? *Landscape and Urban Planning*, **40**:9–20.

Buck, S. J. (1998). *The Global Commons: An Introduction*. London, UK: Earthscan.

Buckland, J. (2004). *Ploughing up the Farm. Neoliberalism, Modern Technology and the State of the World's Farmers*. London, UK: Zed Books.

Bueren, van M. S. and Pannell, D. J. (1999). *Literature Review: Regional Economic Studies of Dryland Salinity*. Sustainability and Economics in Agriculture, Working Paper 99/05. general.uwa.edu.au/u/dpannell/dpap9905f.htm (Accessed 14 August 2003).

Burbidge, A. (1988). The why and how of managing biological resources. In Saunders, D. A. and Burbidge, A. A., editors, *Ecological Theory and Biological Management of Ecosystems. Occasional Paper No. 1/88*, pages 9–14. Perth, Australia: Department of Conservation and Land Management.

Burbidge, A. A. (2004). *Threatened Animals of Western Australia*. Kensington, WA, Australia: Department of Conservation and Land Management.

Burgman, M. (2002). *Remedies for the Scientific Disease. EcoEssay Series Number 4*. National Center for Ecological Analysis and Synthesis. www.nceas. ucsb.edu/frames.html (Accessed 25 November 2003).

Burke, G. (1991). *The Economic and Political Factors Affecting the Viability of Farmland Restoration in the Great Southern Region of Western Australia: A Historical Perspective on the British Economic Paradigm*. Honours degree, Murdoch University, Perth, Australia.

Burley Tobacco Growers Cooperative Association (2003). *The Tobacco Program*. Burley Tobacco Growers Cooperative Association. www.Burleytobacco.com/ website/default.asp (Accessed 4 July 2003).

Burrell, G. and Morgan, G. (1979). *Sociological Paradigms and Organisational Analysis: Elements of the Sociology of Corporate Life*. London, UK: Heinemann.

Burvill, G. H., editor (1979). *Agriculture in Western Australia. 150 Years of Development and Achievement 1829–1979*. Perth, Australia: University of Western Australia Press.

Calas, M. B. and Smircich, L. (1999). Past postmodernism? reflections and tentative directions. *Academy of Management Review*, **24**(4):649–671.

Capp, G. (1997a). Experts warn on environmental threat. *The West Australian*, 28 July 1997, Perth, Australia.

Capp, G. (1997b). House attacked for axing farm review. *The West Australian*, 10 July 1997, Perth, Australia.

Capp, G. (1999). The War on Salt – Let it go may be best way. *The West Australian*, 16 February 1999, Perth, Australia.

Capra, F. (1983). *The Turning Point. Science, Society and the Rising Culture*. Glasgow, UK: Collins Publishing Group.

Capra, F. (1996). *The Web of Life. A New Scientific Understanding of Living Systems.* New York, USA: Anchor Books Doubleday.

Carrier, H. D. and Wallace, W. A. (1994). An epistemological view of decision aid technology with emphasis on expert systems. In Wallace, W.A., editor, *Ethics in Modeling*, pages 37–57. New York, USA: Pergamon.

Carry, A. (1996). Uncertainty in the writings of Kondratiev. In Schmidt, C., editor, *Uncertainty in Economic Thought*, pages 126–145. Cheltenham, UK: Edward Elgar Publishing Ltd.

Cary, J. and Webb, T. (2000). *Community Landcare, the National Landcare Program and the Landcare Movement: the Social Dimensions of Landcare.* Agriculture, Fisheries and Forestry–Australia. Canberra, Australia: Social Sciences Centre Bureau of Rural Sciences.

Cary, J. W., Barr, N., Aslin, H., Webb, T., and Kelson, S. (2001). *Human and Social Aspects of Capacity to Change to Sustainable Managment Practices.* Canberra, Australia: Bureau of Rural Sciences.

Cary, J., Webb, T., and Barr, N. (2002). *Understanding Landholder's Capacity to Change to Sustainable Practices. Insights about Practice, Adoption and Social Capacity for Change.* Canberra, Australia: Agriculture, Fisheries and Forestry–Australia.

Cash, D. W. and Moser, S. C. (2000). Linking global and local scales: designing dynamic assessment and management processes. *Global Environmental Change*, **10**:109–120.

Cavana, R. Y., Davies, P. K., Robson, R. M., and Wilson, K. J. (1999). Drivers of quality in health services: different worldviews of clinicians and policy managers revealed. *System Dynamics Review*, **15**(3):331–340.

Checkland, P. (1984). *Systems Thinking, Systems Practice.* Chichester, UK: John Wiley & Sons.

Checkland, P. and Scholes, J. (1990). *Soft Systems Methodology in Action.* Chichester, UK: John Wiley & Sons.

Chisholm, A. H. and Dumsday, R. G. (1987). *Land Degradation: Problems and Policies.* Cambridge, UK: Cambridge University Press.

Clark, S. (1993). The dilemmas of the legislative process. In *River Basin Management Society Seminar*, La Trobe University, Melbourne, Australia. River Basin Management Society.

Clausen, S. and McAllister, L. M. (2001). An integrated approach to mineral policy. *Journal of Environmental Planning and Management*, **44** (2):227–244.

Clayton, A. M. H. and Radcliffe, N. J. (1996). *Sustainability. A Systems Approach.* Boulder, USA: Westview Press.

Cocks, K. D. (1992). *Use with Care: Managing Australia's Natural Resources in the Twenty-First Century.* Sydney, NSW: NSW University Press.

Commonwealth of Australia (1992). *National Strategy for Ecologically Sustainable Development.* Canberra, Australia: Commonwealth of Australia.

Commonwealth of Australia (1999). *Managing Natural Resources in Rural Australia for a Sustainable Future. A Discussion Paper for Developing a National Policy.* Canberra, Australia: Agriculture, Fisheries and Forestry–Australia.

Commonwealth of Australia (2001). *Our Vital Resources: National Action Plan for Salinity and Water Quality*. Canberra, Australia: Agriculture Fisheries and Forestry–Australia.

Commonwealth of Australia (2002). *Sustaining Our Natural Systems and Biodiversity*. Prime Minister's Science Engineering and Innovation Council, Eighth Meeting 31 May 2002, Canberra, Australia.

Conservation Through Reserves Committee WA (1974). *Conservation Reserves in Western Australia: Report of the Conservation Through Reserves Committee to the Environmental Protection Authority*. Perth, Australia: Environmental Protection Authority.

Cooney, R. (2003). *The Precautionary Principle and Environmental Governanace: Sustainable Development, Natural Resource Management and Biodiversity Conservation*. IUCN–The World Conservation Union, Traffic International, Fauna & Flora International, Resource Africa.

Cortner, H. J., Wallace, M. G., Burke, S., and Moote, M. A. (1998). Institutions matter: the need to address the institutional challenges of ecosystem management. *Landscape and Urban Planning*, **40**:159–166.

Costanza, R. and Farber, S. (2002). Introduction to the special issue on the dynamics and value of ecosystem services: integrating economic and ecological perspectives. *Ecological Economics*, **41**(3):367–373.

Costanza, R. and Jorgensen, S. E., editors (2002). *Environmental Problems in the 21st Century. Toward a New, Integrated Hard Problem Science*. Oxford, UK: Elsevier Science Ltd.

Costanza, R., Cumberland, J., Daly, H., Goodland, R., and Norgaard, R. (1997). *An Introduction to Ecological Economics*. Boca Raton, USA: St. Lucie Press.

Coyle, G. (2000). Qualitative and quantitative modeling in system dynamics: some research questions. *System Dynamics Review*, **16**(3):225–244.

Coyle, R. G. and Alexander, M. D. W. (1997). Two approaches to qualitative modelling of a nation's drug trade. *System Dynamics Review*, **13**(3):205–222.

Cramer, V. A. and Hobbs, R. J. (2002). Ecological consequences of altered hydrological regimes in fragmented ecosystems in southern Australia: Impacts and possible management responses. *Austral Ecology*, **27**:546–564.

CSIRO (2000). *CSIRO Sustainable Ecosystems*. Canberra, Australia: CSIRO.

CSIRO (2001). *Climate Change Projections for Australia. Summary Report*. Canberra, Australia: CSIRO.

Cullen, P. (2000). *River Research 2025*. ABC Four Corners. www.abc.net.au/4corners/water/cullen.htm (Accessed 3 April 2001).

Cumming, D. H. M. (2000). Drivers of resource management practices – fire in the belly? Comments on cross-cultural conflicts in fire management in northern Australia: 'not so black and white' by Alan Anderson. *Conservation Ecology* 4(1): Article 4. www.consecol.org/vol4/iss1/art4.

Cumming, G. S. and Collier, J. (2005). Change and identity. *Ecology and Society*, **10**(1):29. www.ecologyandsociety.org/vol10/iss1/art29/.

Daily, G. C. (1997). *Nature's Services: Societal Dependence on Natural Ecosystems*. Washington, DC, USA: Island Press.

Daily, G. C. (2000). Management objectives for the protection of ecosystem services. *Environmental Science & Policy*, **3**:333–339.

Daly, H. E. (1991). *Steady-State Economics*. Washington, DC, Island Press, USA: 2nd edition.

Davidson, B. R. (1981). *European Farming in Australia. An Economic History of Australian Farming*. Amsterdam, The Netherlands: Elsevier Scientific Publishing Company.

Davidson-Hunt, I. J. and Berkes, F. (2003). Nature and society through the lens of resilience: toward a human-in-ecosystem perspective. In Berkes, F., Colding, J., and Folke, C., editors, *Navigating Social-Ecological Systems. Building Resilience for Complexity and Change*. Cambridge, UK: Cambridge University Press.

De Greene, K. B. (1993). *A Systems-Based Approach to Policy Making*. Boston, USA: Kluwer Academic.

De Greene, K. B. (2000). *Revolution, Now! The New Scientific Basis*. 1stBooks. (Electronic book). www.1stbooks.com.

Department of Agriculture (1996). *Salinity: A Situation Statement for Western Australia. A Report to the Minister for Primary Industry, Minister for the Environment*. Perth, Australia: Agriculture Western Australia.

Department of Agriculture, Fisheries and Forestry-Australia (2002). *Investigating New Approaches: A Review of Natural Resource Management Pilots and Programs in Australia that Use Market-Based Instruments*. National Action Plan for Salinity and Water Quality, Canberra, Australia.

Department of Conservation and Land Management (2005). *Annual Report 2004–2005*. Perth, Australia: Department of Conservation and Land Management.

Department of Environment, Housing and Community Development (1978). *A Basis for Soil Conservation Policy in Australia. Commonwealth and State Government Collaborative Soil Conservation Study 1975–77. Report 1*. Canberra, Australia: Commonwealth of Australia.

Department of Foreign Affairs and Trade (2003). *Globalisation: Keeping the Gains*. Canberra, Australia: Economic Analytical Unit.

Diamond, J. (2005). *Collapse: How Societies Choose to Fail or Succeed*. New York, USA: Viking.

Dore, J., Keating, C., Woodhill, J., and Ellis, K. (2000). *Sustainable Regional Development Kit. A Resource for Improving the Community, Economy and Environment of Your Region*. Canberra, Australia: Greening Australia.

Dorner, D. (1997). *The Logic of Failure: Recognizing and Avoiding Errors in Complex Situations*. New York, USA: Perseus Press.

Dovers, S. (2000a). Still settling Australia: environment, history and policy. In Dovers, S., editor, *Environmental History and Policy: Still Settling Australia*. Melbourne, Australia: Oxford University Press.

Dovers, S., editor (2000b). *Environmental History and Policy: Still Settling Australia*. Melbourne, Australia: Oxford University Press.

Dovers, S. (2001). *Institutions for Sustainability*. Canberra, Australia: Economics and Environment Network.

Dovers, S. and Wild-River, S., editors (2003). *Managing Australia's Environment*. Annandale, Australia: Federation Press.

Dowrick, S., Dunlop, Y., and Quiggin, J. (2003). Social indicators and comparisons of living standards. *Journal of Developmental Economics*, **70**(2):501–529.

Doyle, T. J. and Kellow, A. J. (1995). *Environmental Politics and Policy Making in Australia*. Melbourne, Australia: Macmillan Education Australia.

Dunlop, M., Turner, G. M., and Howden S. M., (2004). *Future Sustainability of the Australian Grains Industry*. Canberra, Australia: Grains Council of Australia and Grains Research and Development Corporation.

Edwards, V. M. and Steins, N. A. (1999). A framework for analysing contextual factors in common pool resource research. *Journal of Environmental Policy and Planning*, **1**:205–221.

Emery, F. (1969). *Systems Thinking: Selected Readings*. Harmondsworth, UK: Penguin Books.

Environmental Protection Authority (2000). *Environmental Protection in Native Vegetation in Western Australia. EPA Position Statement No. 2*. Perth, Australia: Environmental Protection Authority.

ESRC Global Environmental Change Programme (2000). *Risky Choices, Soft Disasters: Environmental Decision-Making Under Uncertainty*. Brighton, UK: University of Sussex.

Ewing, S.A., Grayson R.B., and Argent, R.M. (2000). Science, citizens and catchment: Decision support for catchment management in Australia. *Society and Natural Resources*, **13**:443–459.

Fey, W. R. (2002). Organizational change from a new perspective: pattern feedback control in human systems. In *20th International Conference of the System Dynamics Society. 28 July–1 Aug 2002*. Palermo, Italy: System Dynamics Society.

Fletcher, A. and Davis, J. (unpublished). A dialectical framework for the representation and managment of complex systems.

Fletcher, A. J. P. and Davis, J. P. (2003). Dialectical evidence assembly for discovery. In *Proceedings of 6th International Conference on Discovery Science, 17–19 October 2003*, Sapporo, Japan: Hokkaido University.

Folke, C., Colding, J., and Berkes, F. (2002). Synthesis: Building resilience and adaptive capacity in social-ecological systems. In Berkes, F., Colding, J., and Folke, C., editors, *Navigating Social-Ecological Systems. Building Resilience for Complexity and Change*, pages 352–387. Cambridge, UK: Cambridge University Press.

Ford, A. (1999). *Modeling the Environment. An Introduction to System Dynamics Modeling of Environmental Systems*. Washington, DC, USA: Island Press.

Forrester, J. W. (1961). *Industrial Dynamics*. Cambridge, USA: Productivity Press.

Forrester, J. W. (1971). *World Dynamics*. Cambridge, USA: Wright-Allen Press.

Forrester, J. W. (1989). *The Beginning of Systems Dynamics*. Massachusetts Institute of Technology. (Accessed 5 September 2000).

Forrester, J. W. (1992). *System Dynamics and Learner-Centered-Learning in Kindergarten Through 12th Grade Education*. Massachusetts Institute of Technology. ftp://sysdyn.mit.edu/ftp/sdep/Roadmaps/RM1/D–4337.pdf (Accessed 5 September 2000).

Forrester, J. W. (1995). *Counterintuitive Behavior of Social Systems*. Massachusetts Institute of Technology. ftp://sysdyn.mit.edu/ftp/sdep/Roadmaps/RM1/D–4468–1.pdf (Accessed 5 September 2000).

Fowler, F. G. and Fowler, H. W. (1969). *The Pocket Oxford Dictionary of Current English*. 5th edn. Oxford, UK: Clarendon Press.

Fox, C. J. (1990). Implementation research: why and how to transcend positivist methodologies. In Palumbo, D. J. and Calista, D. J., editors, *Implementation and Policy Process: Opening Up the Black Box*, pages 199–212. Westport, USA: Greenwood Press.

Frost, F. and Burnside, D. (2001). Appreciating and creating history. In Viv Read and Associates, editor, *Wheatbelt Valley Floors Conference, 30 July–1 August 2001*, Merredin, Australia: Water and Rivers Commission.

Funtowicz, S. O. and Ravetz, J. R. (1990). *Uncertainty and Quality in Science and Policy*. Dordrecht, The Netherlands: Kluwer Academic Publishers.

Funtowicz, S. O. and Ravetz, J. R. (1992). Three types of risk assessment and the emergence of post-normal science. In Krimsky, S. and Golding, D., editors, *Social Theories of Risk*, pages 251–273. Westport, USA: Praeger.

Funtowicz, S. O. and Ravetz, J. R. (1993). Science for the post-normal age. *Futures*, **25**(7):739–755.

Gaarder, J. (1994). *Sophie's World: A Novel About the History of Philosophy*. London, UK: Phoenix.

Gallopin, G. C. (2002). Planning for resilience: scenarios, surprises, and branch points. In Gunderson, L. H. and Holling, C. S., editors, *Panarchy. Understanding Transformations in Human and Natural Systems*, pages 361–392. Washington, DC, USA: Island Press.

Gauch, H. G. J. (2003). *Scientific Method in Practice*. Cambridge, UK: Cambridge University Press.

George, R. J., McFarlane, D. J., and Speed, R. J. (1996). The consequences of a changing hydrologic environment for native vegetation in southwestern Australia. In Saunders, D. A., Craig, J. L., and Mattiske, E. M., editors, *Nature Conservation 4: The Role of Networks*, pages 9–22. Chipping Norton, Australia: Surrey Beatty & Sons Pty Limited.

Gharajedaghi, J. (1999). *Systems Thinking: Managing Chaos and Complexity: A Platform for Designing Business Architecture*. Boston, USA: Butterworth-Heinemann.

Gibbons, M., Nowotny, H., Limoges, C., *et al.* (1994). *The New Production of Knowledge: The Dynamics of Science and Research in Contemporary Societies*. London, UK: Sage.

Gill, R. (1996). An integrated social fabric matrix/system dynamics approach to policy analysis. *Systems Dynamics Review*, **12**(3):167–181.

Gill, R. (1999). *Sustainable Agriculture*. Centre for Ecological Economics and Water Policy Research, University of New England. (Accessed 27 September 2002).

Gill, R. (2001). *Planning for Sustainable Agro-Ecosystems: A Systems Approach*. Centre for Ecological Economics and Water Policy Research. (Accessed 14 March 2001).

Gladwell, M. (2002). *The Tipping Point: How Little Things Can Make a Big Difference*. Boston, USA: Back Bay Books.

Goulburn Broken Catchment Management Authority (2002). *Draft Region Catchment Strategy Goulburn Broken*. Shepparton, Australia: Goulburn Broken Catchment Management Authority.

Government of Western Australia (1996a). *Salinity. A Situation Statement for Western Australia, A Report to the Minister for Primary Industry and Minister for the Environment.* Perth, Australia: AWA, CALM, DEP, Water and Rivers Commission.

Government of Western Australia (1996b). *Restoring Nature's Balance. The War on Salt.* Perth, Australia: Department of Premier and Cabinet.

Government of Western Australia (2000). *Natural Resource Management in Western Australia. The Salinity Strategy.* State Salinity Council.

Government of Western Australia (2001). *Natural Resource Management in Western Australia. Western Australian Government Framework to Assist in Achieving Sustainable Natural Resource Management.* Perth, Australia: Department of Premier and Cabinet.

Government of Western Australia (2002a). *Focus on the Future. The Western Australian State Sustainability Strategy. Consultation Draft.* Perth, Australia: Department of Premier and Cabinet.

Government of Western Australia (2002b). *Media Release, 23 May 2002. State Government Signs National Salinity and Water Quality Plan.* Perth, Australia: Department of Premier and Cabinet.

Government of Western Australia (2003). *Hope for the Future: The Western Australian State Sustainability Strategy.* Perth, Australia: Department of Premier and Cabinet.

Grant, W. E. (1998). Ecology and natural resource management: reflections from a systems perspective. *Ecological Modelling*, **108**:67–76.

Grant, W. E., Pederson, E. K, and Marin, S. L. (1997). *Ecology and Natural Resource Management. Systems Analysis and Simulation.* Chichester, UK: John Wiley & Sons.

Gresser, C. (2002). *Mugged: Poverty in Your Coffee Cup.* Washington, USA: Oxfam International.

Guba, E. G. (1990). The alternative paradigm dialog. In Guba, E. G., editor, *The Paradigm Dialog.* Newbury Park, USA: Sage Publications.

Guerin, T. F. (2000). Overcoming the constraints to the adoption of sustainable land management practices in Australia. *Technological Forecasting and Social Change*, **65**(2):205–237.

Gunderson, L. H. and Holling, C. S. (2002). *Panarchy. Understanding Transformations in Human and Natural Systems.* Washington, DC, USA: Island Press.

Gunderson, L. H. and Pritchard, Jr., L. (2002). *Resilience and the Behavior of Large-Scale Systems.* SCOPE 60. Washington, DC, USA: Island Press.

Gunderson, L. H., Holling, C. S., and Light, S. S., editors (1995). *Barriers and Bridges to the Renewal of Ecosystems and Institutions.* New York, USA: Columbia University Press.

Gunderson, L. H., Holling, C. S., and Peterson, G. D. (2002a). Surprises and sustainability: cycles of renewal in the everglades. In Gunderson, L. H. and Holling, C. S., editors, *Panarchy. Understanding Transformations in Human and Natural Systems*, pages 315–332. Washington, DC, USA: Island Press.

Gunderson, L. H., Holling, C. S., Pritchard, Jr., L., and Peterson, G. D. (2002b). Resilience of large-scale resource systems. In Gunderson, L. H. and Pritchard, Jr., L., editors, *Resilience and the Behavior of Large-Scale Systems*, SCOPE 60, pages 3–20. Washington, DC, USA: Island Press.

Gunderson, L. H., Pritchard, Jr., L., Holling, C. S., Folke, C., and Peterson, G. D. (2002c). A summary and synthesis of resilience in large-scale systems. In Gunderson, L. H. and Pritchard, Jr., L., editors, *Resilience and the Behavior of Large-Scale Systems*. SCOPE 60, pages 249–266. Washington, DC, USA: Island Press.

Guvenen, O., Labys, W. C., and Lesourd, J. (1991). *International Commodity Market Models: Advances in Methodology and Applications*. London, UK: Chapman and Hall, 1st edition.

Habermas, J., Rorty, R., Niznik, J., Sanders, J. T., and Kolakowski, L. (1996). *Debating the State of Philosophy: Habermas, Rorty, and Kolakowski*. Westport, USA: Praeger.

Hamblin, A. P. and Kyneur, G. (1993). *Trends in Wheat Yields and Soil Fertility in Australia*. Canberra, Australia: Bureau of Resource Sciences, Australian Government Publishing Service.

Hamilton, C. (2003). *Growth Fetish*. Crows Nest, Australia: Allen and Unwin.

Hanna, S. and Munasinghe, M. (1995). *Property Rights and the Environment: Social and Ecological Issues*. Washington, DC, USA: Beijer International Institute of Ecological Economics and the World Bank.

Hansson, S. O. and Helgesson, G. (2003). What is stability? *Synthese*, **136**(2):219–235.

Harris, G. (2002). Integrated assessment and modelling: an essential way of doing science. *Environmental Modelling & Software*, **17**(3):201–207.

Hartley, R. E. R., Riches, J. R. H., and Davis, J. K. (1992). *A Systems Approach for Landcare*. Sydney, Australia: International Soil Conservation Organisation.

Hathaway, D. E. (1963). *Government and Agriculture*. New York, USA: Macmillan.

Hatton, T. J. and Ruprecht, J. (2001). Watching the rivers flow: Hydrology of the wheatbelt. In *Wheatbelt Valley Floors Conference*, Merredin, Australia. Water and Rivers Commission.

Hatton, T. J., Ruprecht, J., and George, R. J. (2003). Preclearing hydrology of the Western Australian wheatbelt: target for the future? *Plant and Soil*, **257**:341–356.

Hayles, N. K. (1995). Searching for common ground. In Soulé, M. E. and Lease, G., editors, *Reinventing Nature?: Responses to Postmodern Deconstruction*. Washington, DC, USA: Island Press.

Heal, G. M. (2000). *Nature and the Marketplace: Capturing the Value of Ecosystem Services*. Washington, DC, USA: Island Press.

Hickman, S. and Andrews, C. (2003). *Rethinking Australian Agriculture*. The Reid Group. www.reidgroup.org/articles/2003/rethinkingaustralianagriculture.pdf (Accessed 7 December 2003).

Hilborn, R. (1992). Can fisheries agencies learn from experience? *Fisheries*, **17**:6–14.

Hill, S. B. (1998). Redesigning agroecosystems for environmental sustainability: a deep systems approach. *Systems Research and Behavioral Science*, **15**:391–402.

Hobbs, R. J. (1988). What is ecological theory and is it of any use to managers? In Saunders, D. A. and Burbidge, A., editors, *Ecological Theory and Biological Management of Ecosystems*, Occasional Paper No. 1/88, pages 15–27. Perth, Australia: Department of Conservation and Land Management WA.

Hobbs, R. J. (1997). Future landscapes and the future of landscape ecology. *Landscape and Urban Planning*, **37**:1–9.

Hobbs, R. J. (1998). Managing ecological systems and processes. In Peterson, D. L. and Parker, V. T., editors, *Ecological Scale: Theory and Applications*, pages 459–484. New York, USA: Columbia University Press.

Hobbs, R. J. and Kristjanson, L. J. (2003). Triage: How do we prioritize healthcare for landscapes. *Ecological Management & Restoration*, **4** Suppl:39–45.

Hobbs, R. J. and Yates, C. J. (1997). Moving from the general to the specific: remnant management in rural Australia. In *Natural and Altered Landscapes: The Rural Perspective*. Oxford, UK: Elsevier Science Ltd.

Hobbs, R. J., Cramer, V. A., and Kristjanson, L. J. (2003). What happens if we can't fix it? Triage, palliative care and setting priorities in salinising landscapes. *Australian Journal of Botany*, **51**:647–653.

Hodgson, G. A., Hatton, T. J., and Salama, R. B. (2004). Modelling rising groundwater and the impacts of salinisation on terrestrial remnant vegetation in the Blackwood Basin. *Ecological Management & Restoration*, **5**:52–60.

Hogwood, B. W. and Gunn, L. A. (1992). *Policy Analysis for the Real World*. Oxford, UK: Oxford University Press.

Holland, J. H. (1992). *Adaptation in Natural and Artificial Systems: An Introductory Analysis with Applications to Biology, Control, and Artificial Intelligence*. Cambridge, USA: MIT Press.

Hollick, M. and Mitchell, B. (1991). *Integrated Catchment Management in Western Australia: Background and Alternative Approaches*. Perth, Australia: Centre for Water Research.

Holling, C. S. (1973). Resilience and stability of ecological systems. *Annual Review of Ecological Systems*, **4**:1–24.

Holling, C. S., editor (1978). *Adaptive Environmental Assessment and Management*. International Series on Applied Systems Analysis. Chichester, UK: John Wiley & Sons.

Holling, C. S. (1995). What barriers? What bridges? In Gunderson, L. H., Holling, C. S., and Light, S. S., editors, *Barriers and Bridges to the Renewal of Ecosystems and Institutions*. New York, USA: Columbia University Press.

Holling, C. S. (2000). Theories for sustainable futures. *Conservation Ecology* **4**(2) Article7. www.consecol.org/vol4/iss2/art7.

Holling, C. S. (2003). Foreword: the backloop to sustainability. In Berkes, F., Colding, J., and Folke, C., editors, *Navigating Social-Ecological Systems. Building Resilience for Complexity and Change*. Cambridge, UK: Cambridge University Press.

Holling, C. S. and Gunderson, L. H. (2002). Resilience and adaptive cycles. In Gunderson, L. H. and Holling, C. S., editors, *Panarchy. Understanding Transformations in Human and Natural Systems*, pages 25–62. Washington, DC, USA: Island Press.

Holling, C. S. and Meffe, G. K (1996). Command and control and the pathology of natural resource management. *Conservation Biology*, **10**(2):328–337.

Holling, C. S., Folke, C., Gunderson, L., and Maler, K.-G. (2000). *Resilience of ecosystems, economic systems and institutions. Final Report*. Resilience Alliance. www.resalliance.org (Accessed 30 May 2002).

Holling, C. S., Carpenter, S. R., Brock, W. A., and Gunderson, L. H. (2002a). Discoveries for sustainable futures. In Gunderson, L. H. and Holling, C. S., editors,

Panarchy. Understanding Transformations in Human and Natural Systems, pages 395–417. Washington, DC, USA: Island Press.

Holling, C. S., Gunderson, L. H., and Ludwig, D. (2002b). In quest of a theory of adaptive change. In Gunderson, L. H. and Holling, C. S., editors, *Panarchy. Understanding Transformations in Human and Natural Systems*, pages 3–22. Washington, DC, USA: Island Press.

Holling, C. S., Gunderson, L. H., and Peterson, G. D. (2002c). Sustainability and panarchies. In Gunderson, L. H. and Holling, C. S., editors, *Panarchy. Understanding Transformations in Human and Natural Systems*, pages 63–102. Washington, DC, USA: Island Press.

Holmes, K. J. and Wolman, M. G. (2001). Early development of systems analysis in natural resources management from man to nature to the Miami conservancy district. *Environmental Management*, **27**(2):177–193.

Homer, J. and Oliva, R. (2001). Maps and models in system dynamics: a response to Coyle. *System Dynamics Review*, **17**(4):347–355.

Hooper, S., Barrett, D., and Martin, P. (2003). *Australian Grains Industry 2003. Grains Industry, Performance and Outlook*. Canberra, Australia: Grains Research & Development Corporation, ABARE.

Hopper, S. D., Harvey, M. S., Chappill, J. A., Main, A. R., and Main, B. Y. (2001). The Western Australian biota as gondwanan heritage – a review. In Hopper, S. D., Harvey, M. S., Chappill, J. A., and George, S. A., editors, *Gondwanan Heritage: Past, Present and Future of the Western Australian Biota*, pages 1–46. Chipping Norton, Australia: Surrey Beatty and Sons.

Horton, D. R. (1994). Special article - Unity and diversity: The history and culture of aboriginal Australia. abs catalogue no. 1301.0. In *Year Book Australia, 1994*. Canberra, Australia: Australian Bureau of Statistics.

House MLA (1997). *Ministerial Statement on Natural Resource Management and Viability of Agriculture in Western Australia*. Perth, Australia: Government of Western Australia.

Howlett, M. and Ramesh, M. (1998). Policy subsystem configurations and policy change: Operationalizing the postpositivist analysis of the politics of the policy process. *Policy Studies Journal*, **26**(3):466–483.

Hull, R. B., Robertson, D. P., Richert, D., Seekamp, E., and Buhyoff, G. J. (2002). Assumptions about ecological scale and nature knowing best hiding in environmental decisions. *Conservation Ecology* **6**(2):12. www.consecol.org/vol6/iss2/art12.

Industry Commission (1998). *A Full Repairing Lease. Inquiry into Ecologically Sustainable Land Management*. Report No. 60. Canberra, Australia: Industry Commission.

ISAAA (2003). *Crop biotechnology in Oceaneus*. www.isaaa.org/kc/Bin/News/index.htm (Accessed 26 October 2003).

Ison, R. L., Maiteny, P. T., and Carr, S. (1997). Systems methodologies for sustainable natural resources research and development. *Agricultural Systems*, **55**(2):257–272.

Jackson, M. C. (1991). *Systems Methodology for the Management Sciences*. New York, USA: Plenum Press.

Jackson, M. C. (1993). Social theory and operational research. *Journal of the Operational Research Society*, **44**(6):563–577.

Jacobsen, V., Mays, N., Crawford, R., *et al.* (2002). *Investing in Well-Being: An Analytical Framework*. Working paper 02/03. Wellington, New Zealand: New Zealand Treasury.

Janssen, M. A., Scheffer, M., and Kohler, T. A. (2002). *Sunk-Cost Effects Made Ancient Societies Vulnerable to Collapse*. SFI Working Paper 02-02-007. Santa Fe, USA: Santa Fe Institute.

Jansson, B. and Jansson, A. (2002). The Baltic Sea: reversibly unstable or irreversibly stable. In Gunderson, L. H. and Pritchard, Jr, L., editors, *Resilience and the Behavior of Large-Scale Systems*, pages 51–70. Washington, DC, USA: Island Press.

Jasanoff, S. (1990). *The Fifth Branch: Science Advisers as Policymakers*. Cambridge, USA: Harvard University Press.

Jasanoff, S., Colwell, R., Dresselhaus, M. S., *et al.* (1997). Conversations with the community: AAAS at the millennium (American Association for the Advancement of Science). *Science*, **278**(5346):2066–2067.

Jayaratna, N. (1994). *Understanding and Evaluating Methodologies. NIMSAD-A Systemic Framework*. London, UK: McGraw-Hill Book Company.

Jones, C. (2004). *International Service for the Acquisition of Agri-Biotech Applications Briefs 32*. New York, USA: International Service for the Acquisition of Agri-Biotech Applications.

Karacapilidis, N. (2000). Integrating new information and communication technologies in group decision support systems. *International Transactions in Operations Research*, **7**:487–507.

Kay, J. and Schneider, E. D. (1994). Embracing complexity, the challenge of the ecosystem approach. *Alternatives*, **20**(3):32–38.

Kay, J. J., Regier, H. A., Boyle, M., and Francis, G. (1999). An ecosystem approach for sustainability: addressing the challenge of complexity. *Futures*, **31**(7):721–742.

Keating, B. A. and McCown, R. L. (2001). Advances in farming systems analysis and intervention. *Agricultural Systems*, **70**:555–579.

Keighery, G. (2000). Wheatbelt wonders under threat. *Landscope, Summer 2000–2001*.

Kington, E. A. (2000). *The application of policy analysis to evaluate dryland salinity management in Western Australia. 'Why is dryland and water salinisation still a major environmental problem?'*. Ph.D. thesis, University of Western Australia, Perth, Australia.

Kinzig, A. P., Antle, J., Ascher, W., *et al.* Nature and society: An imperative for integrated environmental research. A report from a workshop held June of 2000. Arizona State University. lsweb.la.asu.edu/akinzig/report.htm (Accessed 22 October 2003).

Kitchener, D. J., Chapman, A., Muir, B. C., and Palmer, M. (1980). The conservation value of mammals of reserves in the Western Australian wheatbelt. *Biological Conservation*, **18**:179–207.

Kljajic, M., Verna, C. A. L., and Skraba, A. (2002). System dynamics model development of the Canary Islands for supporting strategic public decisions. In *20th International Conference of the System Dynamics Society. 28 July – 1 August 2002*. Palermo, Italy: International System Dynamics Society.

Krugman, P. (1996). What economists can learn from evolutionary theorists. In *Work, Unemployment and Need: Theory, Evidence, Policies*. Antwerp, Belgium: European Association for Evolutionary Political Economy.

Kuhn, T. S. (1970). *The Structure of Scientific Revolutions*. Chicago, USA: University of Chicago Press.

Lackey, R. T. (1998). Seven pillars of ecosystem management. *Landscape and Urban Planning*, **40**:21–30.

Lal, P., Lim-Applegate, H., and Scoccimarro, M. (2001). The adaptive decision-making process as a tool for integrated natural resource management: focus, attitudes, and approach. *Conservation Ecology* **5**(2) Article 11. www.consecol.org/vol5/iss2/art11.

Lambin, E. F., Turner, B. L., Geist, H. J., *et al.* (2001). The causes of land-use and land-cover change: moving beyond the myths. *Global Environmental Change*, **11**:261–269.

Land and Water Resources Research and Development Corporation (1999). *Social and Institutional Research Plan 1999–2004*. Canberra, Australia: LWRRDC.

Lane, D. C. (1999). Social theory and system dynamics practice. *European Journal of Operational Research*, **113**:501–527.

Lee, K. N. (1993). *Compass and Gyroscope. Integrating Science and Politics for the Environment*. Washington, DC, USA: Island Press.

Lee, K. N. (1999). Appraising adaptive management. *Conservation Ecology* **3**(2) Article 3. www.consecol.org/vol3/iss2/art3.

Lefroy, E. C. and Hobbs, R. J. (1997). Agriculture as a mimic of natural ecosystems. In *Workshop Report for the RIRDC/LWRRDC/FWPRDC Joint Venture Agroforestry Program*, Williams, Australia.

Legislative Assembly, Western Australian Parliament (1990). *Select Committee into Land Conservation. Discussion Paper No. 2, Agricultural Region of Western Australia*. Perth, Australia: Legislative Assembly Western Australian Parliament.

Legislative Assembly, Western Australian Parliament (1991). *Select Committee into Land Conservation. Final Report*. Perth, Australia: Legislative Assembly Western Australian Parliament.

Lessard, G. (1998). An adaptive approach to planning and decision-making. *Landscape and Urban Planning*, **40**:81–87.

Lester, J. P. and Goggin, M. L. (1998). Back to the future: the rediscovery of implementation studies. *Policy Currents. Newsletter of the Public Policy Section, American Political Science Association*, **8**:1–11.

Levin, S. (1999). *Fragile Dominion: Complexity and the Commons*. New York, USA: Perseus Press.

Light, S. S. (2000). *Adaptive Environmental Assessment and Management: The Path of Last Resort*. www.adaptivemanagement.net/Pathoflastresort.htm (Accessed 12 July 2003).

Lissack, M. (1997). Mind your metaphors: lessons from complexity science. *Long Range Planning*, **30**(2):292–298.

Lotka, A. (1956). *Elements of Mathematical Biology*. New York, USA: Dover Publications.

Lubchenco, J. (1998). Entering the century of the environment: a new social contract for science. *Science*, **279**:491–497.

Ludwig, D., Hilborn, R., and Walters, C. (1993). Uncertainty, resource exploitation, and conservation; lessons from history. *Science*, **260**(17–18):36.

Ludwig, D., Mangel, M., and Haddad, B. (2001). Ecology, conservation, and public policy. *Annual Review of Ecological Systems*, **32**:481–517.

Lyman Briggs School (2003). *Lyman Briggs School*. Michigan State University. www.msu.edu/~lbs/ (Accessed 28 July 2003).

Lyons, T. J. (2002). Clouds prefer native vegetation. *Meteorology and Atmospheric Physics*, **80**:131–140.

Maani, K. E. (2001). Consensus building through systems thinking. The case of policy and planning in healthcare. In Hutchinson, W. and Warren, M., editors, *Systems in Management. 7th Annual ANZSYS Conference 2001. The Relevance of Systems Thinking in the Contemporary World, 27–28 November 2001*. Edith Cowan University, Perth, Australia.

Maani, K. E. and Cavana, R. Y. (2000). *Systems Thinking and Modelling: Understanding Change and Uncertainty*. Auckland, New Zealand: Prentice Hall.

Mackenzie, S. (2004). Farmers are laughing all the way to the bank. *The Australian Financial Review*:4, Sydney, Australia.

Mann, M., editor (1983). *The Macmillan Student Encyclopedia of Sociology*. London, UK: Macmillan Press.

Manson, S. M. (2001). Simplifying complexity: a review of complexity theory. *Geoforum*, **32**:405–414.

Marsh, S. P. (2001). Social dimensions of landcare. In *State Landcare Conference 2001, Mandurah, Australia, 11–14 September 2001*, pages 117–28. Perth, Australia: Agriculture Western Australia.

Mason, R. O. and Mitroff, I. I. (1981). *Challenging Strategic Planning Assumptions: Theory, Cases and Techniques*. New York, USA: John Wiley & Sons.

McFarlane, D. J., George, R. J., and Farrington, P. (1993). Changes in the hydrologic cycle. In Saunders, R. J. and Hobbs, A. D., editors, *Reintegrating Fragmented Landscapes: Towards Sustainable Production and Nature Conservation*, pages 146–189. New York, USA: Springer-Verlag.

McIntosh, R. P. (1980). The background and some current problems of theoretical ecology. *Synthese*, **43**:195–255.

McNeill, J. R. (2000). *Something New Under the Sun: An Environmental History of the Twentieth-Century World. 1st edn*. New York, USA: W.W. Norton & Company.

McTainsh, G. and Boughton, W. C. (1993). *Land Degradation Processes in Australia*. Melbourne, Australia: Longman Cheshire.

Meadows, D. H. (1970). *Dynamics of Commodity Production Cycles*. Waltham, USA: Pegasus Communication.

Meadows, D. H. (1972). *The Limits to Growth: A Report for the Club of Rome's Project on the Predicament of Mankind*. London, UK: Earth Island Ltd.

Meadows, D. H. (1991). *The Global Citizen*. Washington, DC, USA: Island Press.

Meadows, D. (1999). *Leverage Points: Places to Intervene in the System*. Hartland, USA: The Sustainability Institute.

Meadows, D. H. and Robinson, J. M. (1985). *The Electronic Oracle: Computer Models and Social Decisions*. Chichester, UK: John Wiley & Sons.

Meadows, D. H., Meadows, D. L., Randers, J., and Behrens, W. W. (1972). *The Limits to Growth*. New York, USA: Universe Books.

Meppem, T. and Bourke, S. (1999). Different ways of knowing: a communicative turn toward sustainability. *Ecological Economics*, **30**:389–404.

Milbrath, L. W. (1989). *Envisioning a Sustainable Society: Learning Our Way Out.* New York, USA: State University of New York Press.

Mitchell, B. (1979). *Geography and Resource Analysis.* London, UK: Longman.

Mitchell, B. (1990). Integrated water management. In *Integrated Water Management.* London, UK: Belhaven Press.

Mitchell, B. (1991). *Integrated Catchment Management in Western Australia: Progress and Opportunities.* Perth, Australia: Centre for Water Research, University of Western Australia.

Mobbs, C. and Dovers, S., editors (1999). *Social, Economic, Legal, Policy and Institutional R&D for Natural Resource Management: Issues and Directions for LWRRDC.* Occasional Paper 01/99. Canberra, Australia: Land and Water Resources Research and Development Corporation.

Monbiot, G. (2003). *The Age of Consent. A Manifesto for New World Order.* London, UK: Flamingo.

Morgan, G. (1986). *Images of Organization.* Beverly Hills, USA: Sage Publications.

Mullner, S. A., Hubert, W. A., and Wesche, T. A. (2001). Evolving paradigms for landscape-scale renewable resource management in the United States. *Environmental Science & Policy*, **4**:39–49.

Murray–Darling Basin Ministerial Council (2000a). *Draft Policy – Integrated Catchment Management in the Murray–Darling Basin 2001–2010. Delivering a Sustainable Future.* Canberra, Australia: Murray–Darling Basin Commission.

Murray–Darling Basin Ministerial Council (2000b). *Draft Policy – Basin Salinity Management Strategy 2001–2015.* Canberra, Australia: Murray–Darling Basin Commission.

Myers, N. R., Mittermeier, R. A., Mittermeier, C. G., Fonseca, da G. A. B., and Kent, J. (2000). Biodiversity hotspots for conservation priorities. *Nature*, **403**: 853–858.

National Land and Water Resources Audit (1997). *Australian National Land and Water Audit.* Canberra, Australia: Natural Heritage Trust.

National Land and Water Resources Audit (2000). *Australian Dryland Salinity Assessment 2000. Extent, Impacts, Processes, Monitoring and Management Options.* Canberra, Australia: Natural Heritage Trust.

National Land and Water Resources Audit (2001a). *Australian Dryland Salinity Audit. Extent, Impacts, Processes Monitoring and Management Options.* Canberra, Australia: Natural Heritage Trust.

National Land and Water Resources Audit (2001b). *Australian Agriculture Assessment 2001. Volume 1.* Canberra, Australia: Natural Heritage Trust.

National Land and Water Resources Audit (2001c). *Australian Agriculture Assessment 2001. Volume 2.* Canberra, Australia: Natural Heritage Trust.

National Land and Water Resources Audit (2001d). *Australian Natural Resource Atlas: Dryland Salinity-Risk and Hazard – 2000 to 2050.* Canberra, Australia: Natural Heritage Trust.

National Land and Water Resources Audit (2001e). *Australian Water Resources Assessment 2000. Surface and Groundwater – Availability and Quality.* Canberra, Australia: Natural Heritage Trust.

National Land and Water Resources Audit (2002). *Australians and Natural Resource Management 2002*. Canberra, Australia: Natural Heritage Trust.

Norgaard, R. B. (1989). The case for methodological pluralism. *Ecological Economics*, **1**:37–57.

Odum, E. P. (1959). *The Fundamentals of Ecology*. 2nd edn. Philadelphia, USA: Saunders.

Office of Catchment Management (1995). *Integrated Catchment Management. Progress Report March 1992 to June 1995*. Perth, Australia: Office of Catchment Management.

Oil Mallee Association of Western Australia (2001). The oil mallee project.

Olsson, C. A., Bond, L., Burns, J. M., Vella-Brodrick, D. A., and Sawyer, S. M. (2003). Adolescent resilience: a concept analysis. *Journal of Adolescence*, **26**(1):1–11.

O'Neill, R. V., Kahn, J. R., and Russell, C. S. (1998). Economics and ecology: the need for detente in conservation ecology. *Conservation Ecology* **2**(1):4. www.consecol.org/vol2/iss1/art4/.

O'Regan, B. and Moles, R. (2001). A system dynamics model of mining industry investment decisions within the context of environmental policy. *Journal of Environmental Planning and Management*, **44**(2):245–262.

Pannell, D. J. (2000a). *Market-Based Mechanisms, Financial Incentives and Other Institutional Innovations: Assessing their Potential for Addressing Dryland Salinity*. Sustainability and Economics in Agriculture. www.general.uwa.edu.au/u/dpannell/dpap0009.htm (Accessed 14 August 2003).

Pannell, D. J. (2000b). *Salinity Policy: A Tale of Fallacies, Misconceptions and Hidden Assumptions*. Sustainability and Economics in Agriculture, University of Western Australia. Working Paper 00/08. www.general.uwa.edu.au/u/dpannell/dpap0008.htm (Accessed 12 July 2005).

Pannell, D. J. (2001). *Public Funding for Environmental Issues: Where to Now?* Sustainability and Economics in Agriculture. Working Paper 01/12, Perth, Australia: School of Agricultural and Resource Economics, University of Western Australia.

Pannell, D. J. and Glenn, N. A. (2000). A framework for the economic evaluation and selection of sustainability indicators in agriculture. *Ecological Economics*, **33**(1):135–149.

Pannell, D., McFarlane, D., and Ferdowsian, R. (2001). Rethinking the externality issue for dryland salinity in Western Australia. *Australian Journal of Agricultural and Resource Economics*, **45**(3):459–475.

Parker, I. (2002). Managing change on an Australian landscape, Einstein vs. Macchiavelli. In Bennett, S. J. and Blacklow, M., editors, *International Conference on Prospects for Biodiversity and Rivers in Salinising Landscapes. 20–27 October 2002*, Albany, Western Australia. Perth, Australia: Centre for Excellence for Natural Resource Management, CRC for Plant-Based Management of Dryland Salinity.

Parliamentary Liberal Party (2002). *Position Statement: Tackling Western Australia's Salinity Crisis. Defining the Difference*. Perth, Australia: Parliamentary Liberal Party.

Parsons, T. (1959). General theory in sociology. In Merton, R., Broom, L., and Cottrell L. S., editors, *Sociology Today: Problems and Prospects*, pages 3–38. New York, USA: Basic Books.

Passioura, J. B. (2002). Environmental biology and crop improvement. *Functional Plant Biology*, **29**:537–546.

Patterson, M. E. and Williams, D. R. (1998). Paradigms and problems: the practice of social science in natural resource management. *Society & Natural Resources*, **11**:297–295.

Peeters, M. (2001). Worth their salt. *Synergy, Murdoch University*, **5**(1).

Penm, J., Gleeson, T., Barrett, D., *et al.* (2003). *2002–03 Drought Review of Its Impact on Australian Agriculture.* Canberra, Australia: Australian Bureau of Agriculture and Rural Economics.

Petrie, M. (2002). *Institutions, Social Norms and Well-being.* Working Paper 02/12. Wellington, New Zealand: New Zealand Treasury.

Pinstrup-Andersen, P., Pandya-Lorch, R., and Rosegrant, M. W. (1999). *World Food Prospects: Critical Issues for the Early Twenty-First Century. Food Policy Report.* Washington, DC, USA: International Food Policy Research Institute.

Pirsig, R. M. (1976). *Zen and the Art of Motorcycle Maintenance: An Inquiry Into Values.* London, UK: Transworld.

Pretty, J. and Frank, B. R. (2000). Participation and social capital formation in natural resource management: achievements and lessons. In *International Landcare 2000 Conference, 2–5 March 2000, Melbourne, Australia.* Canberra, Australia: Agriculture, Fisheries and Forestry–Australia.

Pretty, J. and Howard, H. (2001). Social capital and the environment. *World Development*, **29**(2):209–227.

Pretty, J., Brett, C., Gee, D., *et al.* (2001). Policy challenges and priorities for internalizing the externalities of modern agriculture. *Journal of Environmental Planning and Management*, **44**(2):263–283.

Prime Minister of Australia (2002). *Prime Minister of Australia, John Howard. Media Release. New Drought Support.* Canberra, Australia: Government of Australia.

Productivity Commission (2003). *Social Capital. Reviewing the Concept and Its Policy Implications.* Canberra, Australia: AusInfo.

Productivity Commission (2005). *Trends in Australian Agriculture.* Canberra, Australia: AusInfo.

Quinn, R. E. (1996). *Becoming a Master Manager: A Competency Framework.* 2nd edn. Chichester, UK: John Wiley & Sons.

Quinn, R. and Rohrbaugh, J. (1983). A spatial model of effectiveness criteria: towards a competing values approach to organisational analysis. *Management Science*, **29**:363–377.

Raskin, P., Banuri, T., Gallopin, G., Gutman, P., Hammond, A., Kates, R., and Swart, R. (1998). *Great Transition. The Promise and Lure of the Times Ahead. A Report of the Global Scenario Group.* Stockholm, Sweden: Stockholm Environment Institute, Global Scenario Group.

Ravetz, J. R. (1997). The science of 'what if'? *Futures*, **29**(6):533–539.

Ravetz, J. (2002). *Models as Metaphors: A New Look at Science.* (Accessed 24 September 2002).

Reeve, I. (2001). *Australian Farmers' Attitudes to Rural Environmental Issues, 1991–2001. Final Report to Land and Water Australia.* Canberra, Australia: Land and Water Australia.

Resilience Alliance (2002). *Resilience*. The Resilience Alliance. www.resalliance.org (Accessed 17 September 2003).

Richardson, G. P. (1991). *Feedback Thought in Social Science and Systems Theory*. Philadelphia, USA: University of Pennsylvania Press.

Richardson, G. P. (1996). Definition of system dynamics. In Glass, S. I. and Harris, C. M., editors, *Encyclopedia of Operations Research and Management Science*, pages 656–660. Boston, USA: Kluwer Academic Publishers.

Rintoul, J. (1964). *Esperance. Yesterday and Today*. 4th edn. Perth, Australia: Esperance Shire Council.

Rittel, H. and Webber, M. (1973). Dilemmas in a general theory of planning. *Policy Sciences*, **4**:155–159.

Robertson, D. P. and Hull, R. B. (2003). Public ecology: an environmental science and policy for global society. *Environmental Science & Policy*, **6**(5):399–410.

Robertson, R. (1974). Towards the identification of the major axes of sociological analysis. In Rex, J., editor, *Approaches to Sociology*. London, UK: Routledge and Kegan Paul.

Roe, E. (1998). *Taking Complexity Seriously. Policy Analysis, Triangulation and Sustainable Development*. Boston, USA: Kluwer Academic.

Röling, N. G. and Wagemakers, M. A. E., editors (1998). *Facilitating Sustainable Agriculture: Participatory Learning and Adaptive Management in Times of Environmental Uncertainty*. Cambridge, UK: Cambridge University Press.

Romesburg, H. C. (1981). Wildlife science: gaining reliable knowledge. *Journal of Wildlife Management*, **45**:293–313.

Rosenberg, A. (2000). *Philosophy of Science: A Contemporary Introduction*. London, UK: Routledge.

Rosenberg, A. A., Fogarty, M. J., Sissenwine, M. P., Beddington, J. R., and Shepard, J. G. (1993). Achieving sustainable use of renewable resources. *Science*, **262**(5135):828–829.

Ross, D. (1993). *Metaphor, Meaning, and Cognition*. New York, USA: P. Lang.

Rosser, J. B. (2001). Complex ecologic-economic dynamics and environmental policy. *Ecological Economics*, **37**:23–37.

Royal Commission on the Agricultural Industries of Western Australia (1917). *Commission on Tour in South Australia En Route to Port Augusta, March/April 1917. Progress Report of the Royal Commission on the Agricultural Industries of Western Australia on the Wheat-Growing Portion of the South-West Division of the State, Together with Minutes of Evidence, Indices, and Appendices*. Perth, Australia: Government of Western Australia.

Royal Commission on the Agricultural Industries of Western Australia (1918). *Second Progress Report of the Royal Commission on the Agricultural Industries of Western Australia on the Settled Portions of the South-West Coastal Districts, Including Minutes of Evidence, Indices, and Appendices, Together with a Final Review of the Operations of the Commission*. Perth, Australia: Government of Western Australia.

Ruef, M. (2002). Ecological perspectives on industrial decline and resurgence. In *25th Anniversary Celebration of Organizational Ecology, December 13–14, 2002*, Graduate School of Business, Stanford University.

Runciman, W. G. (1963). *Social Science and Political Theory*. Cambridge, UK: Cambridge University Press.

Sabatier, P. A. and Jenkins-Smith, H. C. (1993). *Policy Change and Learning: An Advocacy Coalition Approach*. Boulder, USA: Westview Press.

Sabatier, P. and Mazmanian, D. (1980). The implementation of public policy: a framework of analysis. *Policy Studies Journal*, **8**, Special No. 2(4):538–560.

Saeed, K. (1998). Sustainable trade relations in a global economy. *System Dynamics Review*, **14**(2-3):107–128.

Sala, M. and Conacher, A. J. (1998). *Land Degradation in Mediterranean Environments of the World: Nature and Extent, Causes and Solutions*. Chichester, UK: John Wiley & Sons.

Saunders, D. A. and Ingram, J. A. (1995). *Birds of South-western Australia. An Atlas of Changes in the Distribution and Abundance of the Wheatbelt Fauna*. Chipping Norton, Australia: Surrey Beatty and Sons.

Saunders, D. A., Smith, G.T., Ingram, J. A., and Forrester, R. I. (2003). Changes in a remnant of salmon gum *Eucalyptus salmonophloia* and York gum *E. loxophleba* woodland, 1978 to 1997. Implications for woodland conservation in the wheat-sheep regions of Australia. *Biological Conservation*, **110**:245–256.

Sawin, B., Hamilton, H., Jones, A., *et al.* (2003). *Commodity System Challenges. Moving Sustainability into the Mainstream of Natural Resource Economies*. Hartland, USA: Sustainability Institute.

Sayer, J. A. and Campbell, B. (2001). Research to integrate productivity enhancement, environmental protection, and human development. *Conservation Ecology* **5**(2): Article 32. www.consecol.org/vol5/iss2/art32.

Scheffer, M., Westley, F., Brock, W. A., and Holmgram, M. (2002). Dynamic interactions of societies and ecosystems – linking theories from ecology, economy, and sociology. In Gunderson, L. H. and Holling, C. S., editors, *Panarchy. Understanding Transformations in Human and Natural Systems*, pages 195–240. Washington, DC, USA: Island Press.

Schumpeter, J. A. (1950). *Capitalism, Socialism and Democracy*. New York, USA: Harper and Row.

Senge, P. M., Kleiner, A., Roberts, C., Ross, R. B., and Smith, B. J. (1994). *The Fifth Discipline Fieldbook. Strategies and Tools for Building a Learning Organisation*. New York, USA: Doubleday.

Sewell, S. (2003). *Myth, Propaganda and Disaster in Nazi Germany and Contemporary America*. Playbox Theatre, Melbourne, Australia.

Sexton, W. T. (1998). Ecosystem management: expanding the resource management tool kit. *Landscape and Urban Ecology*, **40**:103–112.

Shea, S., Butcher, G., Ritson, P., Bartle, P., and Biggs, P. (1998). The potential for tree crops and vegetation rehabilitation to sequester carbon in Western Australia. In *Carbon Sequestration Conference*, Melbourne, Australia.

Soulé, M. E. (1995). The social siege of nature. In Lease, G., editor, *Reinventing Nature?: Responses to Postmodern Deconstruction*. Washington, DC, USA: Island Press.

Standing Committee on Soil Conservation (1971). *Study of Community Benefits of and Finance for Soil Conservation*. Canberra, Australia: Australian Publishing Service.

Stein, S. M. and Gelburd, D. (1998). Healthy ecosystems and sustainable economies: the federal inter-agency ecosystem management initiative. *Landscape and Urban Planning*, **40**:73–80.

Stephens, P. (1986). *Aboriginal Influences on Australian Ecosystems*. Honours degree, Murdoch University, Perth, Australia.

Sterman, J. D. (2000). *Business Dynamics. Systems Thinking and Modeling for a Complex World*. Boston, USA: Irwin McGraw-Hill.

Sterman, J. D. (2002). All models are wrong: reflections on becoming a systems scientist. Jay Wright Forrester Prize Lecture, 2002. *System Dynamics Review*, **18**:501–531.

Stokes, G. (1998). *Popper: Philosophy, Politics, and Scientific Method*. Cambridge, UK: Polity Press.

Swart, J. (1990). A system dynamics approach to predator prey modeling. *System Dynamics Review*, **6**:94–98.

Syme, G. J. and Sadler, B. S. (1994). Evaluation of public involvement in water resources planning. A researcher-practitioners dialogue. *Evaluation Review*, **18**:523–542.

Syme, J. S., Butterworth, J. E., and Nancarrow, B. E. (1994). *National Whole Catchment Management: A Review and Analysis of Process*. Occasional Paper Series No 01/94. Canberra, Australia: The Land and Water Resources Research and Development Corporation.

Szaro, R. C., Bcrc, J., Cameron, S., *et al*. (1998). The ecosystem approach: science and information management issues, gaps and needs. *Landscape and Urban Ecology*, **40**:89–101.

Tainter, J. A. (1988). *The Collapse of Complex Societies*. Cambridge, UK: Cambridge University Press.

Tainter, J. A. (1996). Complexity, problem solving, and sustainable societies. In Tainter, J. A., editor, *Getting Down to Earth: Practical Applications of Ecological Economics*. Washington, DC, USA: Island Press.

Tansley, A. G. (1935). The use and abuse of vegetational concepts and terms. *Ecology*, **16**:284–307.

Task Force for the Review of NRM and Viability of Agriculture in Western Australia (1996). *Review of NRM and Viability of Agriculture in Western Australia: A Discussion Paper*. Perth, Australia: Minister for Primary Industry, Western Australia.

Task Force for the Review of NRM and Viability of Agriculture in Western Australia (1997). *Review of NRM and Viability of Agriculture in Western Australia: Draft Report*. Perth, Australia: Minister for Primary Industry, Western Australia.

Tengerdy, R. P. and Szakács, G. (1998). Perspectives in agrobiotechnology. *Journal of Biotechnology*, **66**:91–99.

Thompson, I. and Heffer, K. (2000). What is happening after Landcare? Future directions in natural resource management. In *Emerging Technologies in Agriculture: From Ideas to Adoption. 25–26 July 2000*. Canberra, Australia: Bureau of Rural Science.

Tognetti, S. S. (1999). Science in a double-bind: Gregory Bateson and the origins of post-normal science. *Futures*, **31**:689–703.

Tonts, M. and Black, A. (2002). *The Impact of Changing Farm Business Structures on Rural Communities*. Canberra, Australia: Rural Industries Research and Development Corporation.

Toyne, P. and Farley, R. (2000). *The Decade of Landcare. Looking Backward – Looking Forward*. Discussion Paper No. 30. Canberra, Australia: The Australia Institute.

Van Dyne, G. M., editor (1969). *The Ecosystem Concept in Natural Resource Management*. New York, USA: Academic Press.

Vayda, A. P. and McCay, B. J. (1975). New directions in ecology and ecological anthropology. *Annual Review of Anthropology*, **4**:293–306.

Vennix, J. A. M. (1999). Group model-building: tackling messy problems. *System Dynamics Review*, **15**:379–401.

Virtual Consulting Group and Griffin nrm Pty Ltd (2000). *National Investment in Rural Landscapes. An Investment Scenario for NFF and ACF with Assistance from LWRRDC*. Canberra, Australia: Land and Water Resources Research and Development Corporation.

Vitousek, P. M., Lubchenco, J., Mooney, J., and Melillo, H. A. (1997). Human domination of earth's ecosystems. *Science*, **277**:494–499.

Waldrop, M. (1992). *Complexity: The Emerging Science at the Edge of Order and Chaos*. New York, USA: Simon & Schuster.

Walker, P. M. B., editor (1995). *Dictionary of Science and Technology*. Edinburgh, UK: Larousse.

Walker, B. (2000). *Analysing Integrated Social-Ecological Systems. Report on a Workshop Funded by the Marcus Wallenberg Foundation for International Cooperation in Science. 12–14 September 2000*. Resilience Alliance. www.resalliance.org/reports/wallenberg–report.dec00.html (Accessed 23 May 2002).

Walker, B. and Abel, N. (2002). Resilient rangelands – adaptation in complex systems. In Gunderson, L. H. and Holling, C. S., editors, *Panarchy. Understanding Transformations in Human and Natural Systems*, pages 293–314. Washington, DC, USA: Island Press.

Walker, B., Carpenter, S., Anderies, J., *et al.* (2002). Resilience management in social-ecological systems: a working hypothesis for a participatory approach. *Conservation Ecology* **6**(1) Article 14. www.consecol.org/vol6/iss1/art14

Wallace, K. J. (2003). Confusing means with ends: a manager's reflections on experience in agricultural landscapes of Western Australia. *Ecological Management & Restoration*, **4**(1):23–28.

Wallace, N. and Evans, J. (1993). *International Commodity Markets: An Australian Perspective*. Canberra, Australia: Australian Bureau of Agricultural and Resource Economics.

Wallington, T. J., Hobbs, R. J., and Moore, S. A. (2001). Implications of current ecological thinking for biodiversity conservation: a review of salient issues. *Ecology and Society* **10**(1): Article 15. www.ecologyandsociety.org/vol10/iss1/art15.

Walmsley, D. J. (1972). *Systems Theory: A Framework for Human Geographical Enquiry*. Research School of Pacific Studies, Canberra, Australia: Australian National University Press.

Walters, C. J. (1986). *Adaptive Management and Renewable Resources*. New York, USA: Macmillan.

Waltner-Toews, D. (1996). Ecosystem health: a framework for implementing sustainability in agriculture. *Bioscience*, **46**:686–689.

Waring, A. (1996). *Practical Systems Thinking*. London, UK: International Thomson Business Press.

Water Studies Pty Ltd (2000). *Moora Flood Management Study*. Perth, Australia: Water and Rivers Commission, Western Australia.

Weber, M. and Schwaninger, M. (2002). Transforming an agricultural trade organization: a system-dynamic-based intervention. *System Dynamics Review*, **18**(3):381–401.

Western Australian Commission on Agriculture (1891). *First Progress Report and Final Report 1888–1891 (Venn Report)*. Government of Western Australia.

Western Australian Fishing Industry Council (2003). *Lobsters*. Western Australian Fishing Indusry Council. www.wafic.com.au/lobsters/index.html (Accessed 4 July 2003).

Westley, F., Carpenter, S. R., Brock, W. A., Holling, C. S., and Gunderson, L. H. (2002). Why systems of people and nature are not just social and ecological systems. In Gunderson, L. H. and Holling, C. S., editors, *Panarchy. Understanding Transformations in Human and Natural Systems*, pages 103–120. Washington, DC, USA: Island Press.

White, M. E. (1994). *After the Greening: The Browning of Australia*. Kenthurst, Australia: Kangaroo Press.

Williams, M. (1976). The perception of hazard of soil erosion in South Australia: a review. In *National Hazards Symposium*. Canberra, Australia: Academy of Science.

Williams, J., Hook, R. A., and Hamblin, A. (2002). *Agro-Ecological Regions of Australia. Methodologies for their Derivation and Key Issues in Resource Management*. Canberra, Australia: CSIRO Land and Water.

Wilson, E. O. (1988). *Biodiversity*. Washington, DC, USA: National Academy Press.

Wilson, E. O. (1999). *Consilience: The Unity of Knowledge*. London, UK: Little, Brown and Company.

Wolfenden, J. A. J. (1999). *A Transdisciplinary Approach to Integrated Resource Management: A Pragmatic Application of Ecological Economics*. Ph.D. thesis, Centre for Water Policy Research, University of New England, Armidale, Australia.

Wolstenholme, E. F. (1983). A methodology for qualitative system dynamics. In *Proceedings of the System Dynamics Society Conference*, Denver, USA.

Wolstenholme, E. F. (1990). *System Enquiry: A System Dynamics Approach*. Chichester, UK: John Wiley & Sons.

Wood, W. E. (1924). Increase of salt in soil and streams following destruction of native vegetation. *Journal of the Royal Society of Western Australia*, **X**(7): 35–47.

World Bank (1998). *The Initiative on Defining, Monitoring and Measuring Social Capital: Overview and Program Description. Social Capital Initiative*. Working Paper No. 1. Washington, DC, USA: The World Bank.

World Commission on Environment and Development (1989). *Our Common Future.* Oxford, UK: Oxford University Press.

Wynne, B. (1974). *Sociology of Science.* SISCON Project, Manchester, UK.

Wynne, B. (1992). Misunderstood misunderstandings: social identities in public uptake of science. *Public Understanding of Science,* **1**:281–304.

Yaffee, S. L. (1997). Why environmental policy nightmares recur. *Conservation Biology,* **11**(2):328–337.

Yearly, S. (2000). Making systematic sense of public discontents with expert knowledge: two analytical approaches and a case study. *Public Understanding of Science,* **9**:105–122.

Young, M. D. and Gunningham, N. (1997). Mixing instruments and institutional arrangements for optimal biodiversity conservation. In Hale, P. and Lamb, D., editors, *Conservation Outside Nature Reserves,* pages 123–135. Brisbane, Australia: Centre for Conservation Biology, The University of Queensland.

Young, M. D. and McCay, B. J. (1995). Building equity, stewardship, and resilience into market-based property rights systems. In Hanna, S. and Munasinghe, M., editors, *Property Rights and the Environment: Social and Ecological Issues,* pages 87–102. Washington, DC, USA: Beijer International Institute of Ecological Economics and the World Bank.

Young, M. D., Gunningham, N., Elix, J., *et al.* (1996). *Reimbursing the Future. An Evaluation of Motivational, Voluntary, Price-Based, Property-Right, and Regulatory Incentives for the Conservation of Biodiversity. Part 1 A Report to the Biodiversity Unit of the Department of the Environment, Sport and Territories.* Biodiversity Series, 9. Canberra, Australia: Department of Environment, Sport and Territories.

Zagonel, A. A. (2002). Model conceptualization in group model building: a review of the literature exploring the tension between representing reality and negotiating a social order. In *20th International Conference of the System Dynamics Society,* 28 July–1 August 2002. Palermo, Italy: System Dynamics Society.

Ziman, J. (2000). *Real Science: What It Is, and What It Means.* Cambridge, UK: Cambridge University Press.

Index

National Action Plan for Salinity and Water
  Quality in Australia (NAP), 28–38
National Dryland Salinity Program, 30
National Farmers Federation, 25
National Heritage Fund, 26
National Landcare Program, 25
  attitudinal change, 27
  criticism, 28
  goals, 26
National Soil Conservation Strategy, 25
native vegetation
  decline, 126
  degradation, 41
natural resource degradation, 5
natural resource management
  adaptive environmental assessment and
      management, 29
  catchment management approach, 29
  integrated catchment management, 29
  integrated natural resource management, 29
  integrated resource management
      approach, 29
  landscape management, 29
  options, 184
  partnerships, 35
  persistent problems, 181
  regional groups, 35
  regional scale, 35
  risk, 30
  systems approach, 29
  uncertainty, 30
Natural Resource Management
    Council, 31
natural resource management policy
  scientific paradigm, 6
Natural Resource Zones of the South West
    Land Division, 33
normal science methodology, 6
normative variables
  desired ecological capacity, 162
  desired social capacity, 162

Office of Catchment Management, 29
ontology, 55–56
organisational analysis, 8, 52–53, 56, 58
organisational ecology, 58

panarchy, 109, 115, 119, 183–184, 186
paradigm, 51, 54–58
  normal science, 52, 56–58, 67, 68, 179
    assumptions, 56

equilibrium-centred, 57
  in relation to the Precautionary
      Principle, 179
  post-normal science, 54, 69, 92–94, 178
  sociological, 59, 60
  systems thinking, 97
  traditional scientific, 6
pathological states, 137, *see also* Poverty
    Trap, Rigidity Trap
philosophy, 52
policy
  command and control (CCP), 52, 67–68, 74
  constraints, mental models, 192
  difficulties of complex systems for, 179
  effectiveness and boundary
      selection, 186
  failure, 47, 49–50
    causes, 47
  impacts of spatial and temporal scales, 173
  incremental change, 192
  land, 24
  natural resource management, 13–39, 53
  paradigmatic change, 192–193
  resistance, 145
  response, 145
  Restoring Nature's Balance, the War on
      Salt, 44
  rural adjustment, 48
  soil conservation, 23–25
  statutory, 32
  wetlands, 32
positivist sociology, 60
post-normal science, *see* paradigm,
    post-normal science; science,
    post-normal
postmodern deconstructivism, 55
Poverty Trap, 137–138
prices
  commodity, 36
  wheat, 19, 21
problem, the, 51, 68, 74
problem articulation, 122
problem situation, 85–87
problem solver, 88
problem-solving process, 85–89
problems
  ill-structured, 89
  messy, 89
  resistant, 47
  wicked, 89